HANDTOOL HANDBOOK
FOR WOODWORKING
by R. J. DeCristoforo

Publisher: Bill Fisher; Editor-In-Chief: Carl Shipman; Editor: Jon Latimer; Editorial Assistance: Jackie Craver; Art Director: Josh Young; Book Design & Assembly: Chris Crosson; Typography: Frances Ruiz, Mary Kaye Fisher, Cindy Coatsworth; Drawings: Dan Thrapp; Cover Photography: Naurice Koonce.

Published by H.P. Books, P.O. Box 5367, Tucson, AZ 85703 602/888-2150
ISBN: 0-912656-53-0 H.P. Book Number 53
Library of Congress Catalog Card Number: 77-89289 ©1977 H.P. Books. Printed in U.S.A.

Contents

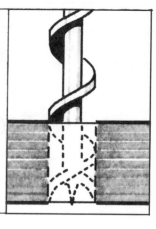

4 Drills

1 Measuring & Marking

5 Screwdrivers

2 Saws

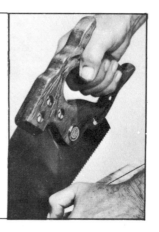

6 Knives & Chisels

3 Hammers

7 Planes

8

Shaping & Finishing

Getting A Handle On Files, Rasps, Formers, Scrapers, Sandpaper and Wood Tape for That Fine Finish.

Page 84

12

Putting Pieces Together

Joints, Splices, Glues, Nails, Brads, Tacks, Screws and Bolts Made Easy.

Page 119

9

Vises & Clamps

Hold That Project: Wood Vises, Handscrews, C-Clamps, Bar and Pipe Clamps, Web Clamps and Miter Clamps.

Page 96

13

Tools You Can Make

How To Make Your Own Saw Horses, Tote Boxes and a Workbench.

Page 145

10

Special Tools

For Special Needs: Pliers, Wrenches, Nut Drivers, Snips, Wood Threading Tools and Workmate™.

Page 106

14

Projects

Easy Plans For Five Board Bench, Coffee Cup Tree, Cutting Board, Modern Bench, Butcher Block End Table, Magazine Stand, Planter, Bird Feeder, Kitchen Rack, Toy Truck, Bobbing Robot Toy, Toy Train.

Page 156

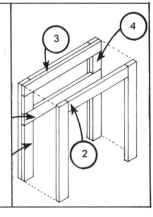

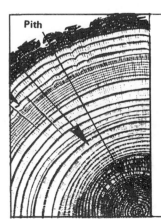

11

Materials

Everything You Need to Know About Lumber, Plywood, Hardboard and Particle Board.

Page 111

Introduction

Wouldn't it be great if you could stare at your fingers and they would become a plane or a chisel or a hammer? Actually, this is what happens when you hold a tool—your fingers form an intimate bond between you and the tool. It is a marriage of intellect and an inanimate object. Suddenly the tool comes alive and performs . . . a miracle *anyone* can accomplish. The keys are not secret or a question of native ability. Interest plus Dedication equal Skill. The prime movers are in all of us.

Tools don't care whether their handler is an amateur or a professional. A plane held and moved a certain way will make the same cut for anyone. The experienced worker has the advantage of trial-and-error knowledge. If a plane skips and jumps, or a saw chatters, or a screw refuses to set properly, stop and examine the problem. Don't force the tool. Find the reason for your trouble. This book can help. Are you planing against the grain? Is the piece you are sawing properly gripped and supported? Are the lead holes for your screw properly aligned? If you use your head as well as your hands, you will find woodworking a creative, relaxing avocation.

I have no doubt if you have not handled tools yet—you can start right off and produce a project you can be proud of. It may take you more time than a neighbor who has been doing woodworking for years, but there is no guarantee his project will be better than yours.

Education is merely a foundation you build on. It is necessary because no one is born with built-in knowledge in any field. What you do with what you learn is up to you. One thing is sure: Knowledge doesn't choose special individuals. You—the individual—make the knowledge something special.

SAFETY—COUNT YOUR FINGERS

Any of the tools talked about in this book can cut, scrape or bang you. You can read a book full of do-and-don't rules regarding safety and still be in danger unless you accept and respect this simple truth: Tools can't think for you.

Tools are great buddies in a very disinterested sort of way. They don't care at all whether the user is an amateur or an expert or what they are applied to. Efficiency and even a large amount of safety are part of quality tools, but in the final analysis the worker is the most important factor.

I have worked with hand and power tools all my life and like to boast that I am as whole as the day I was born. I am afraid of tools—but it's a healthy fear that keeps me from becoming overconfident and careless. I am aware that speed is not as important as quality, and that *fast* work is often more time-consuming than *slow* work. Your output and quality will increase as you become more proficient with tools, but it will be a natural outcome—not the result of frenzied workshop activities.

The first rules are:

- Work at a comfortable pace
- Be the master of the tools
- Don't ever become overconfident.

DO AND DON'T RULES

Always use the correct tool for the job. Use the tool correctly and, when called for, keep it sharp. Put the tool away when you are through with it. Keep the work area clean and well lighted. Having a special shop uniform is a fine idea. An apron is okay, but remember it does more to protect your clothes than you.

A good first-aid kit should be a part of your basic tool set.

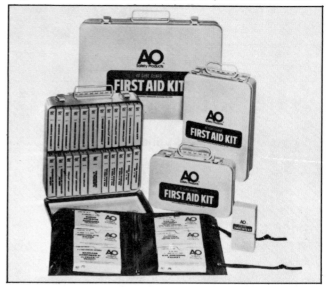

Reach for safety glasses or goggles whenever there is a danger of flying chips. Always protect your eyes when sawing, hammering or grinding.

Don't overdo your workshop stints. You can't do good work or be safe if you are tired. Don't work when you are upset—take a pleasant walk first and calm down. It is not a good idea to work with an audience, especially one who doesn't know what is going on and tries to keep a conversation going. Protect children from tools and tools from children. If youngsters have an interest, *teach* them, and insist they do things the right way to start with. Extend the lessons by example.

Have safety goggles and use them to protect your eyes from dust and flying particles. It is necessary to wear them at some times, optional at others, but being prudent is better than being sorry. Many styles are available—some may be worn over corrective lenses. If you wear glasses, don't regard them as substitutes. It's cheaper to buy new safety glasses than to replace pitted or broken lenses in your prescription glasses.

Remember the most important safety rule of all: Know there is potential danger in *any* tool, not just power tools. We tend to be much too casual with hand tools because of their essential simplicity.

The main reasons for injuries with hand tools are . . .
  • Not using the right tool for the job
  • Not using the tool correctly
  • Not keeping the tool sharp.

BASIC TOOLS

A large number of tools are described in this book, but there are some that must be included in even the most minimal tool kit. Even if you live in an apartment and only want to hang curtains or make minor repairs, your tool kit should include these tools.

• 16-ounce claw hammer
• 4-inch screwdriver
• 6-inch screwdriver with small blade
• Junior jack plane
• Brad awl with 1-1/2-inch blade
• 26-inch hand saw with 8-point blade
• 1/4-inch hand drill and a set of straight-shank carbon drills ranging from 1/16 inch to 11/64 inch in 1/64-inch increments
• Slip-joint pliers
• 8-foot flex tape

These tools will meet your basic needs. As you become more proficient and ambitious in woodworking, add all the tools you need, but let your need be your guide. Too many extra tools are bought on impulse and never used. That's a waste worth avoiding.

Once you have decided, if you haven't already, that you like woodworking enough to want to invest more time and money in your tools, examine the tool list at the end of this book. It describes the kind of tools you are *likely* to need on most woodworking projects. The list has been carefully drawn, but your personal tastes and needs should guide your choices. This list also tells you the location of information on using those tools in this book.

MAINTAINING YOUR TOOLS

Throughout this book you will find suggestions for keeping your tools in good shape. An entire chapter is devoted to sharpening those tools that require it. Maintaining your tools will make them perform more efficiently and safely, and will help you produce better projects.

Clean your tools after use.

Make a proper place for them, either in a tote box or a workbench, both of which can be made from plans in this book.

Make it a habit to return a tool to its place after use. Not only will the tool be there when you need it, there will be less chance of its being damaged accidentally.

Consider your tools extensions of your hands. Properly taken care of, they should give you a lifetime of service.

1

Measuring & Marking

The accuracy of any measuring device depends on the user as much as on the design of the tool. Many of us who work with wood get a little lax because the tolerances are a bit larger than, say, those in a machine shop. Actually, you should strive to be as accurate as possible. Overage or shortage of 1/32 or 1/16 inch on a shelf may not be critical, but it can cause a lot of problems when you are making a joint.

Marking the dimension point or line is as important as placing and reading the rule properly. A common practice is to place the rule flat and then make a heavy, short line to mark the dimension. A better way is to hold the rule on edge and slide the point of the marker down the graduation line so all you get on the work is a small dot. This is easy to do with any rule with incised lines since you have grooves for the point of the marker to slide in. When the grooves are not present, mark with the dot system anyway.

Cut lines may be marked with a hard pencil, but you'll get a finer line if you scribe with a knife. Another advantage lies in letting the knife sever the surface fibers. This helps you produce a smoother line when you get to the sawing. If the knife-line is difficult to see, you can mark over it with a sharp pencil.

Place the square handle against the work edge and slide it until the blade is exactly on the dimension point. Use a sharp pencil or a knife to mark the cut line.

FLEX TAPES

These are the rules made of flexible-steel bands that coil back into a small case. They are probably today's most popular measuring tool because they are available in many sizes and for different applications. Blade widths run from 1/4 up to 1 inch; lengths go up to 100 feet. Common graduations are in inches marked off in 16ths and 8ths, but they are also available in metric or in metric/English so you can make conversions on the job.

Special tapes include those marked in 10ths and 100ths, mason's versions with modular graduations for building block and brick, and even one that tells loggers how many board feet can be cut from a log.

A good tape will retract automatically and smoothly. If it has a lock to hold the tape at any extended position, so much the better. The blade is usually coved, or curved across its width, which gives it stiffness when extended. Wide tapes are bulkier, but, when coved correctly, will span greater distances. This may not be critical for shop work, but can be a boon for on-location jobs. Any tape under 8-feet long is inadequate in a wood shop. You should be able to measure the long dimension on a standard 4- x 8-foot plywood panel. Needless to say, any tape should be clearly readable, with fine, distinct graduation lines.

FLEX TAPES retract automatically, and some can be locked in any extended position. They come in many lengths. This one is a 12-foot tape with a 3/4-inch blade.

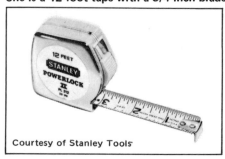

Courtesy of Stanley Tools

Tips can swivel or move to-and-fro, and either type will let you do inside or outside measuring. There are pro and con arguments for each design, but the accuracy of the assembly is most important. The swivel type requires you to move the tip aside when you do a butt measurement—the other automatically recesses into the blade and minimizes the possibility of human error. Be sure the recessing tip is always clean. Sawdust and dirt can jam it and cause errors.

When you read the scale, and this holds true for *any* measuring tool, look directly down on the graduation line. Your line of sight should be at right angles to the point regardless of the work situation. Any other viewpoint can distort the reading and cause inaccuracies. It is like reading a speedometer from the left or right instead of head-on.

An advantage of a flex tape is that you can use it for non-straight measuring. For example, you can wrap it around a circular object and read off the circumference.

FOLDING RULE

These are most often called *zigzag* rules because of the action they follow when opening or closing. Most of them have a maximum length of 6 feet and are 8-inches long in folded position. Many woodworkers, especially carpenters, carry one in addition to a flex tape and use it for most short measurements. An advantage is that you can set the first few blades at right angles to the rest of the tool and reach overhead for a horizontal measurement that might otherwise require standing on a stool or ladder. Metal joints lock the rule in folded or extended positions. When extended, it is rigid enough to span openings.

When you buy, look for a folding rule with a sliding brass extension built into the first blade. This is calibrated and used when taking inside measurements. The reading on the extension is added to the amount of rule that is unfolded. This is useful when measuring the opening of a door or window, the width of an opening for a drawer, and so on.

Like flex tapes, special folding rules are available for engineers, masons and others, and in metric or metric/English versions. Many modern rules have permanently lubricated joints. If yours does not, place a very small drop of light oil in the joints occasionally.

Be sure the tape you buy is replaceable. This model has a drop-in cartridge with a new blade and spring.

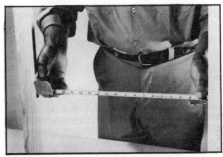

Flex tapes can be used for inside measurements, but you must add the width of the case to the reading on the tape.

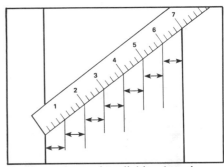

A rule can be used to divide a board into any number of equal spaces simply by setting it at an angle across the piece. Here the board is being divided into 7 equal spaces.

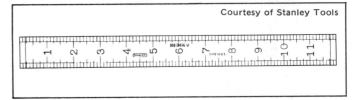

Courtesy of Stanley Tools

BENCH RULES are made of hardwood and have graduations in 16ths of an inch. Select one that is easy to read and has markings that reverse on the opposite side. The 1 is on the right end on the reverse side of the rule shown here.

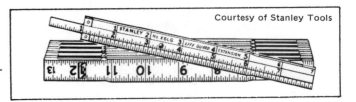

Courtesy of Stanley Tools

FOLDING RULES sometimes have extension slides for inside measurements. The reading on the extension is added to the length of the opened rule.

SQUARES

Squares are good for layout and for checking cuts as well as for measuring and marking. One basic use is as a guide for marking a line at right angles to an edge. Another is checking that line after you have cut it with a saw. In the latter capacity, the blade of the square is placed on the surface of the cut with the handle against an adjacent edge. Both the tool and the work are held so you can sight for openings between the blade and the wood. Hold the pieces so you get backlighting which makes errors more evident.

Try Square—For a long time this was *the* tool to use and the fact that it is still listed in catalogs indicates its continued acceptance. Such tools have a metal blade and a metal or hardwood handle fixed at a right angle. It is pretty much a single-purpose tool unless the blade end of the handle is provided with a 45-degree angle. In that case it's called a *miter square* and has the added feature of being able to indicate 45-degree angles.

Blade lengths run from 6 to 12 inches with handles of 4 to 8 inches. Size selection should be based on intended use. A blade of 8 or 10 inches would be minimum for average use in a wood shop.

Combination Square—This is more widely accepted today for general shop use simply because it is more versatile than a try square. The 12-inch-long blades have handles—or heads—slightly longer than 4 inches. Heads are adjustable longitudinally along the blade and may be locked at any position. This makes the tool usable as a guide for drawing a line parallel to an edge and as a depth gauge. Use it as a depth gauge by placing the end of the blade on the bottom of a cavity and then slide the head down to the surface of the stock. The distance from the head to the end of the blade is the depth of the cavity.

The head is shaped so it may be used to mark or check 90- or 45-degree angles. Because it has built-in glasses or vials, the tool may be used as a level and as a plumb gauge. To top it off, the tool may have a short scriber in the handle. Check though, because some models don't include the scriber.

Incidentally, because the head is removable, you can use the blade alone as a bench rule.

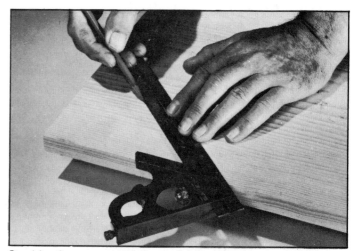

Combination squares can be used to mark lines at a 45-degree angle or to check 45-degree cuts.

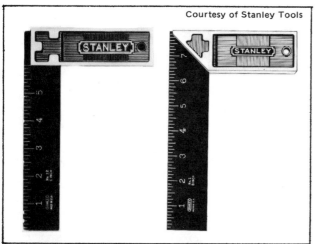

TRY SQUARE blades range from 6 to 12 inches with handles ranging from 4 to 8 inches. MITER SQUARE handles have a built-in 45-degree angle.

Combination squares can be used as edge marking gauges by moving the marker and the square together. Keep the head snug against the edge of the stock.

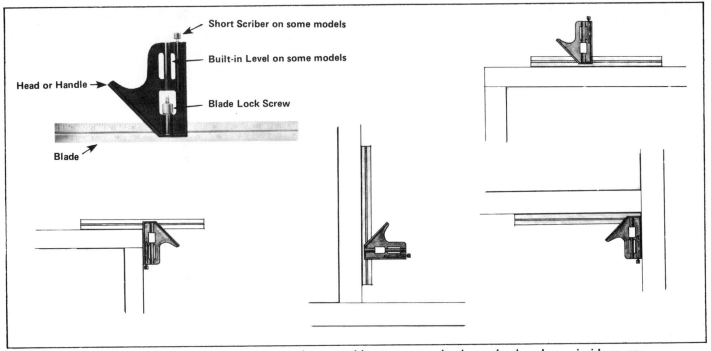

Short Scriber on some models

Built-in Level on some models

Head or Handle ▶

Blade Lock Screw

Blade ↗

COMBINATION SQUARES can be used in many ways: As an outside square; as a plumb; as a level; and as an inside square.

All-In-One Square—This tool is a more elaborate version of the combination square. Its head slides along a steel rule so it can be used to mark lines at right angles to an edge or as a depth gauge. It also has a built-in scriber and vials for testing horizontal levels.

The steel rule has two edges joined in several places with thin connecting strips. This leaves most of the central area open so you can accurately draw several parallel lines without resetting the head. Place the head against an edge with the rule laid across the work. Hold your pencil or scriber in the center of the rule at the desired point and move the square. Repeat this at different points to produce as many parallel lines as you wish.

The steel rule can also be used separately as a ruler and to make arcs. Set the scriber at one end of the rule for a center. Set a pencil through the rule at the desired radius. The rule pivots around the scriber and the pencil traces an arc.

Holes of various diameters are cut into one edge of the head. They can be used either for measuring or laying out holes. There are also gauges in the head for measuring the diameter of nails and screws, and angles listed along the curved edge for use as a protractor.

ALL-IN-ONE SQUARES   Courtesy of Stanley Tools

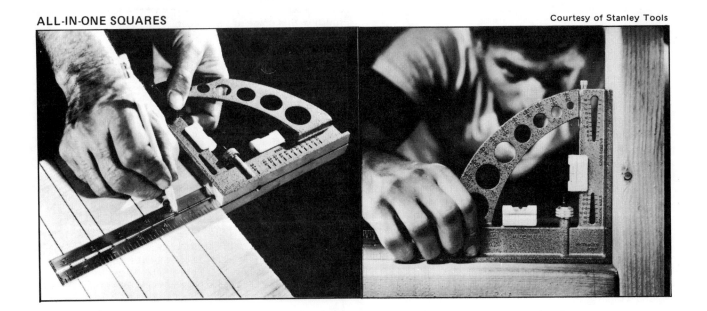

HOW TO DIMENSION AND SQUARE OFF A BOARD

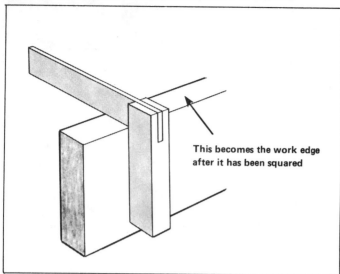

This becomes the work edge after it has been squared

1/Select best edge of the stock and check it for squareness. Make light shaving cuts with a plane to true it if necessary. Check along the full length of the board with the square.

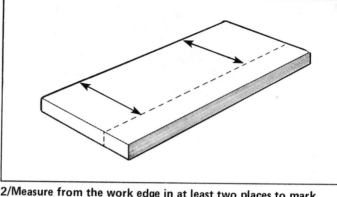

2/Measure from the work edge in at least two places to mark off the width required. Mark across the dimension points with a straight edge. Another procedure is to use an adjustable square as an edge-marking gauge. Carry the cut line over the edge of the stock. In both cases, stay a bit outside the line so the sawed edge can be planed smooth.

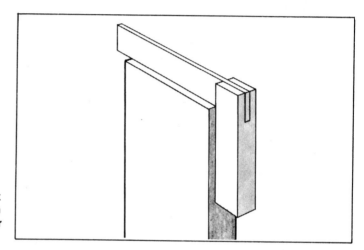

3/Set the handle of a square against the work edge and check one end of the stock for squareness. Minor imperfections can be removed by working with a block plane or with sandpaper wrapped around a block of wood.

4/If the end of the stock is beyond saving, place the head of a square against the work edge and mark a new line. Make the cut with a crosscut saw. Work carefully so the cut may be smoothed by working with sandpaper only. Check the end with a square across the width of the stock and across its thickness.

5/Mark the length required from the new edge and mark a cut line while holding a square against the work edge. Cut and finish with a plane or sandpaper.

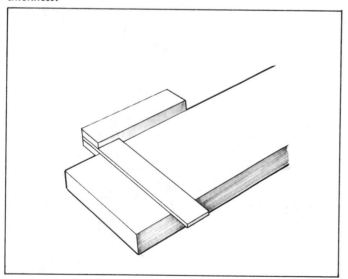

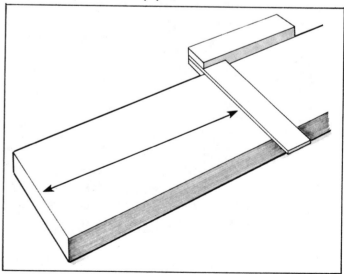

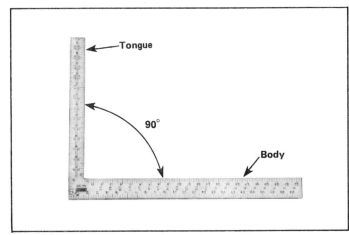

Steel Square—This term has come to cover quite an assortment of tools. There are *flat squares, carpenter's squares, rafter squares* and *mini squares,* among others, and a relative new-comer called a *homeowner's square.* Don't be puzzled if the latter is made of aluminum; it still fits in this group.

Carpenter's squares and, especially, rafter squares are most useful for house construction work. In the hands of someone who knows how to use it, the square becomes a calculator. Its potential is so great, it has been the subject of some good-size how-to-use booklets.

Our interest in the steel square is in its size. The steel square has two long legs. The shorter is called the *tongue* and the longer is called the *body.* It is a fine tool for layout work in the shop. Applications include checking broad surfaces for flatness, testing large inside and outside corners for squareness and being sure of right-angle corners when gluing up frames.

The homeowner's square does for the general woodworker what the other squares do for the house builder. In addition to edge graduations, it

STEEL SQUARES are right angles of metal. The most common size has a 24-inch body and 16-inch tongue. Its large size lets you work accurately with large stock.

is stamped with such information as a metric-conversion table, decimal equivalent table, 30-, 45- and 60-degree angle markings, wood-screw gauges and drill sizes, nail sizes, and other pertinent facts.

A steel square can be used for laying out angles by following the illustration and table below. The pivot point for measuring these angles is the 12-inch mark on the tongue of the square.

ANGLE	TONGUE	BLADE
30°	12″	20-7/8″
45°	12″	12″
60°	12″	6-15/16″
70°	12″	4-3/8″
72°	12″	3-7/8″
75°	12″	3-7/32″
80°	12″	2-1/8″
81°	12″	1-29/32″

MARKING GAUGE

The marking gauge is one of the more accurate tools for marking lines parallel to an edge. The required distance is set by measuring from the point of the marking pin to the face plate, or by taking a reading directly from the scale on the beam. Loosen the lock screw just enough to permit the head to slide. Recheck the setting after securing the head. It's never necessary to really bear down on the lock screw. Doing so can strip the threads which are cut directly in the wood.

Handle the tool with a gentle touch—its only purpose is to mark a guide line. In some situations it's wise to hold the head in your palm with your thumb extended to back up the pin. This doesn't always work because there is a limit to how far you can stretch your thumb. Don't allow the pin to project any more than it must to mark the work. Set it so the flat points away from the head and is parallel to the line you are marking. Be especially careful with pin projection when you are marking cross-grain to avoid tearing surface fibers.

Be sure to keep the head snug against the work throughout the pass. You may find it more convenient to push the tool rather than pull it. The work you are marking and the grain of the wood may have a bearing on this. Make your own judgment—the important thing is to be accurate.

Work gently with the gauge riding on one of the flat faces of the beam. The point projects just enough to mark the work. A piece of lead can be used in place of the metal point.

Marking gauges are excellent for repeating dimension lines as with these cut lines for a tenon.

MARKING GAUGES are used for measuring and marking lines parallel to an edge.

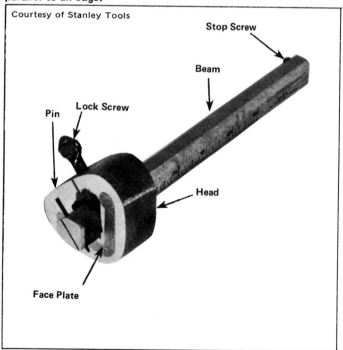

Courtesy of Stanley Tools

Stop Screw

Beam

Lock Screw

Pin

Head

Face Plate

Your fingers can serve as a marking gauge when drawing lines parallel to an edge. Use one finger to ride the edge of the stock and mark by pulling the pencil.

DIVIDERS AND TRAMMELS

Dividers is the name metal workers use for what most of us call a *compass*. If there is a distinction, it's this—dividers have two metal points—a compass has a metal pivot point and uses a pencil or a piece of lead for marking. Some versions can be used either way. No matter what you call them, their basic function is to mark perfect arcs and circles.

They may also be used to step off measurements, to divide distances into equal spaces along a straight or a curved line, and to mark lines to match an irregular surface.

Dividers may be set in one of two ways. One is to mark two dimension points on a piece of wood to equal the radius of the circle you wish to mark. Then set the points of the dividers on the marks. Or you can adjust the tool directly by placing both points on the correct graduation lines of a rule. When you do the latter, don't work from an end of the rule. Instead, place one point on the 1-inch mark and the other where you want it PLUS 1-inch. This is usually more accurate because the ends of rules are sometimes damaged due to use.

There is a limit to how far you can open dividers —that is, the radius you can set—and that is where *trammels* come in. They do dividers' jobs, but are separate points you can mount on a wooden bar of any length. Thus, trammels have unlimited capacity. Some are made with two metal points, others provide for the use of a pencil as a marker.

Actually, trammels are not used every day, so I have included drawings to show how you can improvise for your occasional need.

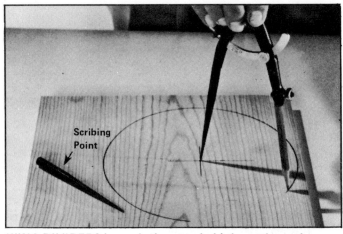

WING DIVIDERS have a lock nut to hold the setting and an adjustment screw for more precise settings. Either a scribing point or a pencil can be used for marking.

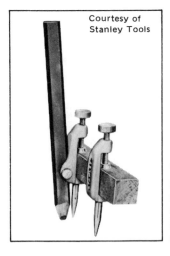

Courtesy of Stanley Tools

TRAMMEL POINTS mounted on a stick are used for making circles too large for dividers. Pencil can be used if desired.

DIVIDERS can be used to mark off any number of equal spaces, as when laying out dowel holes.

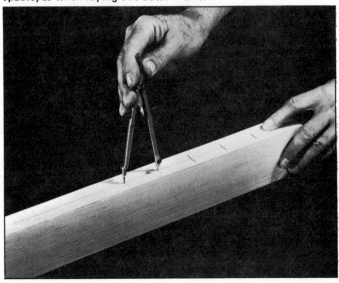

TRAMMELS YOU CAN MAKE: Fixed trammels can be made by driving two nails through a strip of wood. A variable type shown at bottom has a fixed pivot nail and an adjustable scriber nail held by a small C-clamp in a saw-cut groove.

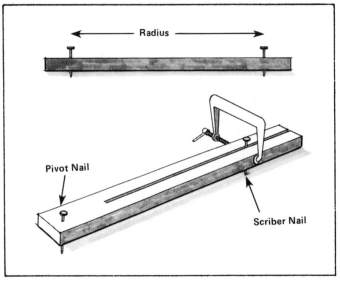

Radius

Pivot Nail

Scriber Nail

LEVELS

You may not require a level often when you are building a piece of furniture, but if the project is a built-in, for example, the level becomes an important tool. In essence, the tool tells the true vertical and horizontal planes of components regardless of angular relationships with mating pieces or attachment surfaces. A couple of examples will point up the concept. Walls, floors and ceilings are seldom square to each other. If you are building-in a bookcase, a level is a better judge of horizontal and vertical surfaces than a square. If you are building an outdoor bench around a tree, a level is about the only tool you can use to establish the plane of the seat.

There are many different types of levels, but the one probably most useful to a woodworker is the homeowner's variety, usually about 24-inches long and made of aluminum. Many of the latest models have built-in magnetic strips on one side that hold to steel surfaces so you can work hands-free. This is not impressive on wood projects, but the tool can be used for other chores around the house such as leveling washing machines and refrigerators.

A level works because it contains vials that hold a liquid and a trapped air bubble. The vials have two marks so you know the reading is correct when the bubble sits exactly between them. Always view the bubble perpendicularly. A lateral viewpoint will cause inaccuracies.

MISCELLANEOUS TOOLS

T-Bevel—Used for marking and checking angles, it has an adjustable blade which can be locked at any angle. The angle can be set by using a protractor or a steel square as a guide. This tool is particularly useful for marking repeating angles such as dovetails. The blade of the T-bevel is protected inside its handle when not in use.

Angle Divider—Used for bisecting angles to determine miter cuts, it can be adjusted to fit any angle from 45- to 90-degrees. Once the angle has been measured, the miter cut required for repeating that angle can be made by holding the body of the divider against the edge of the work and marking along the edge of the blade.

Caliper Rule—This tool is designed for making inside and outside measurements and comes in several sizes. It is also useful for measuring diameters of pipe, dowels and other round stock.

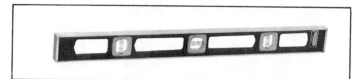

A 24-inch HOMEOWNER'S LEVEL is useful for any job requiring true vertical or horizontal planes.

A TORPEDO LEVEL is handy for on-location jobs. They are usually 6 to 8-inches long.

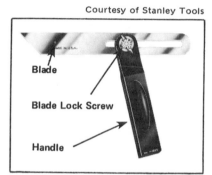

Courtesy of Stanley Tools

Blade

Blade Lock Screw

Handle

T-BEVEL used for marking angles.

ANGLE DIVIDER for bisecting angles. The handle is graduated for marking angles for 4, 5, 6, 8 or 10-sided figures.

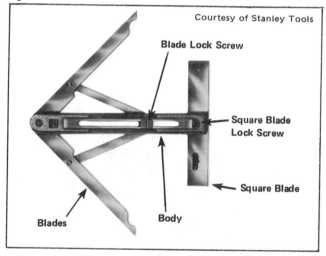

Courtesy of Stanley Tools

Blade Lock Screw

Square Blade Lock Screw

Square Blade

Blades

Body

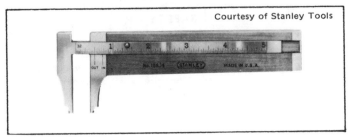

CALIPER RULES are marked for reading either inside or outside measurements directly.

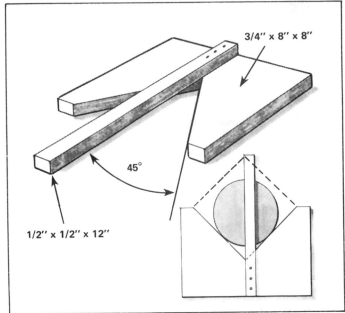

A CENTER FINDER for round stock can be made by cutting a right angle out of a board and tacking a strip so the edge of the strip bisects the V. The work is placed in the V and marked along the edge of the strip that bisects the angle. Then the work is turned 90 degrees and marked again. The center is where these two marks intersect. The same tool can be used to mark diagonals on square stock.

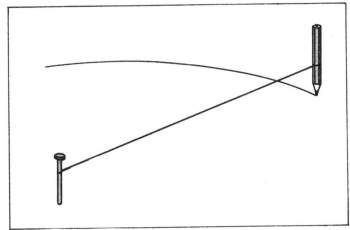

Very large circles or arcs can be made using a string and pencil. Be sure the string is taut as you swing the pencil.

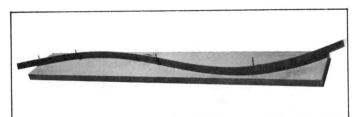

Use a slim strip of wood as a guide to mark irregular curves. Drive the nails lightly to hold the strip in place.

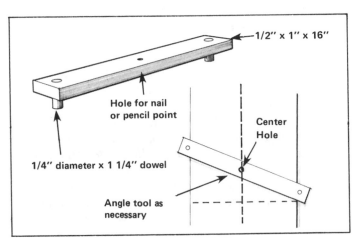

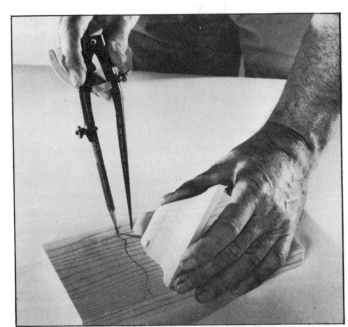

DIVIDERS or a COMPASS can be used to duplicate an *irregular* line. Keep the tool almost perpendicular and make sure both points are moving evenly.

A CENTER FINDER for working across stock can be easily made. Use it as shown for locating centers.

2

Saws

SAFETY TIP

- Blades should be sharp; dull blades slip, stick or skip and cause injuries.

It seems likely that the very first saw was a thin, flat stone with an edge rough enough to abrade through a bone, or a piece of tough meat, or a small branch. The next step was to search for a more suitably shaped stone or, as the innovative member of the group probably did, to chip away at the edge of the original stone to thin it. That brainy person could have been responsible for the first manufactured serrated cutting edge.

Guesswork stops with the introduction of real archeological evidence of saw-forms roughly shaped from flint. Such items have been found among the remains of Neanderthal man and he goes back about 130,000 years. Such finds are not isolated, but cover areas in France, Denmark, Sweden, Switzerland, Northern Italy, and other places.

If the history of the saw were to be well researched, it would show a slow but steady evolution with contributions to its development by the peoples of many nations. An interesting fact that would emerge is how little the basic concept has changed. We may eventually cut wood with laser beams or the like, but as of now, we still use a thin piece of material with a serrated edge.

The modern, efficient saw—and this applies to many other tools as well—did not appear until the advent of the Iron Age. The steps from this to steel, plus the sophisticated technology for handling materials, have resulted in the super products we enjoy today.

IN GENERAL

A saw *cuts* because it has teeth—it cuts more *freely* because the teeth are *set*. This merely means alternate teeth are bent in opposite directions away from the body of the blade. The idea is for the *kerf*—the actual opening made in the wood when you saw—to be wider than the thickness, or gauge of the blade. Sawing is possible without set, but it would be more difficult to stroke the tool because the blade would be rubbing constantly against the sides of the kerf.

The relief provided by the set is increased when the blade is taper-ground. This is evident on a good-quality saw where the blade is thinner at the back edge than at the toothed edge. In essence, this shape puts less blade thickness in the kerf. Top-quality saws have a secondary taper which is wider at the handle-end than at the toe. Taper grinding makes it possible to minimize set and this results in a tool that produces smoother cuts. It also contributes to the proper distribution of thickness and this helps to achieve good balance and flexibility.

POINTS

Whether a saw will cut "coarse" or "fine" is told by the number of points per inch—PPI. The more points, the more teeth per inch. Actually, if you deduct one from the PPI, you will know the number of teeth per inch. What's important to user is this—the more PPI, the smaller the teeth will be. This means *slower* cutting and *smoother* results. Thus finesse tools like the backsaw and the dovetail saw have a lot more PPI than the conventional crosscut saw or ripsaw.

The PPI—and the shape of the teeth—are also affected by the job the tool must do. Crosscut teeth are designed to slick *across* the grain of the wood like so many small, sharp knives. The teeth are bevel-filed and the cutting edges slant at a sharp angle so a shearing action—as opposed to a chiseling action—results.

Ripsaw teeth are filed straight across with cutting edges almost perpendicular to the blade. This is good for cutting *with* the grain of the wood because each tooth acts like a tiny chisel, chipping out its own bit of wood.

Another relevant factor is the less the PPI, the larger each tooth can be. Thus, there are deeper gullets between teeth which provide more room for larger waste chips. This helps to prevent clogging when the tooth takes a big bite, as when you are cutting green or wet wood. You have more choice of PPI in crosscut saws than you do with ripsaws.

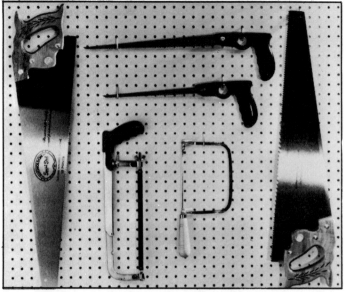

Saws, like all tools, should have enough storage space to guard against damaging cutting edges. Perforated hardboard and standard hangers provide an easy method.

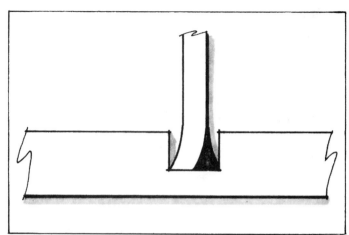

The saw "kerf" equals the gauge of the blade plus the amount of set on the teeth.

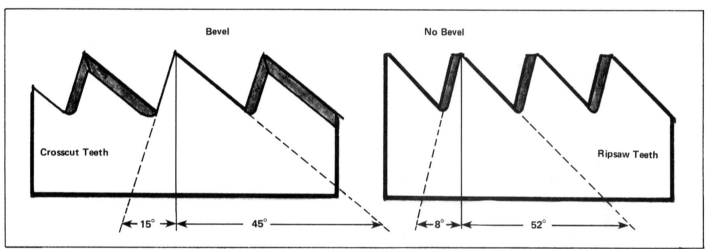

Bevel

No Bevel

Crosscut Teeth

Ripsaw Teeth

15°   45°

8°   52°

CROSSCUT SAWS are beveled to sever wood fibers when cutting *across* the grain. RIPSAW teeth act like small chisels for cutting *with* the grain.

Because of the way the teeth on the saws are designed, the bottom of a kerf formed by a crosscut saw looks like the illustration on the left. A kerf formed with a ripsaw looks like the illustration on the right.

The size of saw teeth depends on the number of Points Per Inch, PPI. This number is often stamped on the heel of the blade. The number of Teeth Per Inch is always one less than PPI. Measurements always begin with a point which is included in the count.

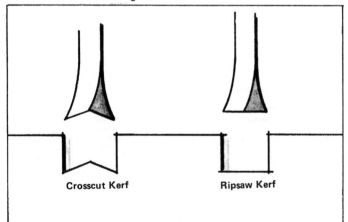

Crosscut Kerf   Ripsaw Kerf

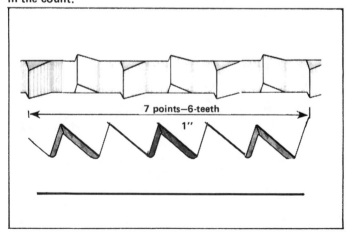

7 points—6-teeth

1"

CROWNED SAWS

You won't find this on all saws, but many experts look for it as an indication of careful designing and super quality. A crowned saw is one where the silhouette of the toothed edge shows a gentle arc rather than a straight line from the *heel* to the *toe*. The reason for the shape is to obtain maximum cutting effect with minimum drag. The arc brings fewer teeth into contact with the wood fibers. While you don't have as many teeth in full contact, those that are cut deeper, faster and easier.

My personal observation, regardless of whether a crowned saw helps you cut faster, is that it contributes a degree of naturalness to the stroke. This reduces fatigue and brings you closer to expertise. In this sense it even contributes to the life of the tool or, at least, to the prolonged sharpness of the cutting edges. Good, clean stroking promotes proper use.

This personal reaction to a product is something you will have to contend with regardless of the tool in question. Quite often, and assuming similar, basic characteristics among an assortment of like tools, the one that looks good, feels good, and mates nicely with your hands as you work is the tool you will swear by.

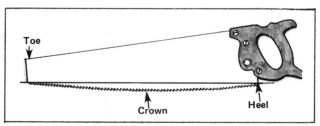

A slight "crown" usually designates good quality. It doesn't have to be much, 1/8 inch at the center of 26 inches is okay.

BUILT-IN TENSION

A necessary degree of flexibility and balance becomes part of a saw when the center portion of the blade is correctly manufactured. Most tools have this, but if not, the saw may cut poorly and will have a tendency to jam or bind when it is being used.

This is how you can check for good, built-in tension before you buy a saw. Brace the toe of the saw against a counter or some convenient stop and bend the blade by pulling the handle upward. Place a straight edge across the blade and sight to see if the blade forms a slight bow across its width. If the bow is there and its arc is uniform from center to outer edges, you can be pretty certain that the saw has proper tension. Poor tension is indicated by an uneven or a lopsided gap. This tension

feature is important because it has spring-back effect that helps to keep the blade straight as you are using it. You will appreciate any help you can get from features built into a saw when the moment of truth—sawing wood—arrives.

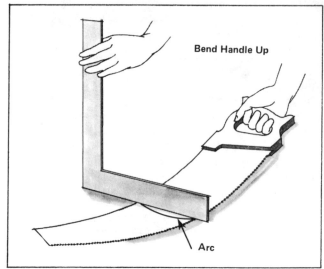

To test for good, built-in tension, the arc of the bow should be an even curve.

HANDLES AND FITTINGS

A saw handle should be easy to grip but still permit a solid union between your hand and the tool. This can play an important role in the way you use the saw and thus in the quality of the cut and how quickly you tire. It doesn't matter if the handle is made of wood, aluminum or plastic—so long as it is not dime-store stuff. It must be contoured to fit the hand and large enough for a four-finger grip without cramping. It should be angled to the blade so correct rhythmic stroke action of both hand and arm will be automatic. This is not something you can see easily, but it is something you can feel when you lift the saw.

What you *can* see is whether the blade is centered in the handle. Just hold the tool with the bottom of the handle "up" and sight along the blade.

The handles on good saws are attached with bolts and tubular nuts. If you broke down the parts you would see the shank of the nut extends more than halfway through the handle and fits precisely into holes punched in the blade. This kind of assembly makes for a fit that is, and stays, tight.

If you discover the handle is secured with wood screws, don't buy the saw.

THE FINISH

Sawing creates friction regardless of the relief created by tooth-set and taper-grinding. Anything done to reduce the friction by the manufacturer, or by you during use, will make the work easier. A properly polished saw blade helps materially and makes the tool more resistant to rust.

Here is an area where you can definitely make a judgement by sight and feel. You can *see* a good polishing job—you can *feel* it with your finger tips. You can maintain it or improve it by keeping the blade coated with a good grade of paste wax rubbed to a high gloss.

Special finishes are available. These can run from a veneer of baked-on plastic to a super blade material such as stainless steel. Most manufacturers are now offering their top-quality saw in either a conventional finish or with a Teflon-S™ coating. The latter treatment brings the price of the saw up a bit, but I think it's worth it. The coating practically eliminates any kind of maintenance attention and contributes considerably to smooth stroking.

THE OVERALL VIEW

Check the field and you will find the price of a saw—like other tools—generally goes up with quality. A big *but* though: the difference between poor and good or good and super is seldom more than a couple of dollars. It's okay to save money by buying a good saw on sale, but the way bargain-counter saws are displayed—thrown into a bin haphazardly along with inferior hammers and screwdrivers and cheap gadgets—should turn anyone off.

A good saw—or a collection of good saws, should the scope of your work require them—is a one-time investment. What I have talked about should help you be a wise judge. Look for a straight blade with teeth set uniformly and sharp to the touch. Check for a centered handle, a comfortable grip and balance that feels right to you. Look for taper-grinding—if you can't see it, ask about it—and an impressive finish. Check several examples even if they are from the same manufacturer. Production variations can create a big difference between similar saws.

SAW MAINTENANCE

A good saw will last as long as you do if you use it correctly, maintain the original finish, and store it safely. I have found from experience that a frequent polishing with a hard paste wax is all the attention the blade needs. If you store the saw for any period of time, be sure to coat the teeth as well as the blade. The wax forms a barrier against rust and reduces drag when you are stroking.

The saw must be sharp—always! A dull saw

BASIC FACTS ABOUT HANDSAWS

Saw size is determined by the length of the blade in inches. 24 and 26 inch are the most popular sizes.

Whether a blade is "fine" or "coarse" depends on the number of points per inch—PPI.

Use a "coarse" saw when you wish to cut fast or when you are working with green wood.

Use a "fine" saw when you need smooth cuts or accurate cuts in dry and seasoned wood.

Most popular ripsaws have 5-1/2 or 6 PPI.

Most popular crosscut saws have 7 or 8 PPI.

Saw teeth are "set" so the kerf will be wider than the gauge of the blade. This prevents the blade from binding in the wood.

A feature that also helps to prevent binding is called *taper-ground.* In such a design, the blade is thinner at the back than at the toothed edge.

Saw blades must be sharp to function correctly. Sharp blades require less effort to use.

makes a poor cut, increases drag and buckling, and contributes considerably to fatigue. Saw sharpening is an art that I personally don't care to get involved in, even though I use hand saws and power saws quite a bit. I don't recommend it for the average craftsperson simply because it's too time consuming and it's too easy to get a quality job done for little money. However, if you want to try it, instructions are found in chapter 15.

CROSSCUT and RIP SAWS look very similar.

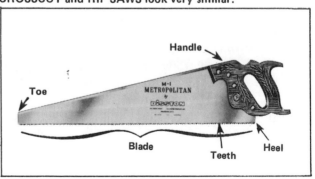

THE BASIC SAWS

Crosscut Saws—The crosscut saw—as the name says—is designed for cutting *across* the grain of the wood. Its teeth are shaped to cut like sharp-pointed knives so they sever wood fibers rather than tear them. If the experienced cabinetmaker or carpenter had to limit himself to one saw, he would probably choose the crosscut design because it comes closest to being all-purpose. It does the optimum job across the grain and when used at an angle to the grain as in miter cuts. It does a respectable job when used *with* the grain although it would lose a speed race if competing with a ripsaw. It is the best saw to use on plywoods because its smaller teeth do minimum damage to surface veneers. For similar reasons, it is a wise choice for cutting hardboards, particle boards and the like.

Average blade-lengths are 16, 20, 24 or 26 inches with PPI running from 7 to 12. The lower the PPI number, the faster the cut, but you pay for speed in cut-quality. More teeth make smoother cuts—a fact that applies generally to all saws.

Blade length also affects speed because you must take shorter strokes with shorter blades. Short saws are good convenience items for working in tight areas, storing in a small tool box, or holding in a tote box for on-location work. Although 24 and 26 inches are the most popular lengths, remember that saw quality has nothing to do with its size.

Incidentally, the length of a saw measures the distance from the toe to the heel along the cutting edge.

Ripsaws—Designed for cutting *with* the grain, ripsaw teeth are much different from those on a crosscut saw both in size and shape. Ripsaws are usually offered in a 26-inch length with a PPI of 5-1/2. Ripsaw teeth have square instead of pointed cutting edges. This creates the chiseling action which is best for cutting along the grain line. You can easily tell the difference between a ripsaw and a crosscut saw if you examine the waste. The crosscut saw spews out sawdust: the ripsaw produces small chips.

While the crosscut saw cuts on both the push and the pull strokes, the ripsaw cuts on the push stroke only. This induces a particular kind of use-action, but it comes naturally if you let the weight of the saw and the correct stroke supply most of the tooth-to-work contact. Generally, any special force you apply should be minimal. Excessive pressure forces the teeth to penetrate more deeply than they are supposed to. This will result in clogging and snagging of the teeth, and buckling in the blade. The truth is, the strength in your arm has nothing to do with the combination of cut-quality and sawing speed you should strive for. The pert, five-foot female can do as well as the husky, six-foot male.

The statement that crosscut saws and ripsaws are interchangeable is erroneous. It is true that a ripsaw will cut in any direction, but when you examine and compare results, you will agree its use should be limited to cutting *with* the grain of the wood.

Backsaws—Average backsaws are 12- or 14-inches long with a PPI of 11 or 13. Because stiffness is important here, blade gauge is uniform throughout and the blade is reinforced with a channeled spine running along the back edge. Use this saw when accuracy and smooth cuts are critical. This automatically places it in the joint-forming category.

Backsaws may be used freehand, but you should take advantage of the assist supplied when the saw is mated with an accurate miter box. The box may be purchased, but I'll show how you can make your own. This accessory is a U-shaped affair with pre-cut kerfs in the vertical members to guide the saw through precise, square cuts or left and right-hand 45-degree miters. While the average box is organized for the 45-degree cuts, there is no reason why you can't make a special one for other angles should the job you are doing call for multiple, similar cuts.

Miter-box Saws—Similar to backsaws, these come in lengths that start at about 22 inches and go up to 30 inches with a spine-to-tooth distance of as much as 6 inches. These are made specifically for use in very sophisticated miter boxes that include protractor adjustments so the saw can be set to cut accurately at any angle. Examples of this special tool are shown later on, but the point here is, miter-box saws can be purchased separately and used in the homemade miter box I just mentioned. One reason for this is the extra length of the saw—longer strokes permit faster cuts. A second reason is the greater blade width which supplies more cutting depth.

Dovetail Saws—This looks like a delicate backsaw. Its handle is in line with the spine and resembles those used with files. The typical dovetail saw has a 10-inch blade with 15 PPI. Blade width from the spine to the toothed edge averages about 1-5/8 inches.

The many small teeth, the thinness of the blade, and the overall lightness of the tool, indicate its precision. The name describes one basic function: To make the slanted shoulder cuts required for dovetail sockets and pins. The name should not prompt any limitation. It's the saw to use for many types of joint cuts whether you are doing dovetailing, tenoning, dadoing or rabbeting.

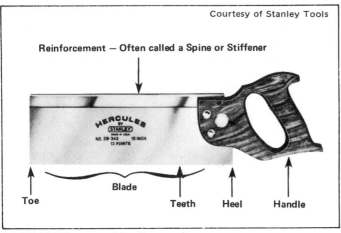

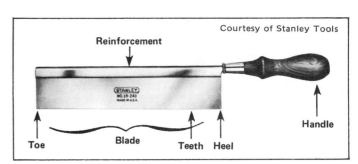

BACK SAWS are used for fine work.

DOVETAIL SAWS are used in making dovetails and for precision work.

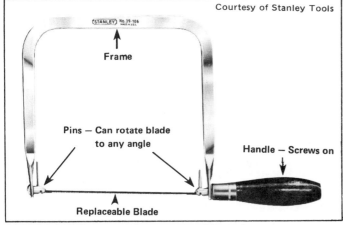

COPING SAWS are used for curves and irregular cuts.

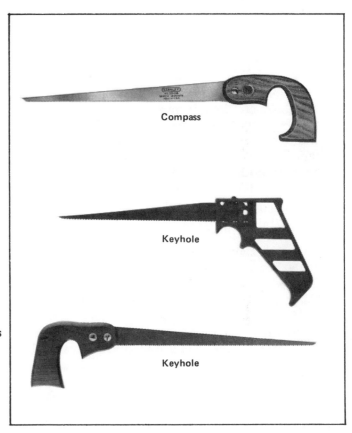

COMPASS and KEYHOLE SAWS look similar, but keyholes have a narrower blade.

HACKSAWS are made with two types of frames: CHANNEL-FRAME and TUBULAR FRAME. Both are adjustable.

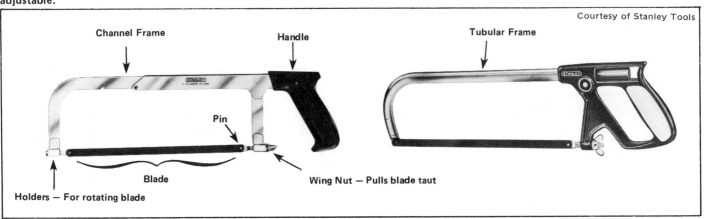

A dovetail saw is called a *hobby saw* because its size and fine kerf make it especially useful for sawing small or thin pieces. Many craftspeople use it to make straight cuts in veneers.

Although it wasn't designed for the backsaw-miter-box technique, there is no reason why the dovetail saw can't be used in similar fashion if the miter box is scaled to suit. This is an area to be explored by anyone who enjoys making models or miniature wood structures of any sort.

Coping Saws—Primarily used to follow uniform or irregular curved lines and to make internal cutouts without the need of a lead-in cut from an edge of the work. The latter technique—often called *piercing*—is possible because the blade is removable from the saw frame. Thus, it's possible to insert the blade through a pre-drilled hole in the work before it is secured in the frame.

Coping-saw blades are about 6-1/2 inches in length, with widths running from 1/16 to 1/8 inch and PPI from about 10 to 20. This gives you the opportunity to select a blade in relation to the work you are doing: finer blades for thin material and smoothest cuts; heavier blades for thick stock and faster going. Because coping-saw blades are rather inexpensive, they are considered disposable. No one bothers to sharpen them, assuming that they don't break before they become dull.

The coping saw permits the blade to be rotated in the frame so you can suit the blade direction to the line of cut. You can do intricate scroll work that would not be possible with a fixed-position blade. Some blades are spiral design.

Compass and Keyhole Saws—These saws have blades much narrower at the toe than at the handle end. Basically they are used to make curved or straight-shaped cutouts so they are popular with electricians, carpenters and plumbers who need to make openings for pipes, cables, electrical boxes, and the like. The average craftsperson will find similar uses for them even though he may never become involved in house building or remodeling. The big advantage of either type saw is that the pointed end of the blade lets you start a cut from a small, drilled hole. Thus, for example, you can make a circular cutout in the center of a full-size plywood panel.

The average compass saw is 12- or 14-inches long and has a PPI of 8 or 9. A typical keyhole saw is 10 or 12 inches with 10 PPI. The principal difference between the two is: The keyhole saw is smaller overall, has a narrower blade, and makes a smoother cut. Thus it is more suitable for intricate, close work.

Nests of Saws—The name describes a set of three interchangeable blades with a single handle. The average assortment includes a compass saw, a key-hole saw, and a similar, specially tempered blade for cutting soft metals, plastics, bone, and the like. Some kits or sets offer broader choices.

One set includes a 16-inch crosscut blade with 8 PPI, a 12-inch compass blade with 8 PPI, and a 10-inch keyhole blade with 10 PPI.

A second example offers a 14-inch compass-saw blade with 8 PPI, a 10-inch finishing blade with 10 PPI, and a 16-inch double-edge, combination blade with 8 PPI crosscut teeth on one edge and special teeth on the opposite edge so the blade may be used for light pruning jobs on shrubs and trees.

It's cheaper to buy a nest of saws than to purchase the same items individually. Check for quality as you would with any saw.

Hacksaws—Designed primarily as a metal-cutting tool, it pays to have one in the wood shop if only for that occasional bolt you wish to shorten or the piano hinge you must cut to length. Of course, the tool may also be used to cut bar stock, tubing or pipe, metal angle, and similar materials.

Like the coping saw, the hacksaw frame takes replaceable blades. Most adjust to take blades either 10- or 12-inches long and have blade holders which turn so you can set the blade position to suit the work. Blade tension is supplied by a wing nut, usually near the handle on the frame.

You'll find using the hacksaw efficiently depends greatly on the blade you choose for the job. All manufacturers offer blades made from different types of steel with different degrees of hardness. The blade type called *flexible,* which is hardened on the tooth edge only, is good to use in awkward cutting situations. A similar blade made of high-speed tungsten steel is described as having a flexible, but shatterproof back and is recommended for general heavy-duty cutting. A third type, of DiMol Molybdenum steel, is designated as *all-hard* and recommended as an economical choice for cutting a wide range of materials.

The point is, read the information on the package before you buy the blade to see if you will be well served. Then you can spend your money wisely.

USING SAWS

The most common error when using any saw is caused by the desire to get the job done quickly. This leads to erratic stroking and excessive pressure that serve only to clog the teeth and cause the blade to buckle. With some saws—for example, the hacksaw and the coping saw—too much speed leads to premature blade breakage. With *all* saws, working too fast leads to difficulty in following the true cut line.

There may be times when you might want to bear down some, but usually the saw's weight and a smooth stroke action gets the job done in efficient fashion with minimum effort. Your intent should be quality and accuracy, even if it requires a few extra seconds to accomplish it.

Be sure the work is supported solidly. If the wood being cut is not firm, you will encounter a chatter that interferes with good sawing. A pair of sawhorses is a must if you are cutting anything that can't be gripped in a vise, or clamped to a workbench, or secured in one of the holding devices I've illustrated in this book.

Don't make the sawhorses too high regardless of how tall you are—24 inches seems to be about right for general work, although an increase of 2 to 4 inches won't cause a crisis. The low height puts you above the work so you have a clear line of sight and maximum freedom to stroke smoothly. It also makes it possible to use a knee as a convenient holddown. Check chapter 13 for more information on sawhorses.

As I show here—and will show again later because it is important—the best cutting-edge-to-work angle when using a crosscut saw is 45 degrees. The angle should be 60 degrees when you are using a rip saw. In either case, the angle between the side of the blade and the work must be 90 degrees—if you intend to produce good, square edges.

Mark all cut lines by using a square or, when necessary, a long straight edge. It's okay to use an ordinary lead pencil as a marker but its hardness ought to be about 4H or 5H. Such a pencil will keep its point and produce clean, thin lines. You can use a sharp scriber, but this will snag surface fibers regardless of whether you are marking across or with the grain. A better marking tool to use when you want a super-thin, clean line, is a sharp knife, especially when you are laying out mating parts for precise joints.

Start cuts by using the knuckle of the thumb on your left hand as a guide for the saw. Make short, backward strokes near the heel of the saw until you have a slight kerf started. Then, gradually increase the stroke length until the full length of the blade is being used. This method is specifically for crosscutting. Some craftspeople suggest that the toe end of the blade be used with short, forward strokes only, to get a kerf started for ripping. No argument—if it works, fine. The important thing is to open a kerf so sawing can get going accurately, and with minimum damage to areas adjacent to the cut line.

Slow up the stroke speed and shorten the length of the stroke as you near the end of the cut. If you do this and support the cutoff with your free hand at the same time, you will avoid the splintering that results when the cutoff falls

Shake hands with the handle of the saw. Be firm but don't put a strain in your hand and wrist.

About 60 degrees between teeth and work is a good cutting angle to maintain when doing ripping. About 45 degrees is best for crosscuts. In either case, the angle between the side of the blade and the surface of the work should be 90 degrees.

Cutting Angle

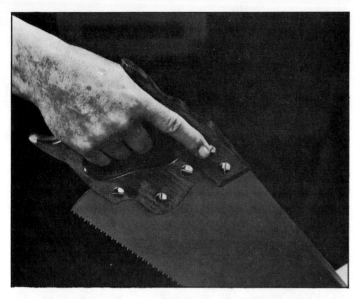

Extending the forefinger on the opposite side of the handle can help make more accurate cuts. You may find it helpful to start the cut this way and then shift to a full grip.

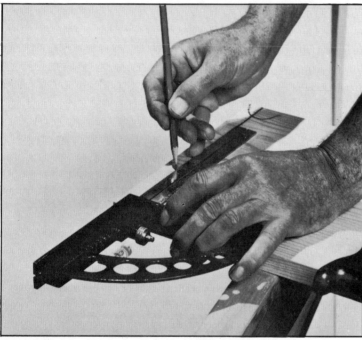

Marking the cut line is the first step before sawing.

When marking stock for either crosscutting or ripping, mark the cut line on both the surface and the edge of the material. This will provide a better guide for getting the cut started accurately. Use a sharp, hard pencil, a scriber, or a knife.

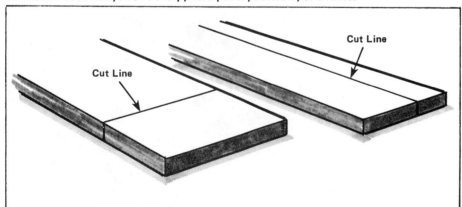

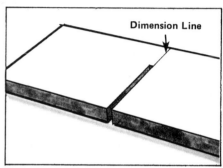

Keep the saw kerf parallel to and abutting the outside edge of the dimension line.

Start crosscutting as shown here. Note how the thumb is used as a guide for the blade. Begin with short draw strokes near the heel of the blade and lengthen your stroke only after you have made a good entry.

of its own weight. This applies to plywood, hard-boards, particle boards and the like—as well as lumber.

Use sawhorses to support the work as near the cut as possible. How you place the work depends on its size and the cut. Try to visualize what is going to happen when you reach the separation point. Quite often, especially when the cut is long or the work is large, you may find it necessary to make changes during the cut or when you near the end.

Check the stock carefully, especially if you are working with used lumber. Be sure there are no nails, pieces of hardware, or embedded pieces of dirt or rocks and the like in the line of cut.

CROSSCUTTING TIPS

Place the lumber so the annular rings on the end of the board arc downward rather than up. This minimizes the splintering that can occur at the edges of the wood. If you are right-handed, take a position that puts your line of sight parallel to and a fraction to the left of the blade. This gives you a clear view of the cut line and the cutting action of each stroke. Left-handers should cut from the opposite edge of the board—the line of sight being a bit to the *right* of the blade.

Place the blade so the cut line will be on the waste side of the dimension line. Use your thumb to guide the blade as shown on page 24. Draw the blade across the wood in a series of short strokes until the kerf is started. Then *gently* push the saw down to deepen the kerf. Too much pressure can cause the blade to buckle or skip. Lengthen your strokes as the kerf deepens, but do not force the saw. It is designed to cut at a certain speed.

Shorten the length of your stroke as you near the end of the cut. It is also wise to stop and make sure the waste is supported. This will prevent splitting the wood when you complete the cut. The guides shown in this chapter can help you crosscut more accurately.

RIPPING

Ripping is done to reduce stock to correct width. Small pieces may be held in a bench vise, but it is wise to work so the sawing is done near the grip area, even if it means repositioning the work as you go. This will minimize work chatter.

Long pieces may be supported on sawhorses, in which case you would take pretty much the same position described for crosscutting. Get the kerf started by using your left thumb as a guide. Use several draw strokes with the teeth near the toe-end of the blade. You want to get the cut

started accurately so don't pressure the saw. After you have made a good entry in the wood, you can gradually increase the length of the strokes until you are using the full length of the blade. Take easy strokes. Forcing the cut creates more chances for mistakes and will tire you more quickly.

Be sure you keep the kerf on the waste side of the guide line. If the edge you are sawing must be a finished one, cut the work a bit oversize so you can smooth the edge with a plane after sawing.

On most long cuts you'll find the kerf tends to close behind the blade. The least that can happen is you get excessive drag on the blade. The most that can happen is the kerf will close enough to grip the blade so stroking becomes impossible. In either case, the solution is to use a thin piece of wood or a wedge in the kerf to keep it open. In some situations you may have to reposition the wedge—keeping it close to the sawing area— as you work. Some workers use a screwdriver as the wedge. It works, but the metal blade can mar the edge of the stock.

It is terribly easy to go off the line when you are ripping, mostly because such cuts are usually rather long and you become impatient. So it is best—maybe even moreso here than when cross-cutting—to work with a guide. A long straight piece of wood held to the work with clamps is all you need. Be sure to put the guide on the "good" side of the line.

The 60-degree blade-to-work angle is a good, general rule. However, it's good practice to de-crease it when you are cutting thin stock. This is because the rip saw has less PPI than other saws and decreasing the angle on thin stock keeps more teeth in contact with the work.

HOW TO USE BACKSAWS

While crosscut and rip saws are used mostly for preliminary sizing cuts, the backsaw comes into play when you start to form the joints de-scribed in chapter 12, and especially for making the precise angular cut called a *miter* used for assembling picture frames and the like. The saw may be used freehand, but it becomes a more pre-cise tool when used in conjunction with a special miter box.

The miter-box design shown in the drawing on page 26 is fairly typical, except the 90-degree guide slots are placed at an end rather than between the 45-degree slots. The argument for centering all the slots is that you get maximum support for the work on each side of the cut. The argument against that design is closely spaced slots create weak areas in the vertical pieces. Both points are valid so the choice is up to you. More important is being careful when you make the box.

Guide strips are even more essential for ripping than for cross-cutting because rip cuts are usually long and there is more chance for human error.

The backsaw may be used freehand when the work is too large for a miter box. Here shoulder cuts are being made for dadoes to be finished with a chisel. Note the clamped-on wood guide that controls the cut depth.

Be sure the side pieces are not higher above the bottom of the box than the width of the blade on your backsaw when measured from the bottom edge of the spine. Note that one of the side pieces is wider than the other and extends about 2 inches below the bottom. This is so you can brace the box against the edge of the workbench or grip it in a vise.

Use a combination square to mark the 45- and 90-degree lines across the top edges of the verticals. Carry the lines down on both the inside and outside surfaces so you will have guides to follow when sawing the slots. Cut the slots with the same saw to be used with the box. When the project is finished, apply two coats of clear sealer with a light sanding between applications.

Mark the cut line on the workpiece and place it in the box, snug against the back. Be sure the cut line is positioned on the correct side of the slot you are going to use. Put the saw in place, hold the work firmly, start the kerf with a couple of back strokes with the handle end of the saw elevated a bit. Lengthen the strokes and bring the saw to full horizontal as you proceed with the cut. It does no harm to cut a bit into the bottom of the miter box, but if you find it objectionable, all you have to do is place a piece of thin scrap under the work.

Like all sawing tools, the backsaw doesn't have to be pressured to make the cut. Let the saw weight and smooth, long strokes do the job. Slow up the speed of the strokes—not the length—when you approach the end of the cut. This minimizes the splintering and feathering that can occur when you break through.

HOW TO MAKE A MITER BOX
Use well-seasoned hardwood. Width of box should suit the scope of work: minimum is about 4 inches. Assemble with glue and flat-head screws. Mark cut lines accurately on edges and vertical surfaces before you saw. The accuracy of the box depends on how well you make the guide marks.

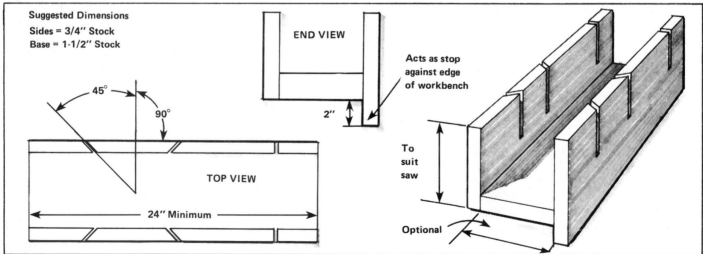

Suggested Dimensions
Sides = 3/4" Stock
Base = 1-1/2" Stock

END VIEW

2"

Acts as stop against edge of workbench

45°

90°

TOP VIEW

24" Minimum

To suit saw

Optional

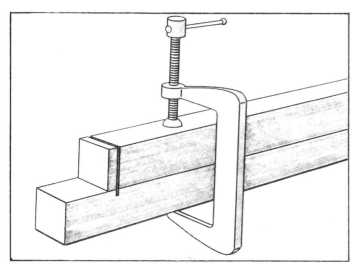

You'll do a better job of cutting off thin strips when you clamp a back-up block to the work. Cut through the work and the back-up at the same time.

On a long rip cut, the kerf can close and bind the blade. You can avoid this by using a slim piece of wood or a wedge to keep the kerf open.

Guides do not have to be designed as jigs. Here a straight piece of wood clamped to the work makes a 45-degree miter cut automatically. It requires a little more time to set up, but the results are worth it.

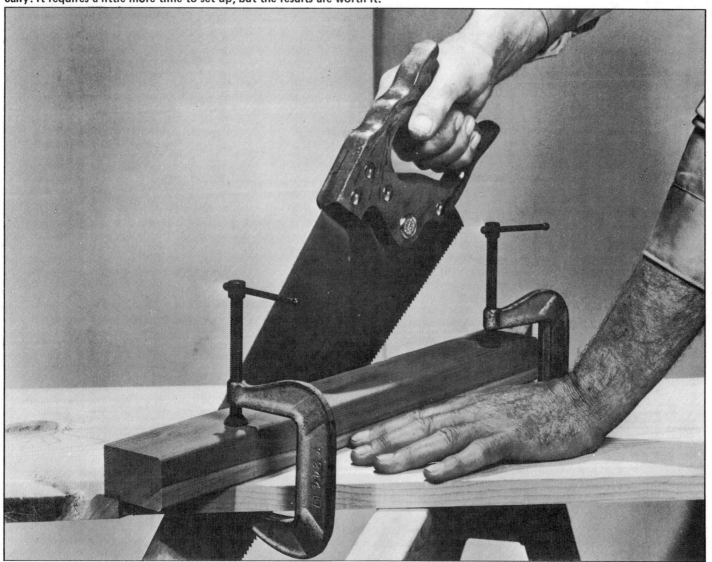

Clamp the miter box in a bench vise whenever possible. Hold the work firmly against the rear. Start the kerf with the handle of the saw slightly elevated. Bring the saw to horizontal as you lengthen your strokes.

To accomplish compound-angle cuts easily, use a strip of wood to brace the work at the slope you want—then make the cut as if you were making a simple 45-degree miter.

DOVETAIL SAW is used with a light touch whenever a minimum-width kerf seems advisable. Here it is used with a guide to make the first cuts required for dovetail work.

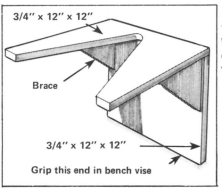

V-BLOCK HOLDER FOR COPING SAW WORK: The dimensions given are not critical, the holder may be sized to suit your own needs.

Use a COPING SAW for jobs like removing the bulk of the waste between initial dovetail saw cuts. This leaves little wood to be removed with chisels.

Work is placed on a special jig for use with a coping saw. Here is one time when it is wise to have the coping saw's teeth pointed toward the handle. Cutting on the down stroke makes this job more convenient. Pressure applied for cutting is in the direction the teeth are pointing.

These are typical jobs you can do with a COMPASS or KEY-HOLE SAW. Note where the saw is working. Corner radii have been formed by drilling holes. At least one hole is needed so the saw can start cutting.

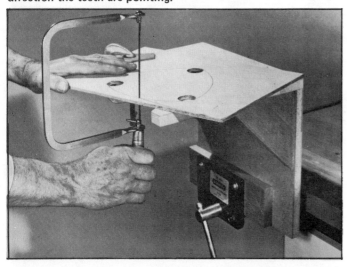

COPING SAW BLADES

Two shapes are available: flat or spiral.

May have "looped" or "pin" ends depending on the design of the coping saw.

Common lengths are 5 or 6-1/2 inches.

Blade widths range from 1/6 to 1/8 inch.

Number of teeth ranges from 10 to 20 per inch.

Blades are considered disposable since they are so cheap. No one bothers to sharpen them.

A good general rule is to choose the widest blade with the least teeth for heavier work. Choose the narrowest blade with the most teeth for thin stock, smoothest edges, and intricate cuts.

HOW TO USE DOVETAIL SAWS

Reach for this tool when you want the most precise joint lines and the finest kerfs. Usually the job of making the preliminary saw cuts for dovetails is done freehand, but more accuracy can be gained by using guides whenever possible. Thus the angle block. The idea seems to make special sense when the job requires many, similar cuts.

Actually, the dovetail saw is much like a lightweight version of the backsaw and is used in similar fashion—even, as I said before, in a miter box if you make one to suit the size of the saw.

HOW TO USE COPING SAWS

Coping saw blades are usually placed in the frame so the teeth point away from the handle. This means cutting occurs on the forward stroke. There is nothing wrong with working that way but the setup can be inconvenient and *should not be regarded as a hard-and-fast rule*. Because changing the cut direction simply requires turning the blade end-for-end, you can make the switch easily and quickly anytime the cut or your work position makes it advisable.

Although coping saw blades can be used for intricate cuts, there is a limit to the smallness of the radius they can turn. Don't force the blade around turns if you feel it binding. Some drag must occur because you are moving a flat blade around a curve, but when it is excessive, just accept that you are asking too much. Back off and make another approach. Twisting the blade just a fraction as you stroke tends to widen the kerf and this gives the blade more room to turn. Spiral blades are available which can cut in any direction, but they tend to be more expensive. Many times, it's a good idea to use pre-drilled holes to form the radii of very tight turns. If you are doing piercing, you need blade-insertion holes anyway.

Be sure you provide maximum support for the work as close to the cut area as possible. That's why the V-block holder is such a good idea—it is held securely in a vise, and the work is shifted about on the platform so cutting can proceed with minimum chatter. The work can be clamped in place when you have intricate cutting to do in a tight area. Working so also gives you a bird's-eye view of the cut area and helps you cut more accurately.

The position of the blade in the frame has to do with convenience in relation to the direction of the cut, and with eliminating interference should the cut be so deep the frame hits an edge of the workpiece. It isn't necessary to remove the blade to change its angle. Loosen the handle just enough to relax the frame tension, turn the blade, and retighten the handle. For internal cutouts, you must pass the blade through a pre-drilled hole before you secure it in the frame. When the design permits, drill the insertion hole so it forms a usable radius. Otherwise, it can be located anywhere in a waste area.

When the thickness of the stock permits, you can form duplicate pieces by using the pad-sawing technique. This is just a matter of making a sandwich of the pieces and then cutting as you would solid stock. There is a limit, of course, to how thick the pad can be, but you should not encounter any critical problems on thicknesses less than 3/4 inch. The hardness—or softness—of the material is a factor along with the size of the blade you use. A wise procedure is to make a test cut on waste stock before sawing the good material.

You can make pads by driving brads in waste areas, or by clamping the pieces together, or even by holding them with tape. Be sure that the pieces are held together firmly.

HOW TO USE KEYHOLE & COMPASS SAWS

These two tools come so close to being interchangeable that work techniques apply to either. Get the saw started in normal fashion when you are cutting in from an edge. That is, execute a few, short draw strokes to open the kerf—then gradually increase the stroke length. Bore a starting hole first when you must do an internal cutout. The size of the starting hole has a lot to do with how much of the saw you can use to get the cut going. It makes sense to bore as large a hole as possible. A 1/2- to 3/4-inch diameter seems adequate to get either saw started efficiently.

The saw blade tapers from handle to toe, so blade width in a given area has a bearing on how tight a turn you can make. If you are doing a straight cut or a very gentle curve, you can use full-length strokes. If the curve is tight, then you'll have to shorten the stroke and use only the blade's narrow part.

Cutting curves requires a lateral as well as a forward pressure. In essence, you are twisting the

An ANGLE or DRILL-PRESS VISE is a handy accessory for gripping metal parts you wish to cut with a hacksaw. Note how this one is bolted to a board that can be gripped in a bench vise.

blade to follow the line. This is one reason why these saws are of comparatively heavy gauge and why they should be made of pretty good steel. If they were not, they would soon bend out of shape. Special carbide blades are available for very hard materials.

Be aware of the saw's limitations. They cut curves but don't come close to the maneuverability of a coping saw. As an example of when to choose one of the straight, curve-cutting saws over a coping saw to cut a project component, consider the reverse curve—the S-shape—you might design as a shelf-support bracket.

HOW TO USE HACKSAWS

The work must be held firmly in a vise and the vise-jaws must bear on the work as close to the cut-area as possible. If you ignore these basic rules you will get a chatter causing poor cuts and premature blade breakage.

You can start a kerf in metal pretty much as you would when using a wood-cutting saw. Use short draw strokes until you form an entry—then gradually increase the strokes until you are using the full length of the blade. You can, if you wish, start the kerf by making a nick with a file. The only argument against such a procedure is its amateurism. If you go that way, I won't tell and neither will the end result.

Hacksaw blades are normally placed in the frame so cutting occurs on the forward stroke. Because metal is so much harder than wood, you do have to exert some pressure so the teeth will cut. This should not be exaggerated though, and should be confined to the forward stroke only. To get an idea of how this works, cut through a 1/4-inch bolt by keeping contact on the forward stroke and lifting completely on the return stroke. This is not what you should do, but it does demonstrate how you should use a hacksaw. Don't really lift the saw free on the back stroke but *do* apply

some pressure on the forward stroke. This may require a conscious effort at the start but it soon becomes automatic.

Keep a full grip on the handle of the hacksaw. Use your free hand at the forward end of the tool to help guide the cut and to apply pressure. Keep the strokes easy enough so you don't twist the blade. Slow up the stroke speed when the work is about to part. You can snag easily when you approach the end of the cut, so be wary and work gently.

Check the chart for the teeth per inch of blades recommended for various materials. You'll note the thinner the material, the more teeth you need. When you use a hacksaw to cut very thin sheet metal, it pays to sandwich the work between thin plywood covers. This makes cutting much easier and will minimize, if not eliminate, rough edges.

Don't use your woodworker's vise to grip metal pieces. If you don't care to buy a machinist's vise—made for gripping metal—clamp the work to a piece of scrap stock and grip the scrap in your bench vise.

You might consider an *angle vise,* or a *drill-press vise* as it's often called. This unit is not too expensive, is quite adequate for the amount of metal cutting that must be done in a woodworking shop, and is small enough to be stored out of the way when not in use.

COMMERCIAL MITER BOXES

I'll tag this *commercial* because it's not the kind of thing you make for yourself—if you want one, buy it.

Elaborate units costing between $80 and $100 let you cut any right- or left-hand angle between 30 and 90 degrees with beautiful accuracy. This is a super feature, especially when you must miter shaped pieces and have to swing the saw on alternate cuts from one side to the other.

The tools are equipped with a long, top-quality backsaw riding on bearings and held in vertical alignment by guides to permit a smooth stroking action with zero lateral motion. Built-in stops keep the saw from cutting too deeply into the wooden bed. Stops are adjustable so you can control depth-of-cut when doing rabbeting, dadoing, or notching.

Such a box should be anchored firmly to a solid base. The base can be a workbench, but, because the tool isn't used constantly, it makes more sense to give it a heavy base of its own to provide a degree of portability. I used a cutout from a heavy, solid core door, but anything similar will do.

The uses shown in these photographs are typical, but don't show all the possibilities by any means. Because these tools come with good owner's manuals there seems little point in repeating information you will get anyway, should you buy.

CHOOSING BLADES FOR HACKSAWS

BLADE	TEETH PER INCH	THICKNESS OF CUT MATERIAL	USED FOR CUTTING
	18	1/4" up to 1"	Aluminum, bronze, copper, high-speed or annealed tool steel. Used for cutting structural shapes.
	24	1/8" to 1/4"	Tubing of copper, brass, steel or iron, BX cable, wrought-iron pipe, conduit, drill rod, sheet steel or metal trim.
	32	1/8" or thinner	Any of the materials above when their thickness is 1/8 inch or less. Used on thin-walled conduit and thin sheet metals.

Compound-angle cuts are easy, even on coved molding, if you brace the work. The cut is then made as if it were a simple 45-degree miter.

Here a V-block guide clamped to the bed of the miter box allows a disc to be sawed exactly in half.

This saw-angle guide can be used with almost any saw to make square cuts or miter cuts at 45, 60, or 75 degrees. It can be assembled for either right or left-hand cuts.

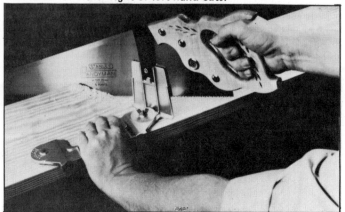

HOW TO CUT A CURVE WITH A STRAIGHT-CUTTING SAW. A curved line can be cut with a regular handsaw by making a series of tangent cuts first. The idea is to remove as much of the waste as possible to give the blade a chance to move around the curve. You should limit the length of the strokes and work with the narrow end of the blade. The less blade width in the kerf, the easier it is to make the turn. Remember, make gentle curves.

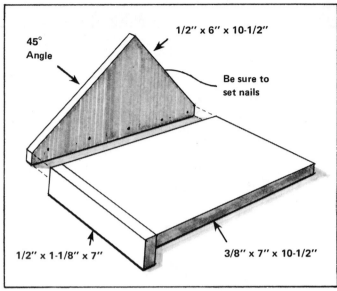

1/2" x 6" x 10-1/2"

45° Angle

Be sure to set nails

1/2" x 1-1/8" x 7"

3/8" x 7" x 10-1/2"

In constructing this guide, be sure the nails on the side facing the saw blade are sunk below the surface of the wood.

You can make this guide to help you do more efficient crosscutting. It can either be held or clamped to the work. It keeps the cut straight and helps maintain the 45-degree blade-to-work angle.

Keep the crosscut saw at a less than a 45-degree angle when cutting plywood. Use a saw with many teeth, as many as 15 points. Position work so the good face is up. These procedures minimize the amount of splintering that can occur on the face veneer.

Clamp a guide block to the saw blade whenever you need to control the depth of cut. This will work with any saw, but is used most often with backsaws and dovetail saws.

Less than 45° angle

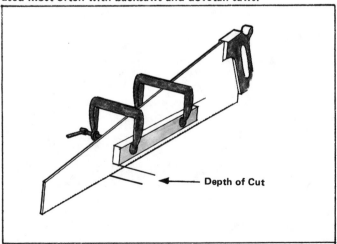

Depth of Cut

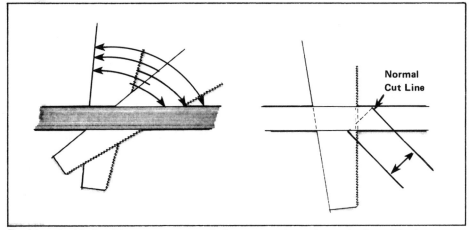

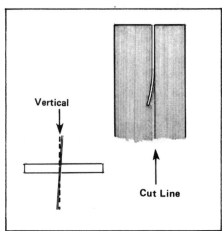

Rocking the blade a bit as you saw can help get you through rough places like knots more easily. When the blade approaches vertical position it is cutting less material but it does make the job easier.

TWO COMMONS SAWING FAULTS are allowing the blade to go off vertical and allowing it to move away from the cut line. In each case you can get back to correct position by applying a gentle twisting action as you continue to saw. Imperfections can be removed later with a file or plane. Avoid such situations by sawing correctly to begin with.

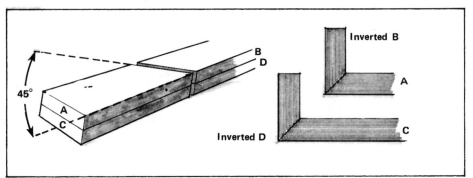

One 45-degree cut will produce stock that makes a 90-degree turn. This works with flat stock that is good on both sides.

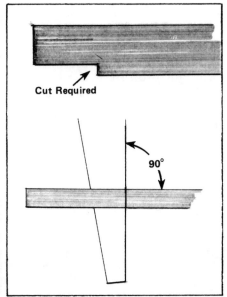

Cutting notches is a matter of making two saw cuts meet exactly. Bring the saw to full vertical at the point where the cuts meet. Never attempt to remove the waste by twisting the blade before the cuts are complete.

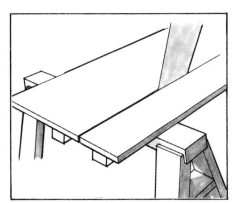

Support thin materials such as plywood on strips of wood. Set support strips close to the kerf. This prevents the springy character of the material from binding the blade.

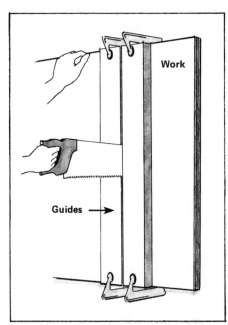

You'll get better, more accurate cuts in plywood if you work with clamped-on guides as shown here. Use straight pieces of 3/4" stock as the guides—space them to equal the width of the kerf.

3

Hammers

If the first sawing tool was a rough-edged, flat stone, then the first striking tool was surely a fist-size rock. Like the person who decided to sharpen the saw by chipping away at its edges, someone thought enough to realize the hammer head could be used more effectively if tied to the end of a small branch. It is logical to assume there were "light" and "heavy" hammers even then.

Like the saw, the basic concept of the hammer hasn't changed too much. It's still a striking surface attached to a handle, even though it has evolved to a super product with specific designs available for particular applications. The latter is a thought to be aware of. A hammer is not an all-purpose tool. You can't—you *shouldn't*—use a nail hammer to bend metal or to split a brick or block. A light hammer is not a good choice for house-framing. A conventional hammer should not be used to drive specially hardened masonry nails or as the striking tool for cold chisels. The nail hammer, or claw hammer—the design most useful for cabinet and furniture making and for general shop use—is not designed for such work. In addition to being inefficient, such usage can present a hazard because of the possibility of chipping that can cause eye or bodily injury.

The eye-injury factor deserves the utmost consideration—to the point of reaching for safety goggles everytime you reach for a hammer. Better to be chicken than sightless.

THE NAIL HAMMER—IN GENERAL

A good hammer contributes to quality work. It's tough and durable, and its head is heat treated for the correct degree of hardness. It has poise, balance and beauty and, unless you just don't give a darn, it forces you to work professionally. The casting blobs attached to rough and often improperly shaped handles seen frequently in bargain-counter trays do little to inspire craftspersonship.

Today's top-quality hammers may have handles of wood, steel or even fiberglass. Technical pros and cons deal mostly with the shock-absorbing qualities of the various materials, and with their resistance to wear. For example, fiberglass can't rust—a steel handle *can* rust, but it can't splinter or crack like a wooden handle—a wooden handle is replaceable, and so on. I know a couple of good construction people who swear by wooden handles because they don't get as cold to the touch as steel handles in inclement weather. Now *that's* a good argument!

In the final analysis, the choice of a hammer is a more personal thing than it is with just about any other tool. Do check the features that I describe. When you find them on several hammers, base your choice on how the hammer feels. Don't go out and buy a hammer—shop for one.

FEATURE CHECK LIST

The overall appearance must be impressive. A good finish will not have rough edges or burrs regardless of the type of hammer. If the handle is wood, it should be straight-grained hickory and attached to the head with a single, diagonally placed wooden wedge, plus two steel wedges. The striking face should be smooth and polished—its edges should have a uniform bevel to guard against chipping. The neck angle should provide sufficient toe-in so the tool will hang properly. The latter may be difficult to see or judge, but if all else is up to par, it will be there.

Look for claws ground at the end so they can fit narrow spaces between nails and between nail heads and wood surfaces. The slot between the claws should have a bevel to allow gripping a nail anyplace along the shank—not just under the nail-head.

Most professionals prefer a bell-face hammer over one with a plain face. The bell curvature is always minimal, so the possibility of skidding off the nail head is slight, but there. It takes a little more getting used to. Its advantage is being able to drive a nail flush with the work surface without doing damage to adjacent areas.

TYPES OF HAMMERS

Claw Hammers—The nail hammer most applicable

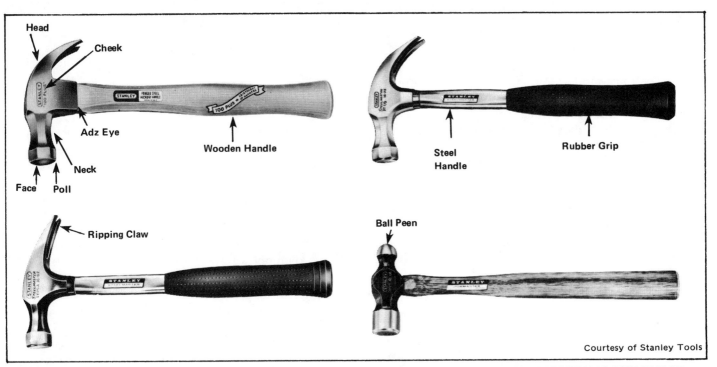

Head
Cheek
Adz Eye
Wooden Handle
Face
Poll
Neck

Steel Handle
Rubber Grip

Ripping Claw

Ball Peen

Courtesy of Stanley Tools

The COMMON CLAW HAMMER has a claw designed for maximum efficiency when pulling nails. The MODERN 16-OUNCE NAIL HAMMER has a shock absorbing rubberized grip which contributes to firmer handling.

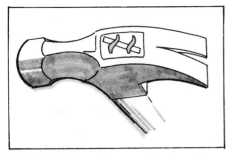

The head of a quality, wooden-handle hammer should be attached with one wooden wedge and two steel ones

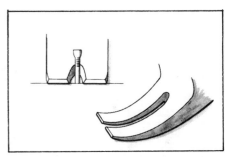

The split in the claw of a hammer should be beveled so it can bite into the shank of a nail.

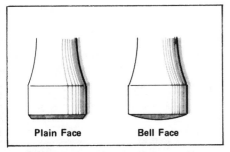

Plain Face   Bell Face

Experienced workers prefer the bell face because it can drive a nail flush or even slightly below the surface of the work without leaving hammer marks.

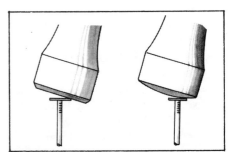

A blow that is slightly off with a plain face is likely to bend the nail. A similar blow with a bell face will still drive the nail straight.

to general woodworking is the 16-ounce *claw hammer*. Weights can differ from as little as 7 to as much as 20 ounces, but you should consider other weights as additions to, not as substitutes for the 16-ounce model. My reasoning here is simple— it's neither wise, nor even possible, to use a single hammer to drive everything from brads to spikes.

When you go above 20 ounces you get into the heavy-duty category where even the length of the hammer changes. A typical 22-ounce heavy-duty hammer with a ripping claw is 16-inches long. Move into areas where the tool is called a *framing hammer* and you find weights like 28 ounces and lengths of 18 inches. This is because the hammer is used constantly to drive 16d and larger nails. Often you can choose between a plain face and a milled, checkered face. The latter is like cross corrugations that guard against nail skid under heavy blows. The fact that the corrugations can mar the wood is not critical because the hammer is used for rough framing.

Ripping claws will pull nails, but the flat curve and heavier cross section adapts them especially for prying apart nailed pieces, breaking down forms, removing siding, and so on.

Ball-Peen Hammers—Sometimes spelled *pein*, these hammers are available for light-touch work as well as for heavy pounding. Sizes range from 2 ounces with a 10-inch handle to 48 ounces with a 16-inch handle. Because the tools are designed primarily for metal working, the heads are—or should be— specifically tempered for maximum hardness and resistance to breakage. This style hammer is not a first-choice tool for a wood shop, but if you are doing hobby work like light metal crafting, or even leather work where you might have some riveting to do, you'll find a 12- or 16-ounce size very handy. An example of when a heavier model is necessary is attaching furring strips to concrete block for the application of wood paneling. The ball-peen hammer can be used to drive specially hardened nails into the masonry. It's not a job you should attempt with a nail hammer.

Tack Hammers—They earn their keep in any wood shop even if you never drive a *tack*. These are the hammers to use for the light fasteners that come under the general category of "brads." Check that the one you buy has a magnetized head so you can tap a small nail to get it started without having to use your fingers. The term *tap* should not be taken literally. The best procedure is to attach the nail to the hammerhead and then exert enough downward pressure to seat the nail where you wish to drive it. Then hit it home in normal fashion. The above procedure assumes the fastener is in the inch-or-less category where it is difficult to hold the nail to get it started without smacking a finger.

Mallets—Regardless of the type you buy, these hammers have soft faces so you can't damage the tool you are striking. The most common application is driving wood chisels. There was a time when mallet was a synonym for wooden hammer and there are many fine workers today who won't use anything else. However, that loyalty has more to do with esthetics than practicality. It doesn't matter which mallet you choose, but you should be aware that modern versions can have faces of rawhide, hard rubber or plastic. All of these materials are adapted to striking finished and polished surfaces of metals without danger of chipping or marring. Many models have replaceable heads—some even have interchangeable tips of various materials.

Heavy Hammers—Here I am talking about blacksmith's hand hammers, hand drilling hammers, engineer's hammers, sledge hammers, and the like. You can do a lifetime of woodworking without needing a tool in this category. If I had to choose one to supplement basic equipment, it would probably be a hand drilling hammer because it comes close to having all-purpose applications in related areas. Weights of typical models are 2, 3, or 4 pounds with overall lengths of 10 to 11 inches. Example applications are striking a star drill to make holes in masonry, driving specially hardened nails and striking a mason's chisel to break brick or concrete block.

HOW TO USE A NAIL HAMMER

Grip the hammer near the end of the handle so you will have maximum leverage which, in turn, provides the most power and drive. The grip must be firm enough to keep the tool from twisting when you strike, but not so tight it contributes to fatigue. Normally your thumb will curl around the handle in natural fashion, but when you want super control, you can extend the thumb in line with the handle. This is done frequently to start a nail, or when using a light hammer, or when a blow that isn't directed perfectly can cause irreparable damage.

You can swing a hammer with your wrist, shoulder or elbow, or all three. Much depends on the force you need to drive the nail. Small nails can be the impact point of an arc that has your wrist as a center. At the other extreme, your shoulder joint might be the center of the swing-arc. Anytime you need to start your swing from somewhere behind your spine, you had better reach for a different striking tool.

The most important consideration is the squareness of the hammerhead to the nail at the moment of impact. If you did a drawing of the procedure you would see the entire action takes place within the arc of a quarter-circle. The length of the arc decreases in proportion to the lightness of the blow

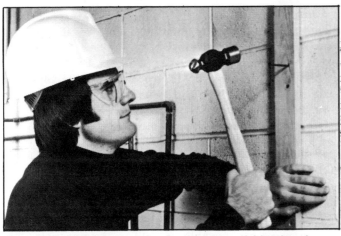

Use a heavy ball-peen hammer for driving special hardened nails into masonry. Note the hard hat and the safety goggles. Hand Tools Institute Photo.

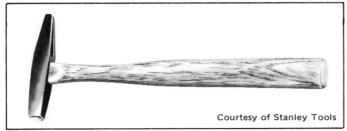

SOFT-FACE HAMMERS may be regarded as modern substitutes for wooden mallets. Head weights range from 1-1/2 to 32 ounces, handle lengths from 8 to 14-1/2 inches. This is the tool to use when you need extra force to drive a wood chisel. Some are available with replaceable plastic tips.

A TACK HAMMER typically has a weight of 5 ounces. The handle length may vary from 10-1/2 to 12 inches. Choose one labeled *magnetic*. A magnetized face is important for holding small tacks and nails in place for driving. When accuracy is important, press the nail into the wood to get it started.

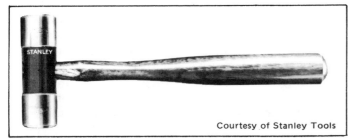

Courtesy of Stanley Tools

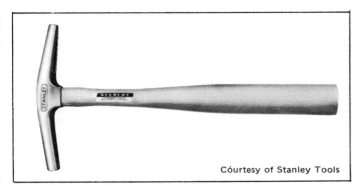

Courtesy of Stanley Tools

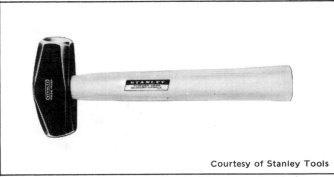

Courtesy of Stanley Tools

HAND DRILLING HAMMER. Used with a mason's chisel or star drill for making holes in masonry; weighs from 2 to 4 pounds.

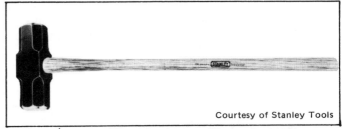

Courtesy of Stanley Tools

SLEDGE HAMMER. Used for driving spikes and other heavy work; weighs from 2-1/2 to 20 pounds.

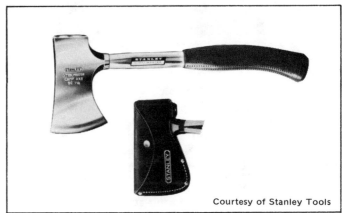

Courtesy of Stanley Tools

AXE—often called a camp axe. Used for chopping wood; 3-inch cut. Cover is especially important for protecting the cutting edge.

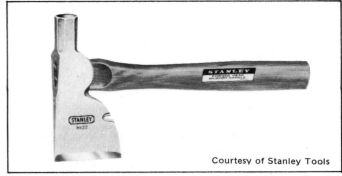

Courtesy of Stanley Tools

HALF HATCHET. Used for rough facing; 3-5/8-inch cut.

UPHOLSTERER'S HAMMER weighs 7 ounces and has a 10-3/4-inch handle.

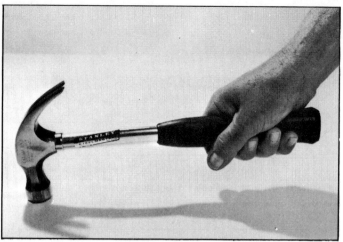

Curl your fingers around the handle close to its end. When the face of the hammer is on a flat surface, the V formed by your thumb and forefinger should point toward the middle of your torso.

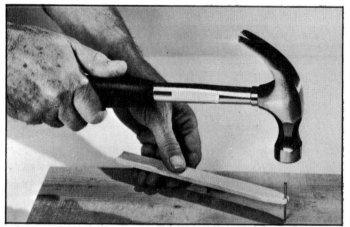

It's okay to extend your thumb when you are doing light work, or to get a nail started correctly. Keep the stroke arc short. A slight kerf in the end of a thin strip of wood makes a good reusable holder for small nails. It is easy to pull away after the nail is seated.

BASIC FACTS ABOUT HAMMERING

Hammering is not a contest. Excessively heavy blows will do more harm than good.

Grasp the hammer firmly near the end of the handle.

Don't use the cheek of the hammer as a striking surface.

Strike the nail gently first. This will help direct the blow accurately.

The face of the hammer should be parallel to the head of the nail when contact is made.

Don't use the hammer to strike material that is harder than it is.

If a nail bends, draw it out and start a new one.

Keep the face of the hammer clean.

you wish to deliver.

Don't ever grab the hammer just behind the head so your forearm substitutes for the handle. This is often done when the worker chooses to substitute his own strength for the leverage supplied by a correct swing. It's a bad idea because it wastes your strength.

Other examples of misuse are striking the nail with the cheek of the hammer instead of the face, and using a hammer to do the job a wrecking bar is designed for. The cheek of a hammer is not hard enough or thick enough to stand up as a striking surface. Wrecking bars are designed to pull large nails, rusted spikes and the like, easily. Once you get to using them, you will learn they can outdo the best ripping hammer.

HOW TO DRIVE NAILS

Nail driving is not a contest. It should not be your intent to do the job with the least number of blows. Working this way can cause you to miss or to strike inaccurately often enough to cause serious damage to the work. Also, nails driven home calmly will hold better because they cause minimum distortion in the wood fibers. Bent fibers spring back more easily to grip than those which are split apart.

Blunt points are less likely to cause splitting than sharp points. That's why you will often see a professional deliberately blunt the point of a nail before he drives it home. There are situations where even this precaution doesn't prevent splitting. Then your only out is to drill pilot holes for the nails before you drive them. Try to keep the pilot-hole size to about 75% of the nail-shank diameter. Its depth can match the length of the nail, but minimize it when you can.

Start a nail with light taps and a minimum stroke arc. This is the way to work accurately and to eliminate the blue thumb. Most people hold the nail near the head between thumb and forefinger. Some say it's better to invert the fingers and to keep them away from the nail head, claiming that should the hammer slip off the nail it will arc away from the fingers. Another claim is, hitting the fleshy tip of a finger is less painful than smacking a thumbnail. The TRUTH is, hitting any part of your fingers is painful and unnecessary. Avoid it by starting a nail with gentle taps regardless of finger position.

There are ways to hold nails so your fingers are not in the impact area at all. Small brads and tacks can be pressed through a strip of thin cardboard about 3 or 4 inches long. Larger nails can be held in a kerf you form in a thin strip of wood. Such ideas can be adopted as standard procedure, or you can just use them when the size of the nail makes finger holding difficult, or when the setup is awkward for routine nailing. In a pinch, double-stick tape can hold a nail by its head on a hammer making an acceptable substitute for a magnetized head. This idea is useful when work position makes it inconvenient to use your free hand to hold the nail.

Let up on the force of the blows when the nailhead approaches the surface of the work to avoid the possibility of hammer dents and broken surface fibers. You can usually straighten a bent nail by tapping it upright gently. If the bend is serious, discard the nail and start a new one. Always drill a pilot hole first when you must drive a nail through a knot.

HOW TO HIDE NAILS

The routine method is to sink the head of the nail—either a finishing or casing nail—below the surface of the wood by using a *nail set*. The hole that remains is filled with a matching wood dough or putty. It's a tried-and-true system but be aware that nail sets come in different sizes. Matching the set to the nail does the job with a minimum size hole. Tip sizes on typical nail sets are 1/32, 1/16, 3/32, 1/8, and 5/32 inch. You can buy the tools individually but they're cheaper in a group. When you shop, look for cupped and chamfered tips and for knurled shanks and a square head. The square head guards against the tool rolling about on the workbench and it also provides a larger striking surface. The knurled shank gives you a firmer finger grip.

Confine the use of these tools to setting nails. They are not designed for use as punches so don't use them, for example, to form holes in sheet metal or to drive hardened pins.

HOW TO PULL A NAIL

This is usually a simple operation. Turn the hammer upside down and grasp the handle firmly. Tilt it forward with the claws pointing away from you. If the head of the nail is above the surface, slip the claws under it and work them around the nail with a slight sideways motion. Pull steadily back until the nail is pulled free. If the nail is extra long, or it is important not to damage the surface of the work, place a block of wood under the hammerhead. This increases your leverage and reduces the strain on the handle. Be sure you are not trying to withdraw a nail that is clinched on the other side.

If the head of the nail is below the surface, place the claws around the head and tap the face of the hammer with a soft face mallet. This will drive the claws down and around the nailhead. Then you can pull the nail as described above.

If the head of the nail pulls off or breaks, drive the claws into the body of the nail. Twist the hammer about one-quarter turn to the right or left and

pull. This should make a cut in the nail which the claws can grasp. If all else fails and it is impossible to get the claws on the nail, drive it through the board with a nail set. Clinch the pointed end over the claws on the other side, and pull it free. This can also be done with nails that are already set, and with surfaces that you do not want damaged. Generally, when a nail that has been set is backed out, the surface of the wood will be split.

If it is impossible to get to the pointed end of the nail, pry up the board and slip in a hacksaw blade to cut the nail. It is advisable to use one of the several prying tools available for pulling spikes, or for prying apart boards with several nails in them. Too much strain can break the handle of your hammer, and can injure you as well. Tools are designed for special purposes. It is best to use them the way they are intended.

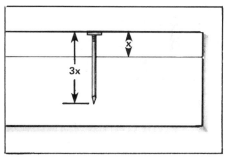

The general rule for choosing nail length is that it must be three times the thickness of the piece it must hold.

A light tap with a hammer is all you need to blunt a nail point. Blunt points make splitting less likely because they bend the wood fibers. Sharp nail points separate the wood fibers and cause splitting.

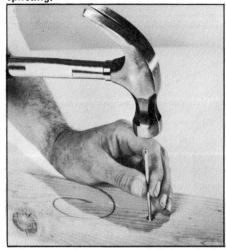

Most people naturally hold a nail this way.

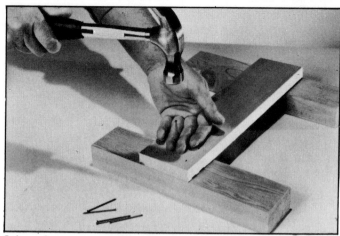

Others, for reasons explained in the text, suggest this method. The important thing is to get the nail started by using light taps. That is the best way to guard against hitting your fingers.

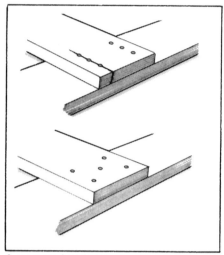

A staggered and spaced nail pattern is much better than nails driven on the same line which can cause splits.

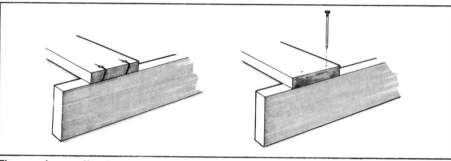

The wood can split when nails are driven close to an edge as shown on the left. In such situations its best to drill pilot holes first. Make the holes slightly smaller than the shank of the nail. Drill them through the piece to be fastened.

Joints designed like this are very strong because they allow the nails to form an interlock.

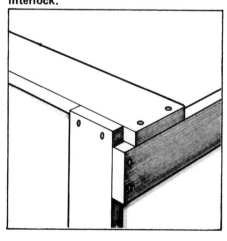

Toenailing is nailing done at an angle to hold a vertical piece in place. It's a good idea to clamp a block in the position shown to provide support for the vertical piece while it is being nailed.

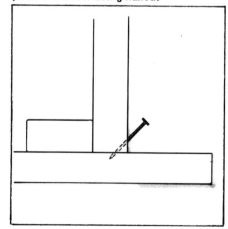

Nails may be clinched when appearance is not important. Be sure that the point of the bend is where the nail emerges. When clinching, you can back the head of the nail with another hammer if necessary.

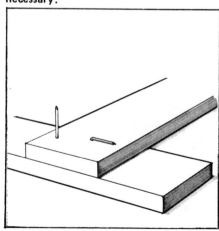

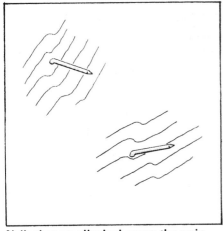

Nails that are clinched *across* the grain are much stronger than nails that are clinched *with* the grain.

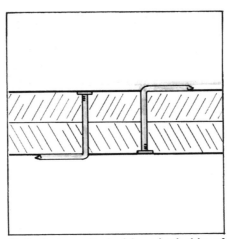

Nails that are clinched from both sides of an assembly make a very strong joint

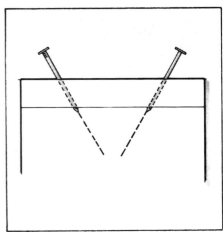

Nails driven at a slight angle will provide a better grip than nails that are driven straight.

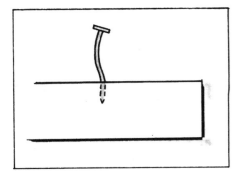

A nail that bends above the surface of the work can be straightened and driven home.

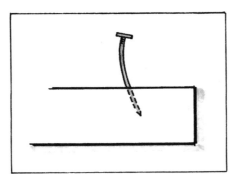

If the nail is bent throughout its length, it can cause problems.

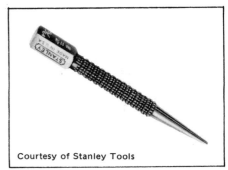

Courtesy of Stanley Tools

A typical, good quality nail set.

HOW A SELF-CENTERING NAIL SET WORKS: The casing of the tool is placed over the protruding nail head and the spring-loaded plunger is struck to set the nail. These sets are available in two sizes, one for brads and another for 4d and 6d finishing nails.

TO SET A FINISHING OR CASING NAIL: Drive the nail in normal fashion but leave the head exposed. Choose a nail set that is a bit smaller than the nail head. Hold the nail set so it has a common vertical centerline with the nail. Strike the set squarely, but only hard enough to sink the nail head 1/16 to 1/8 inch. Fill the hole with a matching wood dough or putty.

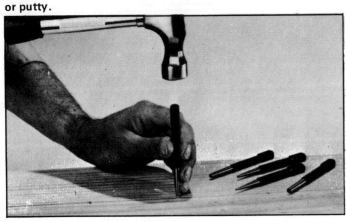

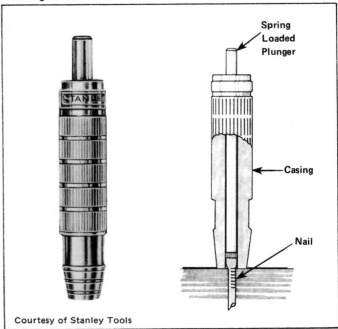

Courtesy of Stanley Tools

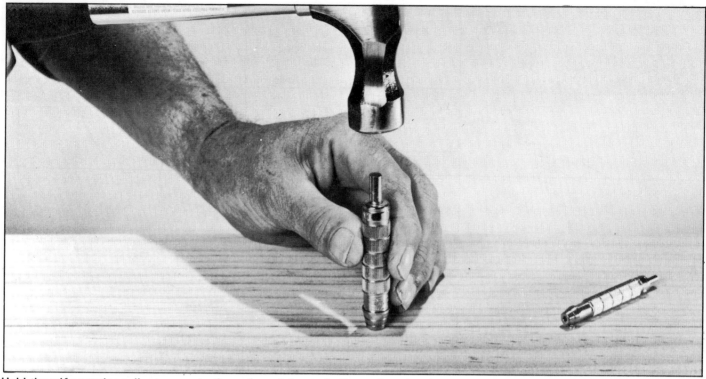

Hold the self-centering nail set square to the surface of the work. Remember, the plunger does the setting, so strike gently. It might pay to practice once or twice on scrap stock.

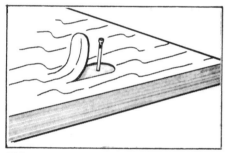

Hide a nail by using a sharp chisel to lift a sliver of wood. Then drive the nail in the depression and glue the sliver back into place.

A special nail set is available for corrugated fasteners. The fastener is placed in the extruded-aluminum housing and hit with a solid-steel driver. This tool can be used with most of the popular sizes of corrugated fasteners.

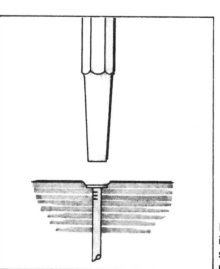

Even a common or box nail can be set if you work with a flat-face punch instead of a nail set. This is not the usual procedure but it does work.

Courtesy of Stanley Tools

Avoid using the tip of the claw to pull nails. This can harm the claw and loosen the handle. Get as much of the claw under the nail head as possible.

A block of scrap wood placed under the hammerhead increases leverage tremendously. The nail is removed easily and the hammer is protected from undue stress.

Use a soft-face mallet to drive ripping claws between pieces that must be pried apart. Never strike two steel hammerheads together.

WRECKING BAR, RIPPING BAR, CROW BAR or GOOSE-NECK BAR are all names for this tool. This is the tool to use when you have to pull many nails. Lengths range from 18 to 30 inches.

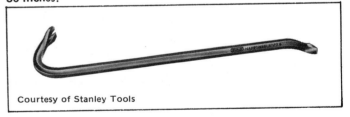

Courtesy of Stanley Tools

WONDER BAR™ is made of steel and is useful for many kinds of pulling, prying, lifting and scraping. It has slots at each end for nail pulling.

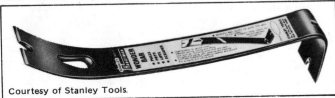

Courtesy of Stanley Tools.

A NAIL CLAW can be used to pull large or very stubborn nails. Beveled slot is specially designed for getting under a nail head close to the surface.

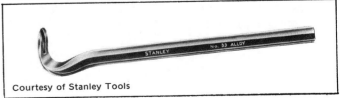

Courtesy of Stanley Tools

4

Drills

Unless you deliberately set out to design otherwise, most woodworking projects call for forming holes for one reason or another. Wood screws are easier to drive and hold most efficiently if you drill pilot and body holes first. Many wood joints are stronger when reinforced with dowels installed in correct-size holes. A mortise cavity can be done more quickly if you first do a series of overlapping holes. Making internal cutouts with a coping saw or keyhole saw requires a predrilled insertion hole. A hole, or part of its circumference, can be planned as part of a design. The list can go on, but the point is, a nice assortment of hole-forming tools will broaden your scope and increase the quality of your output.

The shape of a hole is pretty much the same—round—regardless of whether it is small or big, deep or squat, through or blind. The major consideration is the tool you use to form it.

Holes are either "drilled" or "bored." The distinction is a relationship between hole size and tools. Small holes are *drilled* with a hand drill or a push drill—large holes are *bored* with a brace and bit. The cutoff point between small and large is about 1/4 inch.

HAND DRILLS

A hand drill functions through the rotation of a disc gear with its teeth engaging pinions secured to a central shaft. The shaft terminates in a chuck which is the holding device for the cutter that forms the hole. The mechanical advantages involved provide sufficient power at the working end and adequate rpm for the job. This sounds complicated but all it means is hand drills spin their bits.

All chucks are adjustable to take various size bits or drills, but capacity can vary. A good one for the average shop should be able to handle 1/4-inch shanks, but heavy-duty versions have chuck-jaws that open up to 3/8 inch. Some models have a hi-low drive adjustable crank. This merely means you can adjust the distance from the handle to the center of the speed gear. Use an outer position when you wish to apply more torque—an inner position for more speed.

Most of the tools have a three-jaw chuck to center bits accurately. The chuck works on a thread to open or close the jaws. Be sure the bit is centered between the jaws as you grip the handle with one hand so the speed gear won't turn, and hand-tighten the chuck. Don't ever use another tool, such as pliers, to tighten the chuck.

PUSH DRILLS

Push-drill capacity matches the 1/4-inch hand drill but its rotation action is automatic. When you push down on the handle, an internal spiral spindle rotates the chuck. It's a very handy tool for drilling small holes—especially when you need one hand to hold part of the work. A typical example is holding a hinge while you drill starting holes for the screws.

The chuck on a push drill is special and should not be used to grip conventional, straight-shank bits or "points." Points designed for push drills end in a half circle and have a V-notch cut into the shank.

To insert a point in the chuck of a push drill, you must grasp the chuck sleeve and push it away from the handle end of the tool. Drop in the point and then turn it until you feel it mesh in place inside the chuck—then release the sleeve. You want to make sure the point is seated securely. If it isn't, it can be ejected by a spring contained within the tool and possibly cause injury. Actually, it makes sense not to point the tool in your direction any time you are changing points.

BIT BRACES

Reach for a brace when you need holes 1/4 inch in diameter or larger. Because of the length of the bits used in a brace, you can form deeper holes than you can with other drilling tools. Although the average bit set runs from 1/4 up to 1 inch, the brace can be used with a special expansion bit to drill holes up to 3 inches in diameter.

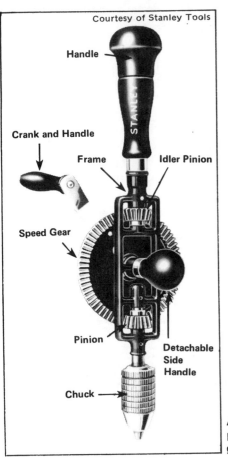

Courtesy of Stanley Tools

Handle

Crank and Handle

Frame

Idler Pinion

Speed Gear

Pinion

Detachable Side Handle

Chuck

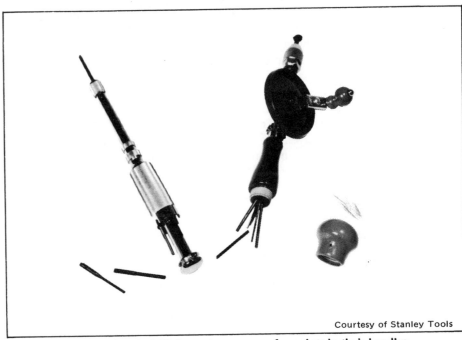

Courtesy of Stanley Tools

Many hand drills and push drills have storage space for points in their handles. Check to see if a set of points is included when purchasing your drill.

A good HAND DRILL has a strong speed gear and double pinions. This one has a two-position crank so you can choose greater torque or higher speed.

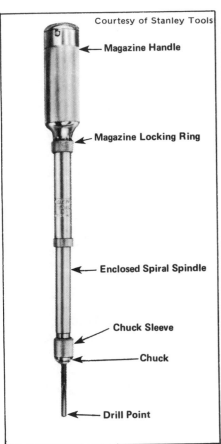

Courtesy of Stanley Tools

Magazine Handle

Magazine Locking Ring

Enclosed Spiral Spindle

Chuck Sleeve

Chuck

Drill Point

The PUSH DRILL has a built-in spiral spindle that rotates the point when you push down on the handle. Extra points are stored in the magazine handle which slides down over the spindle when the locking ring is released.

A good BIT BRACE should have an adjustable ratchet mechanism which allows you to work it either to the left, right, or neutral. Sweep equals the diameter of the handle's full swing.

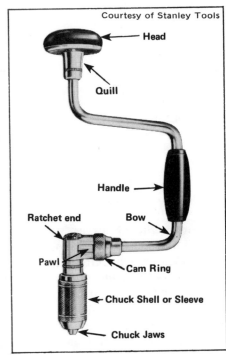

Courtesy of Stanley Tools

Head

Quill

Handle

Ratchet end

Bow

Pawl

Cam Ring

Chuck Shell or Sleeve

Chuck Jaws

The terms *light* and *heavy-duty* are relative. The larger the diameter of the full swing of the handle, its sweep, the more torque you can apply and the heavier the drill must be. Sweep on typical models is 8, 10 or 12 inches.

Most braces have chucks designed to hold bits with taper shanks, but some are available with universal jaws that will grip 1/8- to 1/2-inch straight shank bits as well.

Whatever size tool you buy, do be sure it has an adjustable ratchet mechanism that can work either clockwise or counterclockwise. Ratchet action is convenient in normal use, but is especially desirable when working in close quarters. Because the brace can be used with special bits for screws, the double-direction ratchet helps when removing as well as when driving.

Be careful when placing a bit in the chuck. Even though the chuck-jaws are designed to help center the bit automatically, you can make a mistake. Turn the chuck sleeve lightly as you place the bit. When you are sure the bit is centered, grasp the chuck firmly with one hand and turn the handle with the other.

THE CUTTING TOOLS

Call them *drills, bits, points,* whatever—all are designed to cut holes—each forms a circular cavity by removing a core of wood in its own fashion.

Twist Drills—Designed primarily for forming holes in metal, some are made of carbon steel with a point angle of about 80 degrees for wood drilling. The point on the metal-cutting drills is flatter. While they are not the most efficient way to drill wood, they are usable.

Twist drills do get into large sizes—for power-tool work—but the usual set for home and small shops tops off at 1/2 inch. They may be purchased in letter, number, and fractional sizes to cover just about any diameter from zero-plus up. As a woodworker, your interest will probably lie in a fractional-size set of 29 pieces starting at 1/16 inch and rising in 1/64-inch increments to 1/2 inch.

Drill Points—These are used in push drills and in hand drills. Those designed for push drills have special shanks. Sizes start at 1/16 inch and go up to 11/64 inch in 1/64-inch increments.

Auger Bits—This very special breed of cutting tool should be used and stored like the wood chisel. A good bit will pull itself into the wood with minimum effort on your part. It will cut a clean hole, finish neatly, and remove waste chips easily. Sizes are graded by 1/16ths of an inch and by number. Just remember, the number stamped on the bit tells you the number of one-sixteenths. Thus, a

number 9 bores a 9/16-inch diameter hole. A good size set of bits will include 13 pieces running from 1/4 inch up to 1 inch.

The lead of an auger bit designed for a brace is a screw, not a point. The screw pulls the bit into the wood. Theoretically, the depth of the hole cut by each revolution of the bit is controlled by the screw-thread pitch. A medium screw is best for general woodworking. A steep pitch—fast screw—would cut very thick chips and make the brace harder to turn. A slow pitch—fine screw—may make the job easier because it cuts thin chips, but it may try your patience. The medium screw is a happy compromise.

Expansive, or *expansion bits* are used in a brace to form holes larger than you can make with conventional bits. The tool has adjustable cutters. It can be set up to form odd-size holes, for example, a diameter between 15/16 and 1 inch. Viewed this way, the tool takes on another dimension.

Most types are offered with two interchangeable cutters that overlap in the size holes they can bore. A typical short cutter can bore from 1/2 to 1-1/2 inch holes. Its companion cutter bores from 7/8 to 3 inches. Three inches seems to be the maximum size for all the tools on the market, but there are differences at the minimum end. So, if the smallest hole you can form with the tool is an important factor to you, do some checking before you buy.

DRILLING—IN GENERAL

A certain amount of splintering will occur at the breakout point when you are drilling through stock, regardless of the tool in use. To avoid this, back up the work with a piece of scrap material. The work and the back-up piece can be gripped together in a vise when the work is small. When the work is large you can use clamps to secure the back-up.

With auger bits, or any tool with a point that will break through before the cutting lips, you can avoid breakout splintering by drilling from both sides of the wood. The exposed point will mark the center of the hole so you can complete the job accurately. There won't be very much wood left for the lead-screw to grip when you switch to the opposite side of the work, so work carefully.

It should never be necessary to exert excessive feed pressure with any drilling tool—certainly not with auger bits. The idea is to mate the rotation-speed—which you control—to the cutting action of the bit or drill. The cutter must work constantly, so don't go to the other extreme and just allow the lips to rub. This won't form a hole and it will lead to premature dulling.

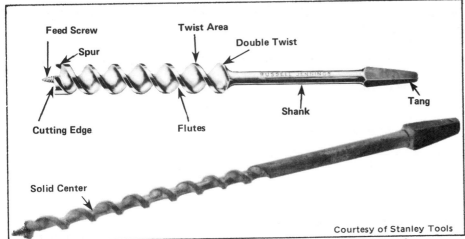

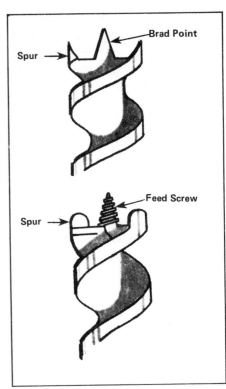

AUGER BITS are made in two styles. The DOUBLE TWIST, which is sometimes called JENNINGS®, leaves a very clean hole. The SOLID CENTER type is stiffer and is useful for very deep holes. Auger bits are sized by 16ths of an inch and run from 3/16ths to 1 inch. Size is identified by a number stamped on the tang which states the number of 16ths.

DRILL POINTS are excellent for use in push drills. Sized by 64ths of an inch, they typically range from 1/16 to 11/64 inches.

AUGER BITS come with two types of tips. A brad point is for use with power tools. A feed screw is essential for work with hand tools. The feed screw pulls the bit down into the work. The spurs make the first contact and outline the hole to assure clean entrance. The cutting edges clean out the waste.

Spurs on the bit should be sharp and long enough to contact the work before the cutting edges to assure clean entry. A complete circle tells you the brace is held square to the work.

Good EXPANSION BITS come with a short and long cutter. Some come with a setting scale. Hole sizes range from 1/2 inch to 3 inches.

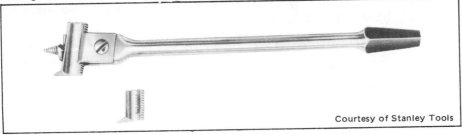

Courtesy of Stanley Tools

FORSTNER BITS are useful for blind or shallow holes on thin stock, or on end grain where the screw of an auger bit may present a problem. They are sized by 16ths of an inch ranging from 1/4 to 2 inches.

TWIST DRILLS for wood are sized by 64ths of an inch as shown on the chart on page 54.

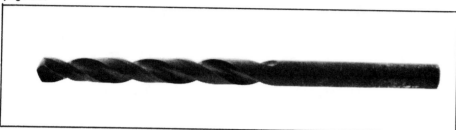

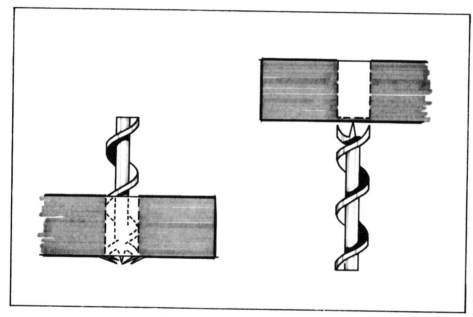

Splintering can be avoided when the bit breaks through by stopping the drill just short of completion, and finishing the job from the opposite side.

Another way to avoid splintering when the bit breaks through is to clamp a backup block to the work.

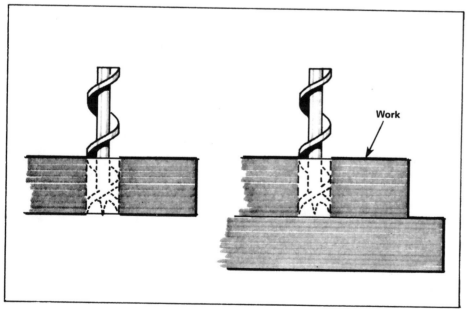

Work

Holding the tool in accurate, vertical position so the hole will be square to the surface is something you should learn to sight. Start by placing the drill point on the mark. Hold the tool at the top with one hand and then step back, and to the side to sight the alignment. Check your judgment with a square the first half-dozen times. Thereafter, use the square occasionally as a spot check to be sure you are not getting careless. Of course, no law says you can't use a square at all times if you find that is a good procedure.

Other ways to achieve good, vertical alignment are shown in the accompanying drawings detailing drilling guides you can make yourself. The jigs take a little time to make and they must be put together accurately, but they then become part of your complement of tools. Those shown are designed for some common drilling chores, but you can adapt the basic concepts to any special requirement you encounter.

It's best to work with an adjustable T-bevel when you must bore holes at an angle. If you lack this tool, you can cut the angle you need in a piece of stiff cardboard and use it as a gauge. If you are working with an auger bit, it's best to start the feed screw as if you were boring a straight hole. Then tilt the tool to the angle described by the gauge you are using. Be careful when the spurs contact the wood. You will be cutting on one side of the hole and it will be easy to move off the mark if you try to force the entry.

Make yourself a guide block when you have a series of holes to drill at the same angle. Make the initial hole through the guide accurately by working with a bevel—or drill a straight hole and then bevel the block with a saw or a plane. Use the guide by slipping it over the bit and then putting the lead screw on the mark. Bring the guide down flat on the work and clamp it in position to control the drilling angle.

HOW TO LOCATE AND START HOLES

The most accurate location method is to draw intersecting lines crossing where the center of the hole must be. This presents a graphic picture and leaves no room for error. Use a hard pencil *lightly* to form lines. Don't use a knife or a scriber for this kind of thing or you will create finishing problems.

All holes, even those to be drilled with a lead-screw bit, should be started with an indentation made with an awl or a punch. Exceptions occur only when you are using a guidance system that will not allow the bit to move off the mark.

When you use an awl, hold it at an angle of about 45 degrees to the work. Put the point exactly on the intersection of the lines, then bring the awl to vertical position before you apply pressure to form the indentation. Follow the same pro-

cedure if you work with a prick punch or a center punch. The difference here is you tap the punch lightly with a hammer to form the indentation. Many of us regard punches as metal-working tools only, but there is no reason why they can't be used to contribute to hole-drilling accuracy in wood as well.

If all this seems like a bit much just to start a hole, remember the intent is to work efficiently and accurately and to get the job done right the first time.

SMALL HOLES

Holes up to 1/4-inch diameter can be made with either a hand drill or a push drill. Start by placing the drill point in the indentation you formed with an awl or punch. Bring the tool to vertical and start the rotation with very little pressure. Once the drill is seated and biting, you can increase both the pressure and the rotation speed.

Usually the bit will clear chips from the hole on its own. When it doesn't, help the process by retracting the bit occasionally. It's *very* imporant to do this when you are drilling a hole deep enough to bury the *flutes* on the bit. When chips can't escape they will clog in the hole and cause overheating and distortion.

If you have trouble drilling a full-size hole in one operation, work up to it by degrees. For example, you can make a 1/4-inch hole in hardwood by starting with a 1/16-inch drill and then enlarging it to 1/8 inch before taking the final step. This procedure should not be used with auger bits, but it works okay with twist or push drills.

LARGE HOLES

What's a *large* hole? Let's just assume its diameter is beyond the capacity of the maximum size bit contained in a routine set of augers—a hole you would form with an expansion bit.

The expansion bit is used in a brace, but it takes a good deal more torque to drive than the average auger. For one thing, you must remove a large amount of waste. For another, this bit is a one-sided cutter and this makes it likely that you will be removing heavier chips.

Choose the shorter of the two cutters that will do the job. Lock it in the bit so the distance from the lead-screw center to the outside edge of the spur equals the radius of the hole. Make a test cut in scrap stock first before cutting good material if the hole diameter is critical.

Start the cut by feeding in the lead screw, and then apply as much pressure as you need to keep the cut going. Normally, the brace is held in vertical position, but there are times when tilting it just a bit to put a little more pressure on the cutter, makes the job go better. The tilt, of course, must change with the rotation, but it should never be extreme. Whether to use tilt and to what degree depends on the size of the hole and the material you are cutting. You can always make a logical decision just by trying the idea.

One point—which applies to all auger bits as well as expansion bits—the lead screw will bite more strongly when penetrating surface grain than when going into end grain. Boring into end grain always requires greater pressure.

DEEP HOLES

A "deep" hole is one deeper than the length of a conventional bit. An example is drilling a hole through a lamp base for the electrical cord. Extension bits and extra-long augers are available for such work—as is a *bit extension* which lets you work with conventional-size augers. This has a locking device for the auger bit at one end and a taper shank at the other end so it can be secured in a brace. It does have limitations. If you want the extension to follow, the bit has to be at least 11/16-inch diameter. If the deep hole you need must have a smaller diameter, then you have to think in terms of extra-long, individual bits. Quite often, the special long items are made for particular functions and are called special names—for example, *car bits* and *electrician bits*.

Be careful when drilling such holes because it's possible for the grain of the wood to throw the bit off course without your being aware of it. The best precaution is to drill from both ends of the stock. Most times it won't matter if the two holes don't meet exactly.

BLIND OR STOPPED HOLES

These are holes of limited depth needed, for example, when drilling for screws or dowels. Drilling techniques are normal, but some device must be placed on the bit to indicate where you should stop boring. The "stop" doesn't have to be more than a slim square of wood, drilled to slip over the bit, or a length of tape wrapped around the bit at the correct point.

Two items you can buy for use on auger bits are shown in photos.

HOLES FOR SCREWS

The most unacceptable way to drive a screw is to start it going with a hammer. You might as well—in fact you would be better off—just using a nail. If the screw is to hold as it should, and if it is to drive with minimum effort, you must drill *lead* holes and *body* holes first. When the wood is soft and the screw is small, you might get by using an awl to form a lead hole. In some situations you can get by with just a body hole, but generally you should follow the correct procedure described here. See chapter 12 for more information.

First, mark the location of your holes and make an indentation with an awl or punch. Drill a lead hole to the desired depth. Remember, unless the screw is properly started, it may enter at an angle, or the screwdriver tip may slip and mar the work surface. When joining two pieces of hardwood, a body hole the same diameter as the screw shank should be drilled in the piece to be attached. If you are using a flat-head screw, countersink the hole to the diameter of the screwhead. When fillister-head screws are used, or when a plug will conceal the screw, the hole is counterbored so the entire screw head can fit below the surface. Counterboring may be done with a proper size twist bit, a counterbore with a pilot, or an auger bit.

Special combination cutters are available so you can form correct-size screw holes with either a countersink or a counterbore in one operation. These great time savers should be considered by anyone doing any kind of woodworking.

COUNTERSINKING

Countersinking is done with a specially shaped bit that forms an inverted cone shape so a flat-head screw can be set flush with the wood surface. Various types are available so you can do the work with either a hand drill, push drill, or a brace.

Most times, countersinking is done after the lead and body holes are formed. Reverse the procedure if you wish. Many people who work this way claim the countersink is an excellent guide for the holes that follow. Anyway, the countersink depth should be just deep enough to seat the screwhead. It's okay to be a bit on the minus side, especially in soft woods because the screw will pull itself in. Going too deep is considered sloppy work.

COUNTERSINK BITS, sometimes called *rose head* bits, are used to widen screwholes so the heads of flat-head screws will fit flush with, or slightly below the surface of the work. Properly tempered, they may be used with soft metals such as aluminum or brass.

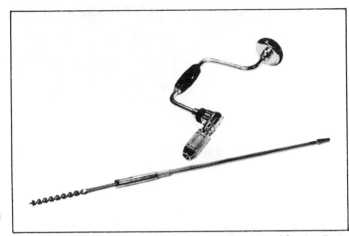

BIT EXTENSIONS can be 12- to 18-inches long. They are used to drill deep holes and to reach places you could not get to with an ordinary bit. Hole must be at least 11/16-inch diameter if the bit extension is to enter the hole behind the bit.

Courtesy of Stanley Tools

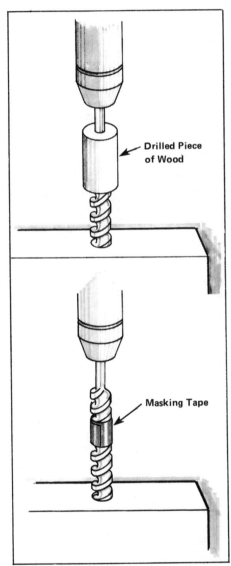

Drilled Piece of Wood

Masking Tape

BIT GAUGE at left can control hole depth. It is attached by a clamp to the shank of the bit and can be used with any size cutter. The stop at right locks to the bit with a thumb screw.

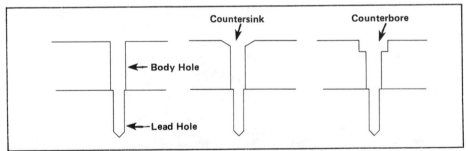

Countersink   Counterbore

Body Hole

Lead Hole

TWO WAYS TO MAKE DEPTH INDI-CATORS. You can drill a block of wood and slip it over the bit, or wrap a length of tape around the bit at the desired hole depth.

TYPES OF HOLES FOR SCREWS: For round-head screws, drill the lead hole first and then open the top to body hole size. For flat-head screws, drill the lead hole first and then *countersink* to the diameter of the screwhead. To hide screws with plugs, drill the *counterbore* first, then the lead hole and finally the body hole.

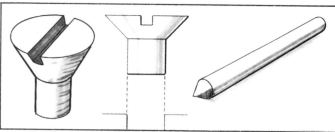

TWO WAYS TO IMPROVISE COUNTERSINKING: On the left the head has been cut from a screw. It can be tapped into place with a hammer and, when removed, will leave a counter-sunk hole. On the right a length of drill rod has been shaped to match the desired screwhead, and it can also be used like a punch. These ideas work best with softwoods, but can be used with hardwoods when the screwhead is not too large.

COUNTERSINKING is done to form a beveled seat for the head of a flat-head screw. Be sure to buy one designed for wood screws. Those made for metal fasteners have a different angle. Countersinks can be used with various tools. This one is being driven with a hand drill.

After counterboring, drill the lead hole. Then open up the top portion for the body hole.

A brace and bit can be used to form a counterbore. The counterboring should be done first. Here a stop is used to control the depth of the hole.

Drive the screw and then glue a length of proper size dowel into the counterbore. After the glue dries the excess portion of the dowel may be removed with a chisel and sandpaper. The plug may be sanded flush or allowed to protrude as a decorative detail.

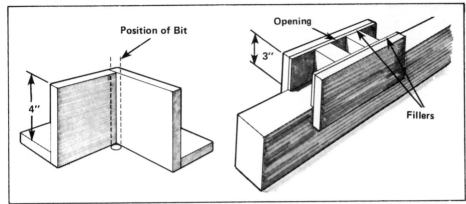

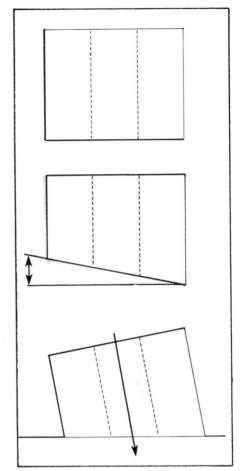

DRILLING GUIDES: These guides may be used on any surface and with almost any size bit. Align the one on the left with the bit after you have placed the point of the feed screw properly, and clamp the guide into place. The one on the right is used for drilling into edges. The opening should have side dimensions to match the diameter of the bit.

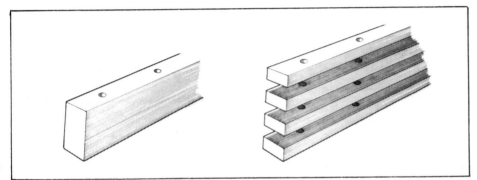

Sometimes production methods can result in more accurate and faster work. Here a thick pre-drilled piece can be cut to produce any number of similar thin pieces with identical hole patterns.

DRILLING AT AN ANGLE: First, drill the correct size hole through a block. Then saw off or plane the block to the correct angle. The block can then be used as a guide for your bit.

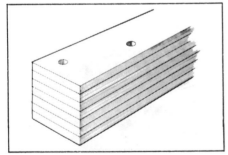

PAD DRILLING: When you want the same hole through several similar pieces, clamp the parts together and drill through the assembly as though it were solid stock.

The AWL looks like an ice pick, but it should be cared for like a quality tool. Don't abuse it.

You can compensate for either an oversize or undersize hole by filling it with a dowel and boring a new hole.

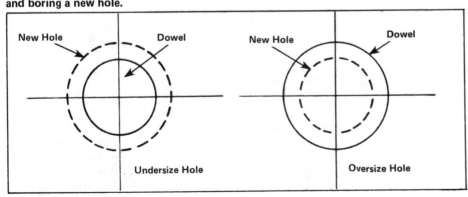

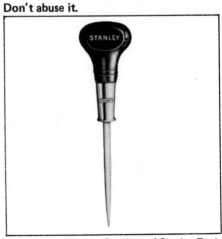

Courtesy of Stanley Tools

STANDARD SIZES FOR TWIST DRILLS					
SIZE IN INCHES	DECIMAL EQUIVALENT	NUMBER OR LETTER	SIZE IN INCHES	DECIMAL EQUIVALENT	NUMBER OR LETTER
1/64	.0156	78	17/64	.2656	G
1/32	.0312	67	9/32	.2812	L
3/64	.0468	56	19/64	.2968	M
1/16	.0625	53	5/16	.3125	N
5/64	.0781	48	21/64	.3281	Q
3/32	.0937	41	11/32	.3437	R
7/64	.1093	36	23/64	.3593	U
1/8	.125	31	3/8	.375	V
9/64	.140	28	25/64	.3906	W
5/32	.156	23	13/32	.4062	Z
11/64	.1719	18	27/64	.4218	—
3/16	.1875	13	7/16	.4375	—
13/64	.2031	6	29/64	.4531	—
7/32	.2187	3	15/32	.4687	—
15/64	.2344	A	31/64	.4813	—
1/4	.250	D	1/2	.5	—

For holes larger than 1/4 inch, it is usually best to switch to an auger bit, even though twist drills are available.

Tools such as these help form holes for screws faster. The type on right, called SCREW-SINK™, combines countersink, body hole and lead hole. The style on the left, called SCREW-MATE®, combines a lead hole and body hole with a counterbore. These are available in sizes to suit screws from #6 x 3/4 inches to #12 x 2 inches. They are easiest to use with a power drill, but can be used in a hand drill.

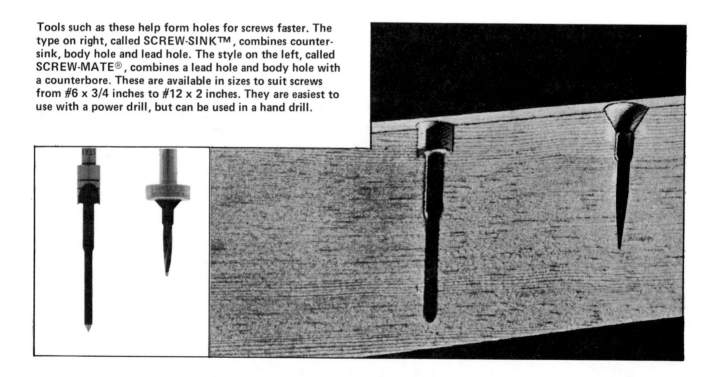

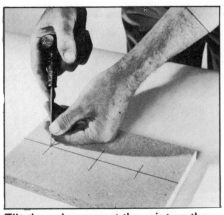

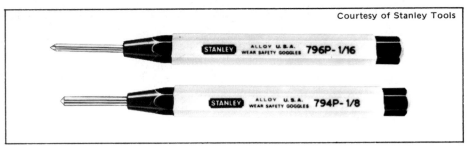

Courtesy of Stanley Tools

The PRICK PUNCH, top, makes a smaller mark than the CENTER PUNCH at bottom. These can be used to make starting indentions for your bit.

Tilt the awl as you set the point on the line intersection, bring it vertical, and then apply pressure. This gives you a clear line of sight for greater accuracy. This procedure should also be used with a prick punch or a center punch.

Hold the hand drill as shown here, at least to get the hole started. When you need more pressure, bring your palm down on the handle. Arrow points to guide mark made with awl.

This is the proper way to hold a brace, but not to hold the work. It should always be gripped with a vise or clamps.

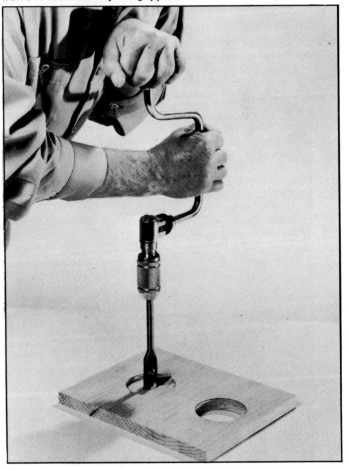

Start a push drill this way. You can't hold the chuck end because it turns with the point. Let the tool come up on its own at the end of each down stroke.

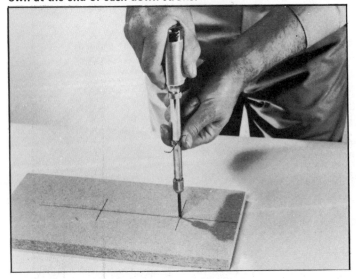

55

HOW TO DRILL FOR DOWELS

Dowels are used quite often to reinforce various types of wood joints, so the holes you drill for them need to be pretty accurate in diameter, depth, and verticalness. Trying to form them by guiding the brace freehand is a rough way to go, especially when you consider most jobs require many similar holes.

You can work by making one of the drill guides shown earlier, or you can buy a commercial doweling jig for use with various stock thickness and different size bits. The jig includes an adjustable stop to lock on the bit so you can control the hole depth. It can be set to gauge the edge distance of holes, but spacing is still a layout job you must do. For example, when you are joining a number of narrow boards edge to edge to make a large slab, mark the hole spacing on the edge of one board and then hold all the pieces together, edge up, in a vise or with clamps. Then use a square to carry the dimension points across all the edges. Mark the same surface of each board lightly with a pencil—it pays to know which side of the board should be "up."

Placing and setting the jig is detailed in instructional materials supplied with the tool so I won't repeat them here. Read them carefully and make the setups accurately.

Methods of using dowels when assembling parts are illustrated in chapter 12.

Typical doweling jigs include sleeves for various size bits and a stop to control hole depth. The jig is adjusted to center the hole in the stock, then clamped in place. The jig also guarantees the hole will be perpendicular.

An off-beat, but practical application for a doweling jig is drilling a deep hole through a pre-fabricated turning for use as a lamp base.

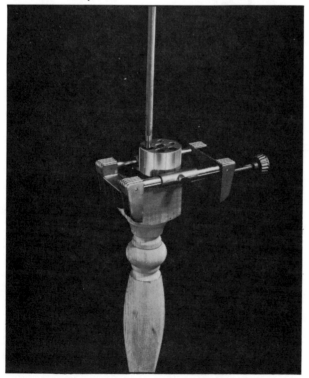

Courtesy of Stanley Tools

Screwdrivers

Screwdrivers are among the most-used tools in the shop. You will seldom find a quality wood project that doesn't call for screws somewhere in the assembly. The reason for screwdrivers is screws. Screws differ in size, shape and application, and so do the tools designed to drive them home. Properly driven screws require two things—the use of proper procedures and the proper matching of screw and screwdriver.

Driving a screw into wood is easy to do with efficient results unless you choose to ignore basic good practices. If you try to do without the body and lead holes—which are discussed in the preceding chapter—and try to turn the screw with an inadequate driver, you can count the following among your frustrations: screws that don't seat at all regardless of how strong you are—marred screwheads—broken screws that are miserable to extract—distorted screwdriver tips—scarred work—blistered palms—fatigue—and the like. Even if you seat the screw, it may not hold because the maximum holding power of any screw is achieved only through correct installation procedures.

The driving force that turns a screw is a twisting action, or torque. You supply this through the handle and down to the tool's tip seated in the screw's head slot. The larger the screwdriver, the more power goes into the twist. You can assume that screwdrivers are heavier and longer in direct relationship to the size of the screw they are designed to drive. The physical size of the driver leads you into a suitable power application. You naturally use only your fingers to turn a slim, delicate-looking driver. When the blade is 12 inches or longer, and the handle is palm size, you lean into the twist direction with biceps and shoulders, forearm and wrist.

Generally, screwdriver sizes are determined by the length of the blade. The longer the blade, the broader and thicker the tip, and the bigger the screw it will drive. To be equipped for general screwdriving in a woodshop, you should have an assortment that includes 3, 4, 6, 8, 10 and 12-inch blades. If you wish to start with a minimum, eliminate at the high side, not the low.

There are so many high-quality brands of screwdrivers available today that it's difficult to make a bad choice unless you buy for price rather than quality. Check for overall appearance and a quality-controlled finish. Rough surfaces and burred edges mean an inferior tool. Handles can be hardwood or of a composition material. The latter usually last longer and should be considered unless you react negatively for esthetic reasons. The handle should fit your palm comfortably and provide for a firm grip, whatever the material. Most handles are round or octagonal, and fluted so the tool won't slip in your hand as you turn it.

SCREWDRIVER TYPES

Conventional Screwdrivers—These have a wing-type blade and are used to drive flat-head, oval-head, and round-head slotted screws. The thickness and width of the tip varies with the length of the blade, so you can base your selection in relation to the size of the screw. This style screwdriver is the most abused and misused of all. It's used as a pry, a punch, a ripping tool, an ice pick, and a can opener. The truth is, the style of the tool makes it handy for such off-beat applications, but those uses can ruin it for its intended purpose. If you wish to use them that way, good practice calls for having a few "specials" tagged for non-screwdriving chores.

Phillips Screwdrivers—Cross-slotted screws are used extensively on home projects as well as commercial ones. For these you need a driver shaped to fit the cross in the screw head. The most common type is known as a *Phillips,* but another—often confused with the Phillips—is called *Frearson.* The difference between the two is in the shape of the cross-slots. A Phillips screw head has modified U-shaped slots of uniform width—a Frearson screw-head has V-shaped slots with tapered sides. You can tell the difference between the two by

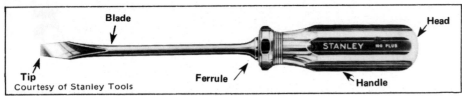

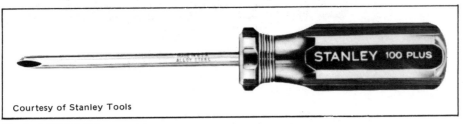

CONVENTIONAL SCREWDRIVER with wing-type blade.

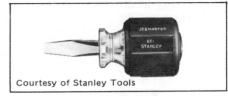

A STUBBY SCREWDRIVER.

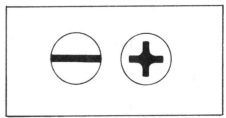

Typical **PHILLIPS** screwdriver.

TYPICAL SCREW HEADS. Slotted head on the left and Phillips head on the right.

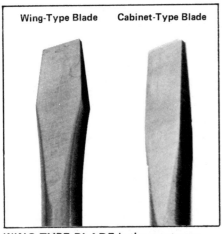

WING-TYPE BLADE is the most common for slotted screws. **CABINET-TYPE BLADE** is often called *wingless*.

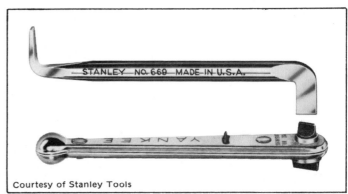

There are several types of **OFFSET SCREWDRIVERS.** Two common types are one with two blades, at the top, and a ratchet type which usually has changeable blades. Both are available for slotted or Phillips-head screws.

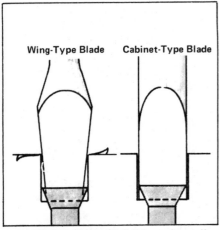

A CABINET-TYPE BLADE works easily in counterbored holes. Conventional wing-type blades must have sufficient room to avoid marring the wood.

A wrench may be used on a square-shank screwdriver to apply more force to the screw. Care should be taken not to apply too much force or the screw might break.

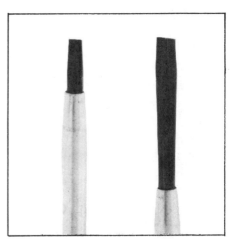

Some screwdrivers have special tips that expand to hold a screw. This is convenient when it is difficult to start a screw by holding it with your fingers.

looking at the screwdriver tips. Cross blades on a Phillips are almost square throughout—on a Frearson, they taper almost to a point.

Other types of cross-slot screws requiring special drivers are called *Reed and Prince* and *Pozidriv®*. The latter is used extensively in automotive and appliance industries.

The Phillips is more than likely the one cross-slot screw you will be involved with in woodworking.

Wingless Drivers—Drivers with cabinet-type blades —often called *wingless*—are useful in woodworking for turning screws in counterbored holes. Sides of the tips are parallel. Their width is equal to the diameter of the shank. Generally, these blades are lighter than those on conventional screwdrivers of similar length. Some people find them more convenient than a wing-type blade for driving oval-head and round-head screws. Because they are light and slim, even in the long lengths, they are widely used in radio, TV, and electronic industries.

Stubby Drivers—When you are working in tight quarters you can turn screws with *stubby drivers.* Stubbies have a very short blade—1 or 1-1/2 inch are common—with fat handles so you can grip them firmly.

Offset Drivers—Also for tight places, offsets come in a variety of styles ranging from a length of rod bent at right angles at each end, to a ratchet type with interchangeable blades.

Spiral-ratchet or Yankee® Screwdriver—Pushing down on this driver's handle automatically provides turning action for the screw. It can be set for retracting as well as driving and may be locked in neutral position so it can be used as a common driver. The tool has a chuck-like end for use with different blade sizes and styles—it may even be used with points for drilling holes.

Sizes range from light-duty to heavy-duty types —overall length in extended position running from about 10 to 28 inches. The automatic screwdriver contains a spring to return the tool to the extended position unless it is secured by turning the locking ring. Be sure to point the tool away from yourself whenever you release the lock. It is best to grasp the chuck with one hand and allow the tool to extend gradually. It's wise to store the tool in its extended position, and to apply a drop of light oil on the spindle and the chuck sleeve periodically.

Special Screwdrivers—Blades made to fit a brace can be used to turn very large screws. You get a tremendous amount of leverage here, so it's very important to choose a blade to fit the screw, and to provide adequate body and lead holes. The brace provides enough torque so you can break a screw easily if you don't follow correct procedures.

This also applies when you are removing a tight screw. Apply only as much leverage as you need to loosen the screw—keep the blade tip snug in the screwhead.

Another way to provide extra torque to drive or to remove a screw is to work with a driver with a square-shank blade. Here you can use a wrench on the square shank to get extra leverage. You can also break a screw this way, so don't bully the job.

HOW TO DRIVE A SCREW

The most common error when starting a screw is applying excessive pressure on the driver. Screws draw themselves into the wood, so down pressure is needed mostly to keep the tip of the driver snugly in the slot.

You can start screws by finger-turning them just enough for them to catch. Then hold the screw vertical with one hand as you put the driver in place with the other. Once you are satisfied the screw is penetrating correctly, shift your free hand to somewhere near the tip of the blade so your fingers act as guides to keep the driver seated correctly.

Another way is to hold the screw on the driver tip with the fingers of one hand while you grasp the handle with the other hand. Retain the grip as you place the point of the screw in the hole, using one hand to guide the screw and the other to do the turning.

Whichever way you go, do be sure the vertical centerline of the screw is at right angles to the work surface, and that the centerline continues up through the screwdriver. Apply minimum torque until the screw is solidly engaged. When the screw is firm, increase the torque, but only enough to do the job. Keep the driver vertical and use as much down pressure as you need to keep the driver engaged with the screw.

THREADING SCREWS

There are times when it is difficult to drive screws even when you have done a good job with body and pilot holes. This occurs most often with hardwoods like maple and birch. Don't enlarge the pilot hole or smack the screw with a hammer. These never work. Sometimes you can get by with scraping the screw threads against a bar of dry soap. This acts as a lubricant to make driving easier. A more professional technique is to make a threading screw by filing off—lengthwise—half the threaded portion of one of the screws you must drive. Turn this screw into each of the holes before you drive the permanent fastener. It will act like a tap to pre-form threads so the regular screw will drive easier. Be sure to store any threading screw you make because it can be used whenever you are in a similar situation.

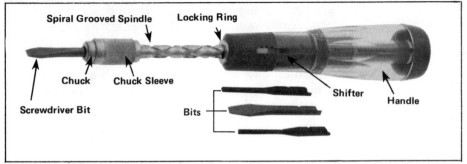

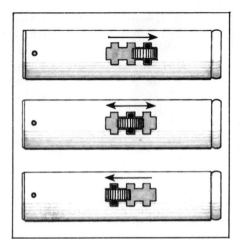

A SPIRAL-RATCHET SCREWDRIVER.

Courtesy of Stanley Tools

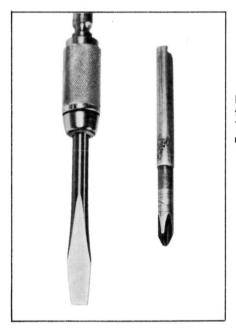

Different style and size tips are available for SPIRAL-RATCHET SCREWDRIVERS. They can also be equipped with points and used like a push drill.

To set a SPIRAL-RATCHET SCREW-DRIVER, move the shifter toward the chuck for driving screws. When the shifter is centered, the tool can be used like a conventional screwdriver. Move the shifter toward the handle for removing screws.

Blades with taper shanks can be used in a conventional brace for heavy-duty screwdriving.

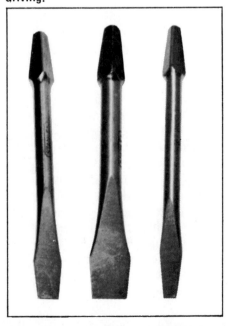

DIMENSIONS OF TYPICAL SCREWDRIVERS IN INCHES

STYLE	OVERALL LENGTH	BLADE DIAMETER	BLADE LENGTH	TIP THICKNESS	TIP WIDTH
REGULAR Wing-Type	6-1/2	7/32	3	.032	7/32
	7-3/4	1/4	4	.037	1/4
	10-1/2	5/16	6	.041	5/16
	13	3/8	8	.050	3/8
	15	3/8	10	.060	3/8
	17-1/2	3/8	12	.060	3/8
STUBBY Regular	3-1/2	1/4	1	.037	1/4
	3-3/4	1/4	1-1/2	.037	1/4
PHILLIPS HEAD	5	1/8	2-3/4		No. 0
	6	3/16	3		No. 1
	7-3/4	1/4	4		No. 2
	10-1/2	5/16	6		No. 3
	13	3/8	8		No. 4
STUBBY Phillips Head	3-5/8	1/4	1-1/2		No. 2
	2-7/8	3/16	1		No. 1
CABINET-TYPE Light Blade	6-1/4	3/16	3	.030	3/16
	9-1/2	3/16	6	.030	3/16
	11-1/2	3/16	8	.030	3/16
	13-1/2	3/16	10	.030	3/16
	15-1/2	3/16	12	.030	3/16
SQUARE BLADE	7-5/8	1/4 square	4	.037	1/4
	10-1/2	5/16 square	6	.041	5/16
	13	3/8 square	8	.050	3/8

Too small a screwdriver tip makes the screw hard to drive and can break the tip. Too wide a tip will mar the wood around the screw.

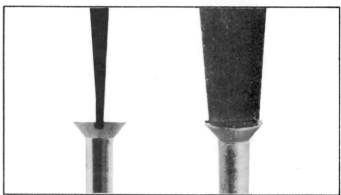

The screwdriver tip should fit snugly in the slot and not be wider than the screw head. The width is less critical when round-head or oval-head screws are used because the tip does not come into contact with the work.

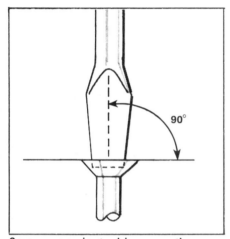

Screws are easier to drive correctly when the screwdriver tip is centered in the slot and properly lined up with the screw.

Once the screw is started, use your free hand as a guide to keep the driver in **vertical** alignment.

Both hands are needed to turn a brace, so you must be extra careful about keeping the blade tip and the screw mated. Use a little more downward pressure on the handle to keep them together.

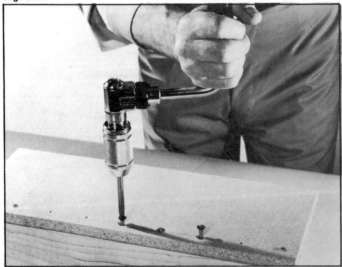

When using a spiral-ratchet driver, keep your free hand on the chuck sleeve and press with the other hand on the handle to turn the screw. Let the ratchet turn under its own power.

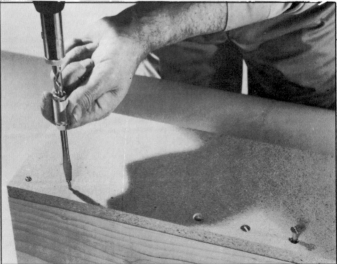

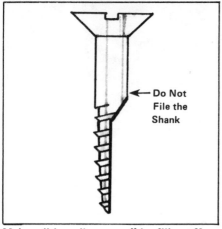

Make a "threading screw" by filing off about half the threaded area of a screw.

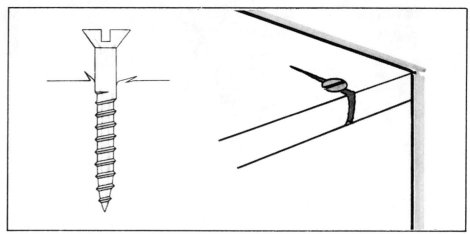

A body hole that is too small for the shank of the screw can cause splits, especially if you are driving through thin wood or near edges.

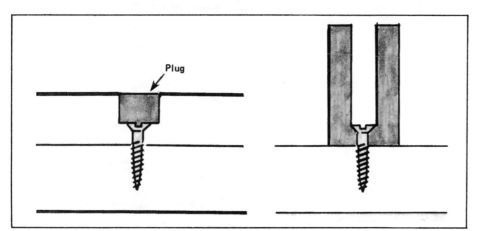

Two uses for counterboring are when you wish to hide a screw with a plug as shown on the left, and when you want to attach thick stock with a short screw.

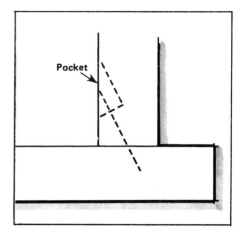

Chisel or bore a pocket for the screw head when you want to drive the screw at an angle.

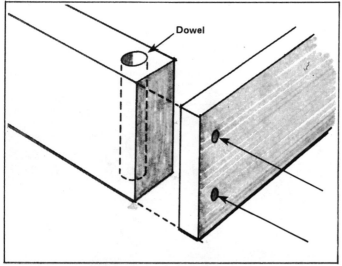

A dowel can be placed in a drilled hole to help hold screws driven into weak end grain.

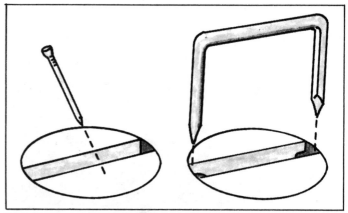

To lock a wood screw; a small hole is drilled through the screw head at a 45-degree angle, and then a brad is driven through it into the wood. Or it can be done with a staple as shown.

Knives & Chisels

KNIVES

I have already mentioned using knives as marking tools. A sharp knife can mark a thin line on wood more exactly than a pencil, but of course knives are cutting and scoring tools as well. They can be used instead of saws for cutting many thin, non-wood materials such as acoustical tile. They can also be used for cleaning areas a chisel cannot reach.

Slim-Line Knives—These have an adjustable, replaceable blade which can be retracted when not in use. They make a narrow, precise cut, but the blade can easily break if used incorrectly.

Utility Knives—More commonly used, they have a wider, heavier blade that is reversible and replaceable. In some models, the blade is retractable and has two cutting positions so a small groove can be made without using the entire blade. There is usually storage space in the handle for extra blades. Utility knives are extremely sharp and should be used with great care.

CHISELS

The chisel probably evolved from the knife. Because its general functions fall into a more heavy-duty category, it is designed to provide more bulk behind the cutting edge, and shaped so the driving force applies to a relatively narrow blade. The intent is to facilitate woodcutting whether the feed pressure is supplied by hand or with a mallet.

Chisels can play primary roles. It is possible to sculpt a chair from a large block of wood by working only with chisels. Usually, however, they are used in associate or accessory roles. Making the chair would go much faster without loss of quality if the bulk of the waste was removed with saw cuts. This example may seem extreme but it does apply. A more reasonable illustration would be using only chisels to make the cavity for a mortise-tenon joint when the job can go faster and be done easier if you remove the bulk of the waste by first drilling a series of overlapping

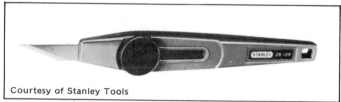

SLIM-LINE KNIFE with a retractable blade.

Courtesy of Stanley Tools

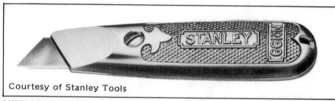

UTILITY KNIFE with fixed blade. Removing the screws allows you to change blades and provides access to spare blades stored in the handle.

Courtesy of Stanley Tools

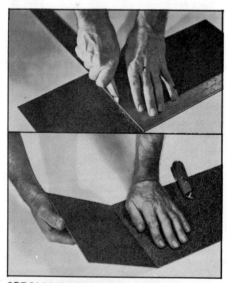

SPECIAL SCORING BLADE may be used in a utility knife. Blade is tempered, high-carbon steel and may be used to score laminates such as accoustical tile. Snapping the material sharply makes a break along the score line.

holes. The chisel comes into play to do the final paring.

There is a joke about these tools which says you must learn to be a chiseler if you are going to be a good woodworker. If there is humor here, it is in the derogatory connotation of chiseler. The statement is true if you take it literally. Being a good chiseler does help you be a good woodworker.

TYPES AND SIZES

There are many types of chisels but those you will find most useful for general woodworking are called *butt* chisels or *pocket* chisels. The butt chisel is the more popular of the two and is the one more generally available. It has the shortest blade, but this factor does not impose severe limitations too often.

The overall length of a chisel is usually deter-

mined by its type. For example, a pocket chisel is longer than a butt chisel. But there is a determination to be made in relation to blade *width* which applies to any type. Usually, blade widths increase from the minimum size up to one inch in 1/8-inch increments. From there they go up to 1-1/2 inches in quarter-inch jumps. Above that they grow in 1/2-inch steps. You probably won't find wood chisels with blades wider than 2 inches listed in any catalog.

I recommend you buy chisels in sets, keeping in mind the fact that not all sets cover the full scope of blade widths. For example, a four-piece set may contain widths of 1/4, 1/2, 3/4, and 1 inch. A six-piece set may go up to 1-1/2 inches. Other sets, regardless of the number of chisels, may provide the normal 1/8-inch size-increase increments. The point is: Don't assume; check before you buy. A decent starter set should

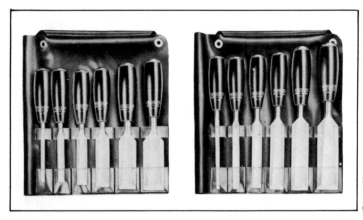

SET OF CHISELS often come in compartmented wrappers. These roll up for storage or can be hung on hooks through grommeted holes.

The WOOD CHISEL has a steel blade heat treated throughout its entire length so that it may be sharpened to hold a keen cutting edge.

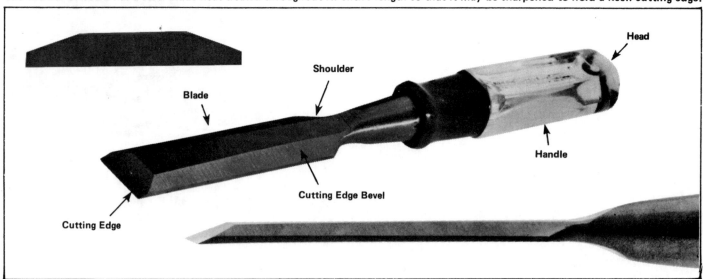

Shoulder

Blade

Head

Handle

Cutting Edge Bevel

Cutting Edge

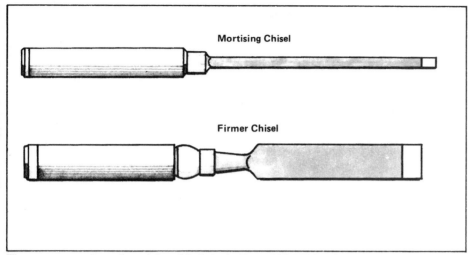

Mortising Chisel

Firmer Chisel

There are a number of specialty chisels including a MORTISING CHISEL with a narrow blade for cleaning out a mortise, above, and a FIRMER CHISEL, at bottom, with a thick blade for heavy cutting.

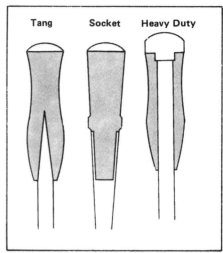

Tang   Socket   Heavy Duty

Three types of chisel handles are TANG, at the left, which is best for hand pressure and light mallet blows; SOCKET, which will take more punishment than the tang and has a replaceable handle; and HEAVY-DUTY, which has a steel head that contacts or connects with the blade and may be struck with a steel hammer.

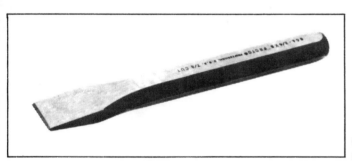

One-piece, all-steel wood chisels are available, although uncommon. They stand up well under heavy use.

contain 1/4, 1/2, 3/4, and 1-inch chisels. If you can buy more right off, great. I approve. If not, you can always add later on.

GET A HANDLE ON IT

Most any chisel may be struck with a mallet or a soft-faced hammer, but the amount of force you use should be governed by the design of the tool's handle. The *tang* chisel, especially when the handle is wood, will take the least punishment and should be used mostly with hand pressure. Be sure to keep the blows light when you must drive it with a striking tool. Modern versions, with plastic handles terminating in a crown-shaped steel cap, permit the tool to hold up under harder use.

Socket-type handles have a round taper fitting a mating cavity at the top of the one-piece blade.

Hardwood handles are still much in evidence here. They are often available with tough leather tips to guard against splitting. You may even find some with a metal crown like a chair glide. In all, the socket chisel is a more durable tool when used on jobs needing a lot of driving with mallets.

The *heavy-duty* chisel has a one-piece blade and shank that passes through the handle and makes direct contact with a steel cap. You can see that any blow on the cap passes directly through the blade to the cutting edge without putting any strain on the handle. This chisel is made for continuous use with striking tools. Just because the design is called *heavy-duty*, you should not think these tools are for rough-and-tough work only. They are good, general-purpose wood chisels and may be used with the same light-fingered finesse as any of the others.

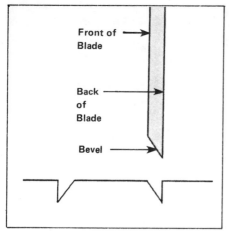

The BEVEL compresses the wood away from the back of the blade. For clean borderlines always point the bevel toward the center of the cavity. Using a mallet is safest when you are cutting across the grain. Be careful to avoid splitting when you are cutting with the grain.

Be careful of splitting at the end of any cut. It is best to stop short of an edge and cut from the other direction.

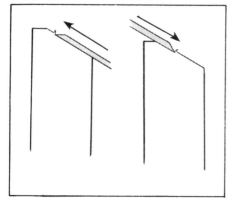

Let the work you are doing determine whether the chisel bevel should be up or down. Keep the bevel up in open areas.

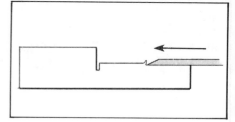

Keep the bevel down in confined areas. A shoulder cut should be made with a saw before you begin chiseling.

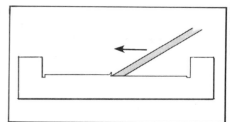

The bevel should be away from you when shaping outside curves.

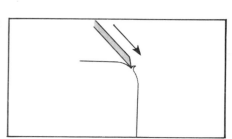

Inside curves are easiest to cut when the bevel is toward you.

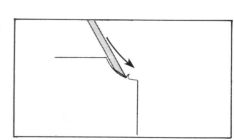

HOW TO USE CHISELS

For most types of work it is best to use one hand to *control* the tool and the other hand to apply the pressure. Assuming you are right-handed, hold the blade in your left hand with your thumb on the beveled side. Keep your thumb as close to the cutting edge as the work will permit. Grasp the handle in your right hand almost as if you were holding a hammer. In situations where you must apply more pressure, work with the end of the handle against your palm.

Remember, the chisel is a cutting tool, a super-sharp one if you maintain it correctly. It will cut you more easily than wood. In *all* situations, make it a rule to keep both hands and the rest of your body in back of the cutting edge.

The chisel may be used with the bevel either up or down depending on the work being done.

Generally, the bevel-down attitude is used for roughing cuts, the bevel-up technique for paring cuts. When possible, make cuts with the chisel held at a slight angle to the pass direction. The resulting shearing action produces smoother results with less effort.

Cut *with* the grain of the wood whenever you have a choice. Making a number of shallow cuts is always better than a single, heavy one. The angle between the tool and the work is determined by the job, and by the amount of material you wish to remove. Regardless of whether you are working with the bevel up or down, the closer to vertical you hold the tool, the deeper it will cut. To form a cavity, for example, work with the chisel almost perpendicular. For a paring cut—just a minimum shaving—hold the chisel almost flat on the work. To form depressed areas you change the tool

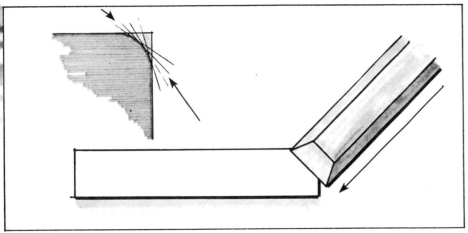

To round a corner, make a series of cuts that are tangent to the arc you want. Work with the chisel at a slight angle with the bevel up.

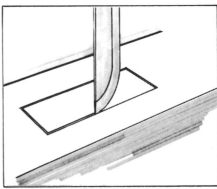

Score outlines with a sharp knife or the chisel itself before starting to cut cavities. This severs the surface fibers and assures a clean entrance.

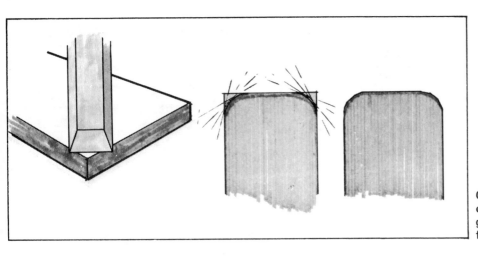

Corners can be rounded by cutting vertically with the chisel. Keep the cuts tangent to the arc. Sandpaper can be used for the final shaping.

When working crossgrain, as in a lap joint, work from both sides and leave a raised center area to be cut down last.

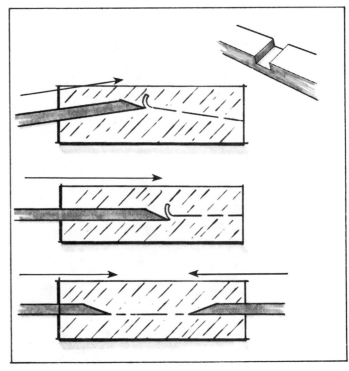

angle as you cut. Start with the tool in near-vertical position and decrease the angle as you push forward. When the bulk of the waste is removed, work with the chisel almost flat with the bevel up to do final paring cuts.

Use mallets only when you must, and then in gentle fashion. Learn to work with finesse rather than force. Don't use chisels to do jobs more easily accomplished with saws, drills, or planes. Bring these other tools into play whenever possible to remove maximum waste before you apply the chisel.

Always be sure the chisels have keen cutting edges. Dull edges do poor work and are actually dangerous because they force you to apply more pressure. This increases the possibility of slipping. Check chapter 15 on sharpening for information about maintaining chisel edges.

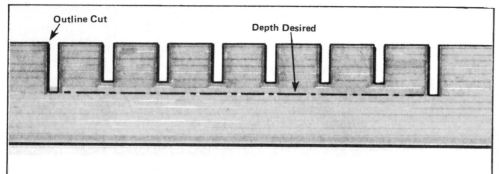

Parallel saw cuts between outline cuts will make removing waste material easier. The outline cuts should be full depth, but the waste cuts not so deep.

Start a MORTISE for a hinge by holding it firmly in the correct position and tracing around it with a hard, sharp pencil.

Use a knife to incise the pencil lines, pressing hard enough to sever the surface fibers. It's a good idea to incise the lines to the full depth of the mortise.

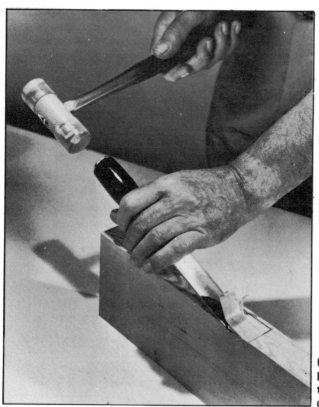

Use the chisel at a low angle with the bevel down, tapping lightly if you use a mallet. The shavings should be uniform and thin. Work from both ends and leave enough side wall so you can clean up with vertical shearing cuts.

Chisel work can be reduced by drilling a series of overlapping holes to remove the bulk of the waste. The cavity is then cleaned with the chisel. Note how the thumb is used as a guide. Round ends of the mortise can be left if you decide to shape the tenon like the one on the left.

Another way to make a MORTISE is to make a series of perpendicular cuts and then clean out the waste. Many people find this method more accurate. Pencil line on edge shows the mortise depth.

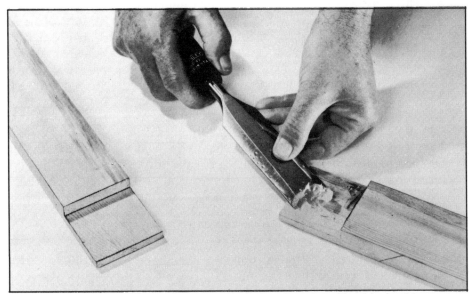

Clean up an end by making paring cuts with the bevel up. Jobs like this should always be started by making shoulder cuts with a backsaw.

Outline intricate cuts with a knife or coping saw and clean with a chisel. Take slight cuts and be sure the chisel is SHARP.

Waste material between saw-cut shoulders on a DADO can be removed if you work bevel down with the chisel at an angle of 45 degrees. Use your left hand to control the depth of cut. Finish with paring cuts.

7

Planes

The plane came about when someone decided he could do a controlled job of smoothing the edge of a board if he secured a chisel at a particular angle in a block of wood. The modern plane has evolved into a very sophisticated piece of equipment, yet the basic concept of a chisel-in-a-holder remains.

A skilled woodworker will rate hand planes on a par with any essential tool, even though much of the wood materials we buy come S4S which means surfaced or finished on four sides. A lot of the material may be used as-is—especially when you take pains to plan for using dimensioned lumber. But it's a rare project that doesn't call for dressing wood to some specific dimensions. Planes are used to reduce widths and thicknesses, and to smooth edges and surfaces cut with other tools. They can square and true edges, do chamfering and beveling, contribute to joints. They can take off a lot of material or a shaving so fine you can almost see through it. The latter application suggests the need for a plane in any minimum tool box, if only to remove a smidgen of material from a drawer or door that doesn't close smoothly. Thus the plane becomes a maintenance tool as well as one to shape components for projects.

BASIC PLANES

Smooth, jack, fore, and *jointer* planes all belong in the bench-plane category. The major physical differences are in length and weight. This may suggest light and heavy-duty applications and that thought is correct to a degree. There is considerable overlap in the functions of bench planes even though each might be more appropriate or easier to handle for a particular job.

A short, light plane might be the choice for some final touches on work that is already level and reasonably smooth. A long, heavy plane makes sense when you are working on a rough surface and wish to remove a lot of material quickly. A long plane also spans high points on irregular work so it's easier to bring the surface to true levelness. The longest plane of all derives its name *jointer* from its ability to smooth and true the edges of boards to such a precise degree they may be joined together in tight-fitting joints.

Smooth Plane—The smallest of the bench planes, this is a favorite among woodworkers. Its length and weight contribute to easy handling and it is a good learner's tool, although experience will soon indicate that a longer, heavier plane is better suited for many woodworking chores. However, the smooth plane will never become obsolete in your shop no matter how much equipment you add in this area. Many experts use the smooth plane to do the final finishing work on surfaces previously dressed with a jack plane. All plane blades must be kept keen, but the smooth's should be maintained razor-sharp constantly, and adjusted to produce an extremely thin shaving. Because this plane is short, the worker must learn to apply equal pressure throughout the pass. Otherwise, hollows may form when smoothing down long work.

BASIC FACTS ABOUT BENCH PLANES

The SMOOTH plane is light and small, only 9-1/4-inches long. It is especially useful for final smoothing.

The JACK plane is longer, 14 to 15 inches, heavier than a smooth plane and is a good tool to use on rough surfaces. A JUNIOR JACK plane is 11-1/2 inches long.

The FORE plane is 18-inches long. While it may be used like a JACK or a JOINTER plane, it is most often selected for flat finishing.

The JOINTER plane is the longest, 22 to 24 inches, and heaviest hand plane and produces the smoothest and flattest surfaces. It is ideal for finishing boards that will be joined edge to edge.

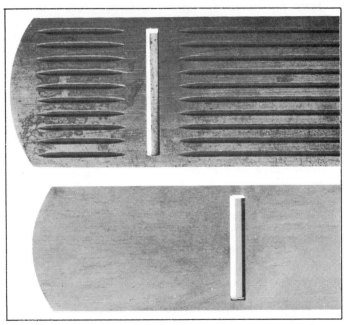

The modern plane, properly used, will produce a smooth, even finish.

A CORRUGATED BOTTOM has less contact with the work than a SMOOTH BOTTOM, and therefore moves more easily because there is less friction.

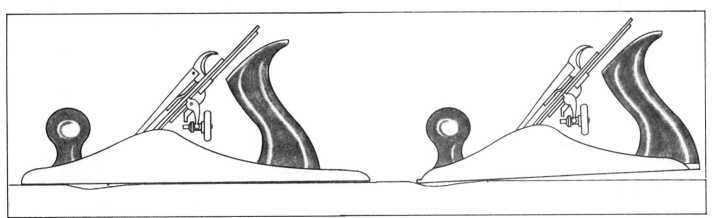

An advantage of a long plane is that it can span the high points on irregular work. A short plane rides the valleys and makes it more difficult to true the edge.

The plane may seem complicated, but a short time spent familiarizing yourself with it will result in finer, more accurate work.

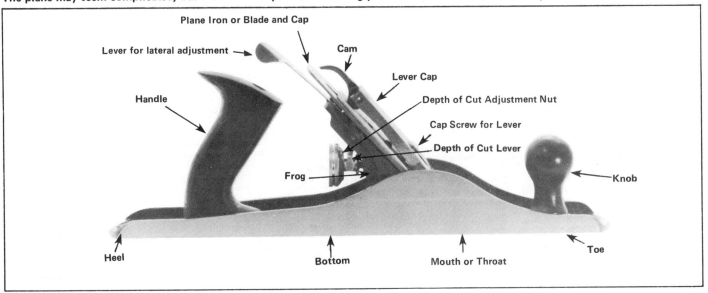

Plane Iron or Blade and Cap

Lever for lateral adjustment →

Cam

Lever Cap

Depth of Cut Adjustment Nut

Handle

Cap Screw for Lever

Depth of Cut Lever

Frog

Knob

Heel

Bottom

Mouth or Throat

Toe

Jack Plane—Longer and heavier than a smooth plane, this is generally a more powerful tool. While it is suitable for obtaining smooth, flat, true surfaces, it is especially good for doing rough, heavy work when you are bringing stock down to size. For such applications, set it to produce a coarse chip because that makes the job go faster. Many times, the blade—or "iron"—ends in a very gentle convex curve so the tool can take deeper bites. The weight of the tool is an asset when you are producing thicker shavings.

Jointer—This is the longest and heaviest hand plane made. It's designed to produce the flattest and truest surfaces possible. Its length enables it to span irregularities a shorter plane might follow like the car on a roller coaster. To picture one of its basic functions, imagine having to even up a length of wood with a scalloped edge. The long plane will ride and gradually take down the high spots until the edge becomes uniform. Another, more frequent application is smoothing and truing boards for edge-to-edge joining. Two boards, clamped or gripped together in a vise, can be dressed so the edges will mate perfectly.

Fore Plane—This falls between jack and jointer planes. Quite often it is referred to as either a *long-jack* plane or a *short-jointer* plane. Like the jack plane, its blade often terminates in a slight convex curve instead of being straight across.

Block Plane—This palm-sized tool, good for many woodworking operations, is especially suited to smoothing end grain and plywood, and doing shaving on oblique hardwood grain. It works in such situations because its blade is set at a smaller angle than those on bench planes and the bevel on the blade points up instead of down. On many of its applications the block plane produces sawdust-like waste instead of shavings. Its design and cutting action also make it the tool to use when you need to trim the end—square or mitered—of moldings, casings, siding, and the like, for planing corners, and for beveling and chamfering across the grain. It is an excellent toolbox plane even if your woodworking is limited to house-maintenance chores. Refitting of drawers and doors are typical uses.

Trimmers—Block planes are available in midget versions where the size might be, for example, 1-inch wide and about 3-inches long. Such tiny tools are useful for odds and ends of light work, breaking edges, smoothing feathered corners, doing wood sculpture, and so forth. Model makers find them extremely useful.

SPECIAL PLANES

Rabbet Plane—An L-shaped cut along an edge or across the end of stock is called a *rabbet*. It is used frequently in joints occurring in case work, drawers, shelves, and the like. A flush cabinet back is an example. The back of the cabinet can be inset when the back edges of the frame are rabbeted. This kind of work can be accomplished with saws and chisels, but the special rabbet plane makes the job easier, especially when you have many similar cuts to make.

Router Plane—This can be considered an all-purpose tool in the area of planing or smoothing the bottom of grooves, or just about any recessed area with a bottom that is parallel to the surface of the work. Various types of cutters are supplied with the plane and these may be positioned to point forward for regular work, or reversed for bull-nose work—"stopped" cuts. A frequent use for a router plane is forming or smoothing the bottom of *dadoes*. These U-shaped cuts, like the *rabbet,* are often required in joint making. A typical example is inserting shelf ends in the vertical members of a bookcase. With the router plane you can make the U-shaped cut for the shelf end straight across the vertical piece, or you can stop short of the front edge so it can't be seen.

TYPES OF PLANES AND TYPICAL DIMENSIONS		
TYPE	OVERALL LENGTH INCHES	CUTTER WIDTH INCHES
SMOOTH	9-1/4	1-3/4
	9-3/4	2
JUNIOR JACK	11-1/2	1-3/4
JACK	14	2
FORE	18	2-3/8
JOINTER	22	2-3/8
BLOCK PLANES	6	1-1/4
	6	1-3/8
	6	1-5/8
	7	1-5/8
TRIMMER	3-1/2	1
RABBET (COMB)	8-1/4	1-1/2
SIDE RABBET	5-1/2	1/2
REGULAR RABBET	5-1/2	1
BULL NOSE RABBET	4	1
	4	1-3/32
ROUTER	7-5/8	1/4 and 1/2
NARROW CUT ROUTER	3	1/4

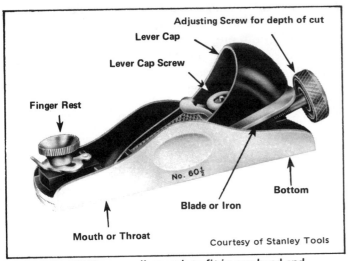

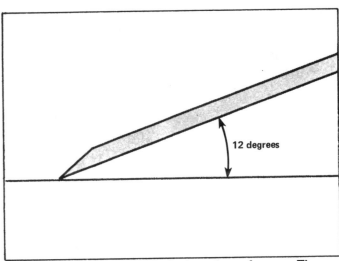

BLOCK PLANES are small enough to fit in one hand and are used for smoothing end grain, especially for beveling and chamfering.

The bevel on the blade of a block plane always faces up. The blade angle is usually about 12 degrees from horizontal because end grain is more difficult to cut.

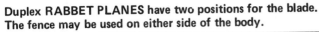

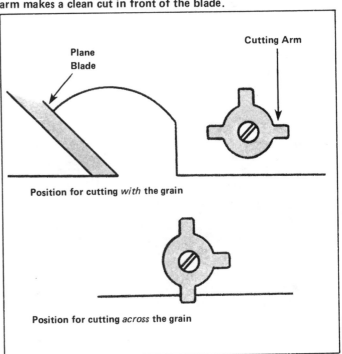

A BLOCK PLANE can be held in one hand, but many jobs require the use of both hands.

The cutting arm of the spur on a RABBET PLANE is held above the work when cutting *with* the grain. The spur is rotated 90 degrees for working *across* the grain so the cutting arm makes a clean cut in front of the blade.

Duplex RABBET PLANES have two positions for the blade. The fence may be used on either side of the body.

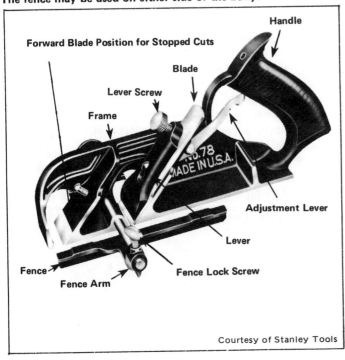

Courtesy of Stanley Tools

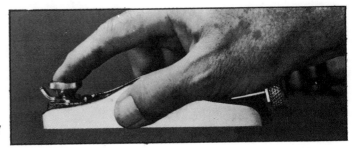

Position for cutting *with* the grain

Position for cutting *across* the grain

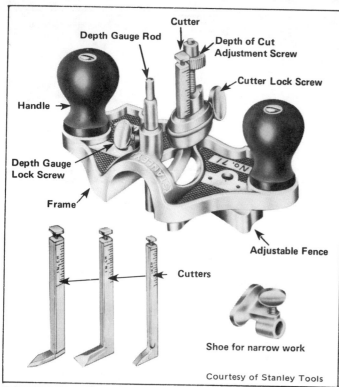

ROUTER PLANE. Note cutter markings to make setting the depth of cut easier. Cutters include 1/4-inch and 1/2-inch routers and V-shaped smoother

PALM-SIZED ROUTER is handy for tight places, small dadoes, recesses for inlays and shallow mortises for lock plates and other hardware.

Spokeshaves—Originally used to form wheel-spoke contours, these are still used today for similar functions on wood projects. They do belong in the plane category even though the basic function is opposite that of a bench plane. While planes are used mostly to make edges and surfaces flat, the spokeshave works to develop, smooth, round off, or chamfer concave or convex shapes.

The most common spokeshave has a straight blade, but special models are available for particular applications. For example, a half-round version has a concave body and blade that may be used to form an edge to a radius. Another model with a convex body and blade forms concave shapes.

SETTING A PLANE BLADE

The assembly consisting of the plane's blade—or *iron*—and the blade cap are often called a *double plane cutter.* While the blade actually does the cutting, the cap breaks the shaving and causes it to curl. The cap also serves as a blade stiffener and, together with the toe of the plane, acts to prevent splitting in front of the cutting edge. You can see the relationship between cap and blade is critical.

To properly set the blade, place the cap on the flat side of the blade at right-angles to it. Hold it in position by finger-tightening the screw. Draw the cap back as you turn it clockwise to align it with the blade. At this point the front edge of the cap should be well behind the front edge of the blade. Slide the cap forward—or bring the blade back—until you have 1/16 inch between the cap and the cutting edge. Be sure the edges of blade and cap are parallel, and then secure the screw. You may change this procedure after a bit to suit your own work habits, but be sure you don't drag the cap across the blade's cutting edge. The 1/16-inch clearance is good for general work, but you can reduce it to as little as 1/32 inch for very fine shavings and cross-grain work, or increase it to as much as 1/8 inch for rough work. Incidentally, block plane caps do not function like those on bench planes because the tool is designed primarily for end-grain work and this does not produce shavings.

Follow the directions supplied with the tool when you are ready to install the double plane cutter in the body of the plane. There can be some slight differences in method or design, so it's best to obey the manufacturer's instructions.

CONTROLLING THE CUT

Three factors are involved—the size of the *mouth,* often called the *throat,* through which the blade projects, the amount of projection, and the horizontal alignment of the cutting edge in relation to the plane bottom.

The rectangular throat opening may be widened or made narrower by adjusting the round adjusting nut that controls the assembly or *frog* on which the blade rests. The throat size can be adjusted further by moving the screws securing the frog. When you get the plane, it will probably be adjusted for general smoothing chores. Work with a narrower throat when you want to do very fine planing and when the wood is very dense and close-grained. When you open the throat, you get thicker shavings. This can be useful when you wish to remove stock quickly, or when you are working on wood that has a coarse grain or is resinous. Remember, there is a relationship between the width of the throat opening and the depth of the cut. Generally, a wide opening goes along with a deeper cut. Splitting can occur when the opening is *too* wide for the cut you are taking.

The actual depth of cut, or thickness of shavings you will produce, is controlled by how much the blade projects beneath the bottom of the plane. The lateral adjustment—that which controls the parallelism of the blade edge to the plane bottom—is what determines the uniformity of the shavings.

Suggestions for setting blade projection and angle often say to sight along the bottom of the plane and use the depth-adjusting frog and the lateral adjusting lever until the cutting edge is horizontal and projects about the thickness of a hair. There is no objection to doing it this way except it leaves much room for human error. A safer, more consistent procedure is to make the blade projection gauge shown in the drawing on page 76. If you make several of these with various thicknesses, you will be organized to achieve various degrees of projection automatically. Use minimum projection in relation to the job you are doing. You will know quickly when you are trying to remove too much material. It will be very difficult to make smooth passes, edges will be rough, and shavings will not curl nicely.

HOW TO PLANE

Always examine the stock to determine the direction of the grain so you can organize the work for planing *with* the grain rather than against it. If you are ever in doubt, you will find the first cuts educational. If made against the grain, they will be rough and pitted and the shavings will not curl smoothly—if at all. Working with the grain makes for easy passes, smooth cuts, and even-curling shavings. If you are working with old or used wood, check it for nails, embedded materials, and defects that can damage the cutter. When you have a choice, avoid planing on a side of the wood containing knots.

Provide adequate work support. Usually you can grip the wood in a vise, but when you can't, take other means to assure the work stays put while you do the planing. Very long work can be clamped to sawhorses placed lengthwise. Shorter pieces in a

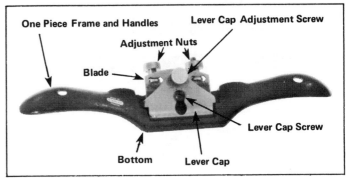

SPOKESHAVE with a flat bottom blade. Not all have blade adjustment nuts. They are a great convenience, so check before you buy.

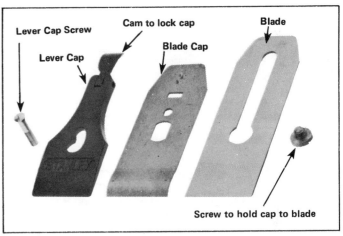

PLANE BLADE assembly.

The blade does the cutting, but the cap breaks and curls the shaving. Cap and toe work together to keep the wood from splitting ahead of the cutting edge.

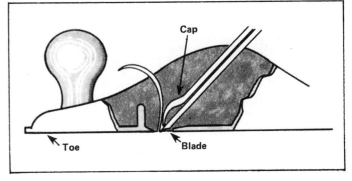

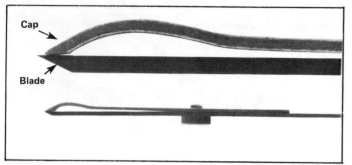

Side view of the cap and blade. Set the cap 1/16 inch from the cutting edge for general work. Bring it as close to the edge as possible when working cross grain.

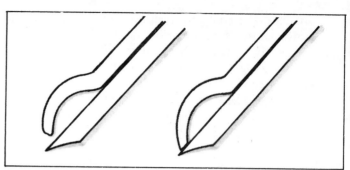

Cap poorly mated to the blade will result in chips piling up and prevent quality work. The correct relationship between the cap and blade is shown at right.

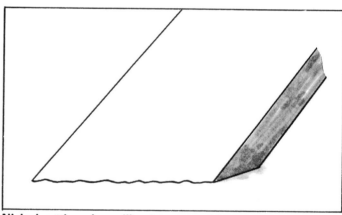

HOW TO MAKE A BLADE PROJECTION GAUGE: A simple gauge can be made by gluing two thin pieces of cardboard, wood veneer, or plastic laminate to the narrow edge of a 2x4. Adjust the blade so it just touches the surface of the board. Be sure to adjust the blade laterally as well as for projection.

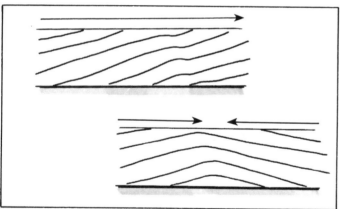

Always plane with the grain of the wood as shown on the right. When you encounter a change in grain direction in the middle of a piece of work, plane from both directions.

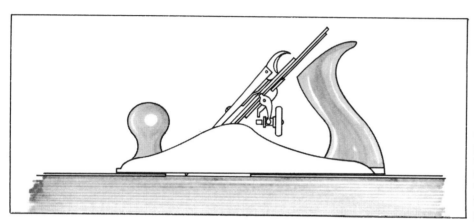

Nicked cutting edges will not cut smoothly.

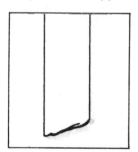

A blunted edge can result from careless or excessive whetting.

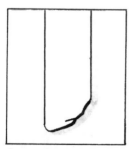

A round edge can result from careless whetting.

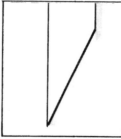

Too long or thin a bevel will nick easily.

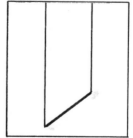

Too short or thick a bevel will make cutting more difficult.

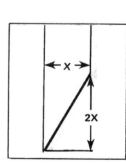

As a rule, the bevel should be a bit more than two times the blade thickness.

vise can be braced against bench stops like those shown in the drawing on page 78. This also works well when you are doing surface-planing. The V-block also can hold stock on edge.

THE PASS

Planing is done most efficiently when you coordinate the swing of your arms and body. Stand with your left foot forward when the pass direction is to the left. Do the reverse when you are planing toward the right. This is suggested so your body can rock forward with the plane action. If you stand flat-footed with your feet together, you will find it awkward to move along with the plane even when you are smoothing short pieces.

Start the pass by placing the toe of the plane flat and firmly on the work. At this point there should be a bit more pressure over the toe of the plane than elsewhere. Distribute pressure equally over toe and heel as you get into the cut. Work this way until the cutter has cleared the stock and you can lift the plane for the return. Never drag the plane back over the work. This dulls the cutting edge quickly.

There may be a tendency to relax pressure and to lift the plane before the cut is complete. Pay special attention to avoid this or you will get a high spot at the end of the stock. It is also possible to create a taper when you increase pressure over the toe and relax it over the heel when you near the end of the pass. Start the pass correctly, maintain uniform pressure, and you will get straight, flat edges.

Beginning planers often find that while they get smooth results, the planed edge is not square to adjacent surfaces. This can happen when you don't start the pass correctly or when you apply pressure unevenly during the pass. It can even be caused by poor lateral blade alignment. Be careful setting the plane, and do some practice plane handling. A couple of ideas can contribute mechanical help. A simple one is to hold a short wooden block under the plane against the side of the work. The block is held in place by the forward hand which grips both the plane and the guide—the guide moves along with the plane. The purpose of the block is to provide additional bearing surface for the bottom of the plane and help keep it flat while you make the pass.

A better system is to make a special right-angle guide attached to the side of the plane with small C-clamps or screws. This leaves both hands free to function in a normal manner. This same guide can be fitted with a V-block to help you do bevels and chamfers more accurately.

PLANING END GRAIN

Work with a block plane set to take a minimum cut when all you are doing is smoothing. If you have to take off some material to bring a board to size, increase the depth of cut and adjust the throat opening accordingly. One of the hazards of planing end grain is the splintering which occurs at the end of the pass, no matter what. One way you can avoid it is by planing from both ends toward the center but this poses the possibility of getting a high spot.

There are better solutions. The best of all is probably the clamped-on end-block. When it is in place you can cut as deep as you wish without worry about splintering. The end chamfer also can do the job, but it calls for a degree of accuracy between the bevel and the amount of material you wish to remove. It's probably okay when you just want to smooth an edge.

SURFACE PLANING

This kind of work should be done with a heavy plane set to take a shallow cut. Be sure the blade is razor-sharp. Don't bear down excessively—you're not going to cut any deeper than the amount of blade-projection allows anyway, so why tire yourself by straining unnecessarily? Remove the bulk of the waste by planing obliquely across the grain. Take strokes that overlap about 50%. Finish up by working with the grain and with the blade projection set to almost nothing. This is probably the hardest kind of planing work to do with optimum results. Even experts don't expect a finish that doesn't require some additional attention with sandpaper. However, that is not an excuse for sloppy work. The intent should be to produce a surface requiring *minimum* additional attention.

This kind of work is often done after narrow boards have been glued edge to edge to form a large slab. Be sure to remove any dried glue that has squeezed out of the joints before you use the plane.

RABBETS

The rabbet plane is equipped with a fence and a stop. The fence is set to control cut width, the stop to control its depth. Because rabbets are usually wide and deep, it takes quite a few passes with the plane to accomplish the full cut. This prompts many users to adjust the blade projection for a very deep cut—a mistake! Better to make 4 or 5 or 6 passes and end up with a good job than to do it in two passes and end up with a mess.

Rabbets should be cut precisely, so be sure to measure carefully when you set the fence and the depth stop. Also, be certain the blade is set correctly in the plane. If it isn't, no amount of expert handling will produce good results.

The most important factor when cutting a rabbet is to keep the plane square to the surface of

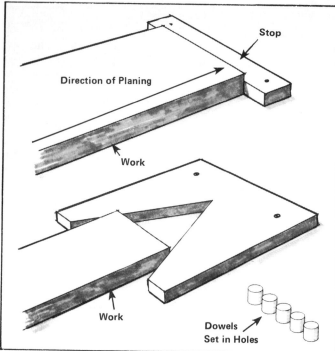

Direction of Planning

Stop

Work

Work

Dowels
Set in Holes

WAYS TO MAKE STOPS FOR PLANING ON A WORK-BENCH: A strip of wood nailed or screwed into the work-bench as shown at the top, or short dowels placed in a series of holes drilled in the bench top, or a V-block that will accommodate various width work, can be used as stops. In all cases the stop should protrude less than the thickness of the work.

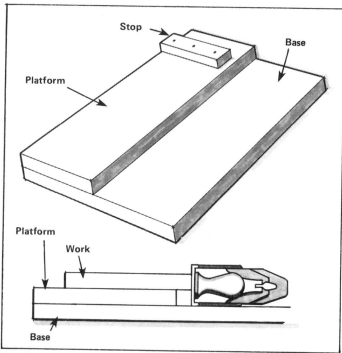

Stop

Base

Platform

Platform

Work

Base

This jig can assure square edges. The work is placed on the platform against the stop. The pass is made with the plane on its side.

As you begin your pass with the plane, hold the tool firmly with the toe flat on the work. Your pressure should be slightly greater on the toe.

Equalize the pressure on both the toe and heel once the tool starts to cut. It is sometimes easier to hold the plane at a slight angle to the work which causes a shearing action. Shavings should be uniform and your motion should be smooth.

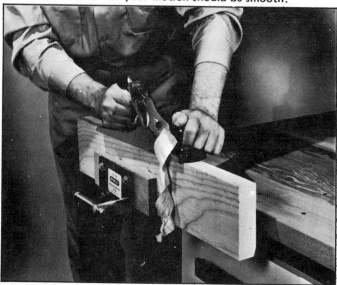

Don't allow the plane to dip when you reach the end of the pass. Continue off the work on the same level you were on during the pass. Lift the plane clear of the work for the return.

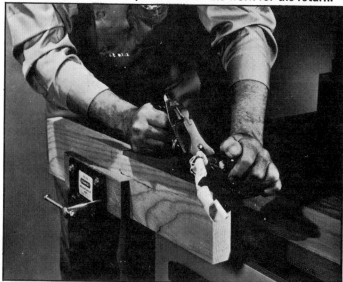

the work and the fence snug against the side throughout the pass. Use one hand to do the feeding while the other hand acts to maintain a good relationship between the plane and the work. Be sure the toe of the plane and the fence are in good position before you make each cut. Maintain just enough pressure throughout the pass to keep the blade cutting evenly.

A rabbet that does not go the full length of the work is called *stopped* or *blind*. This design calls for two special steps. First, a full-size notch is formed at the blind end of the rabbet with a chisel. Second, the plane-blade is set in the forward or "bullnose" position. Then, the cutting proceeds in normal fashion.

The rabbet plane will work across the grain, but be sure the spur is positioned correctly to sever wood fibers in front of the cutter. The blade could not cut cross-grain without considerable splintering and feathering except for the slight pre-cutting done by the spur. The spur is actually a tiny knife that projects below the bottom of the plane. It must be kept sharp. Because it is such a small item, sharpening is easiest to do when you hold the spur with pliers and whet the edges with a small stone.

Set your RABBET PLANE to the proper depth and width for an L-shaped cut. Be sure to make all passes with the fence snug against the side of the work.

DADOES

One of the main functions of the router plane is smoothing the bottom of U-shaped grooves. When the groove is formed *across* the grain it is called a *dado*—when it is formed *with* the grain it is called a *groove*. Often, the cut-action used to form a groove is called *ploughing*. These are technical terms and often ignored. The single word—*dado*—is often used to describe any U-shaped part of a joint regardless of its relationship to grain-direction. I mention them to avoid any confusion you might have with project plans.

The router plane is more of an accessory tool than a complete former. It is very difficult to form dadoes or grooves without making shoulder cuts with a saw first. These are usually made with a backsaw fitted with a block of wood to control the depth of the cut. After the cuts are made, you use the router plane to remove the waste between them. Don't try to do this in one pass unless the U-shape is very shallow. It is usually wise to make several passes, setting the cutter in the plane for a deeper bite each time. How deep to bite depends on the density of the material. For example, it is easier to cut pine than maple or birch. A wise judgment isn't difficult to reach. You are cutting too deep anytime you must force the tool. Minimum-depth cuts are easier to do and usually result in better quality work.

Like the rabbet plane, the router can form stopped cuts. The technique is the same. Work with chisels to form a cavity at the stopped end of the cut and place the plane's cutter in the forward or "bullnose" position. Then plane as you would normally.

Of course, the router plane can be used to smooth the bottom of any depressed area. When the area is too wide for the plane to span, you can work by attaching a piece of plywood to the bottom of the plane. Holes are provided for just such a purpose. This false bottom should be sized to suit the work.

PLANING CURVES

The spokeshave can be used for many jobs, but its main function is to shape or smooth curved surfaces. The tool may be pushed or pulled, but it should always cut *with* the grain. Work with minimum blade projection if you are just smoothing. The depth of cut may be increased when you are using the tool to create a shape. The last passes should be so fine the job will require a minimum amount of sanding for the final smoothing.

Make long, smooth, uninterrupted passes so you will avoid bumps which can result when you hesitate mid-way. Remember, a flat-blade spokeshave makes flat cuts. To produce a rounded edge or a contour, you must constantly change the tilt of the tool to reduce the width of the flat formed on the previous pass. It's like using many tiny straight lines to form a circle. The visual effect is a curve—final smoothing with sandpaper actually makes it so.

An easily made RIGHT-ANGLE GUIDE assures square edges. Cut to fit the shape of the plane, it can be attached with clamps as shown, or with small bolts through holes drilled in the side of the tool.

BEVELS or CHAMFERS can be made by holding the plane at the correct angle throughout the pass using your free hand for extra guidance. Carefully mark the edge of the work with a pencil before cutting.

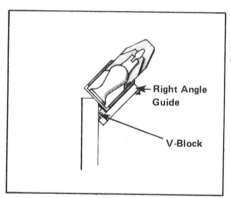

Right-angle guide may be used for bevels and chamfers when you add a V-block as shown here. Width of the guide should be adjusted to suit the work.

To assure a good cut, you can clamp a scrap block to the work as shown on the left, or you can use a scrap piece to control the angle when doing chamfering or beveling.

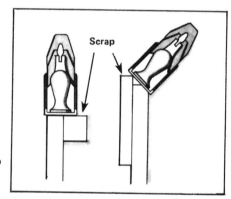

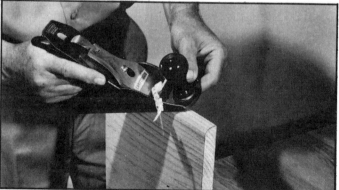

To round off edges, rotate the plane between passes. Each pass makes a flat cut. The narrower the cuts, the rounder the edge.

Splintering may occur at the end of end-grain cuts, even if you decrease the depth of your cut. Prevent it with the methods shown on the next page.

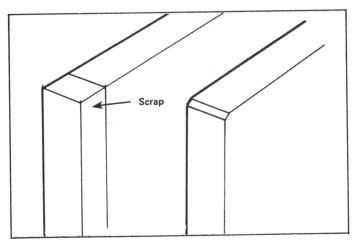

Scrap

Splintering can be avoided in at least two different ways. A piece of scrap can be clamped to the edge of the work as shown on the left. The scrap takes the splintering rather than the work. Chamfering the end of the work as shown at right will also reduce the chances of splintering.

BLOCK PLANES work well smoothing plywood edges. Use minimum blade projection and maintain full contact between plane bottom and work edge.

Block planes can be used to round or chamfer edges on circular pieces. Passes are made across the edge rather than along it.

When you want to remove a lot of material, make oblique passes across the grain. Don't try to cut too deep — make more passes instead.

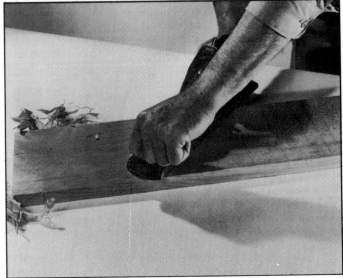

Arrow indicates the part of a stopped rabbit that must be cut with chisels. Note the blade of the plane is in the forward, or bullnose position.

ROUTER PLANES can be used to finish a dado. The job should be started by making shoulder cuts with a saw as shown at left.

Arrows point out the part of a groove that must be cut with a chisel when a router plane is used to make a stopped cut.

Making DADOES can be done quicker if you remove the bulk of the waste with a chisel. Use the router plane with a V-cutter for final smoothing.

Wide depressed areas can be smoothed if you equip the router plane with a special bottom to span the work area. Be sure the plywood is thick so it won't flex.

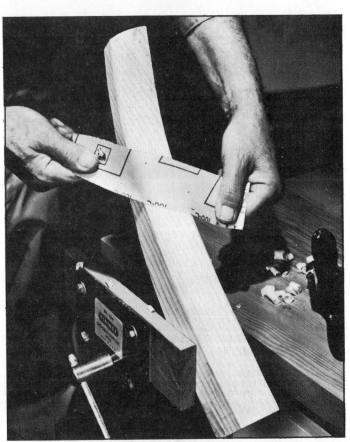

Grip the SPOKESHAVE with both hands and exert force both downward and in the direction of the pass. Hold the tool at a different angle for each pass when you are forming a contour.

A good job with a spokeshave will leave little work to be done with sandpaper. Start by using a strip of sandpaper as if it were a shoe rag. Finish by sanding in line with the grain.

Like a block plane, a spokeshave will do a good job of chamfering or rounding edges of circular pieces. On jobs like this you can not always work with the grain, but try to as much as you can.

83

Tools For Shaping & Finishing

Tools in this area include files and rasps, special formers like the Stanley Surforms™, abrasive papers, and scrapers. Many are designed for final touch-ups or for smoothing surfaces prepared with other tools. Others—rasps and Surforms in particular—may be used to do a considerable amount of shaping and are often used for creating contours other tools can't handle. Examples include handles, spiral forms, contoured arms and legs for furniture projects, sculptured joints, and in-the-round craft or art projects.

As accessory tools they can often right a wrong. For example, they can take off a fraction of material so a tenon fits a mortise—just so—or open up a bored hole that's a little too tight for what it must receive.

FILES AND RASPS

The basic physical difference between a file and a rasp is in the tooth arrangement. Rasp teeth have been cut individually; file teeth are continuous. Rasp teeth are specially designed to cut soft material with minimum clogging. Large spaces between teeth allow waste to escape. Files have nothing but teeth—soft, adhesive waste can collect easily. When this happens, the file clogs. Even though the teeth are still sharp, they can't cut.

The spacing of the teeth and the angle at which they cross the surface of the file is called the *cut.* Teeth that run diagonally in one direction are *single-cut.* Teeth that cross each other are called *double-cut.* Both cuts are classified according to roughness as *coarse, bastard, second-cut* or *smooth.* Roughness is also related to the length of the file. The longer the file, the rougher its cut will be. It is necessary to specify the kind of file you want both by roughness and length. A 16-inch coarse file will be rougher than a 6-inch coarse file. Files can be used for smoothing in a progression of lesser degrees of coarseness. For example, you can start with a 16-inch bastard for rough shaping and work to a 10-inch bastard to bring the form to the point where it can be finished with sandpaper.

Most files are available in two shapes: *Blunt,* with parallel edges, and *taper,* which is narrower at the point. Blunt files cut faster because they have more area, but taper files can be used in smaller places.

There are literally hundreds of types and sizes of files. Many of them should never touch a piece of wood because they clog so easily. Files most useful in a wood shop have a bastard cut and are at least 10-inches long. A few other types are useful for sharpening other tools. These are discussed in chapter 15. You may also have an occasional use for files to smooth metal. Examples are smoothing a cut made by a hacksaw or removing burrs from hardware. The chart on page 86 shows some of the basic types and shapes of files with suggestions about when you might need them.

Files and rasps should never be used without suitable handles; the tang is sharp enough to puncture your hand easily. Handles come in different sizes, but they are fairly interchangeable. For this reason, many shops have a good assortment of files, but few handles. That makes it possible for a casual person who wants to do only a few strokes with a file to skip the chore of mounting a handle. Handles are not that expensive. I recommend you buy a handle each time you add a file or a rasp. Don't mount the handle by smacking it with a hammer. Instead, insert the tang into the handle-socket and set it by rapping the handle smartly on a solid surface. The tang must fit snugly, but if you overdo the rapping you run the risk of splitting the handle.

File work is usually a two-hand operation—one hand on the handle, the other near the point. The stroke is supplied by the hand on the handle while either or both hands contribute feed pressure. You make deeper cuts when both hands are bearing down of course, but excessive pressure should not be necessary, especially when you are using course files and rasps on wood.

Be careful with the hand used near the point. Lacerations can occur when the file moves and the hand does not. You can wear a glove on your

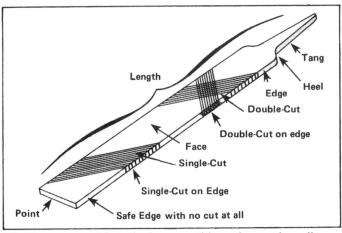

FILES are essential tools for smoothing edges and small curves.

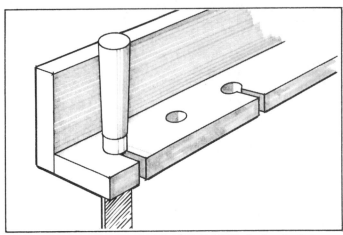

STORAGE RACK FOR FILES AND RASPS: A simple rack can be made to protect your files and rasps. Bore holes in a piece of 3/4-inch stock and make two saw cuts from one edge to each hole. Attach to a piece of 1/2-inch plywood and hang on the wall.

COMMON CUTS OF FILE TEETH

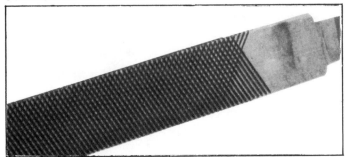

DOUBLE-CUT

SINGLE-CUT

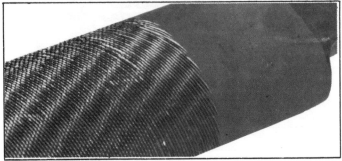

CURVED

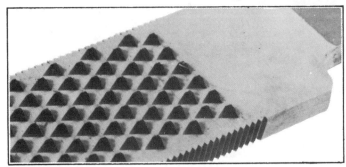

RASP

Wood waste clogs file teeth easily and quickly. Files will not cut if the waste piles up, so clean files frequently as you work.

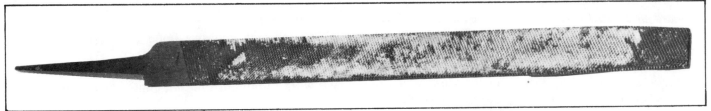

SHOP FILE TYPES

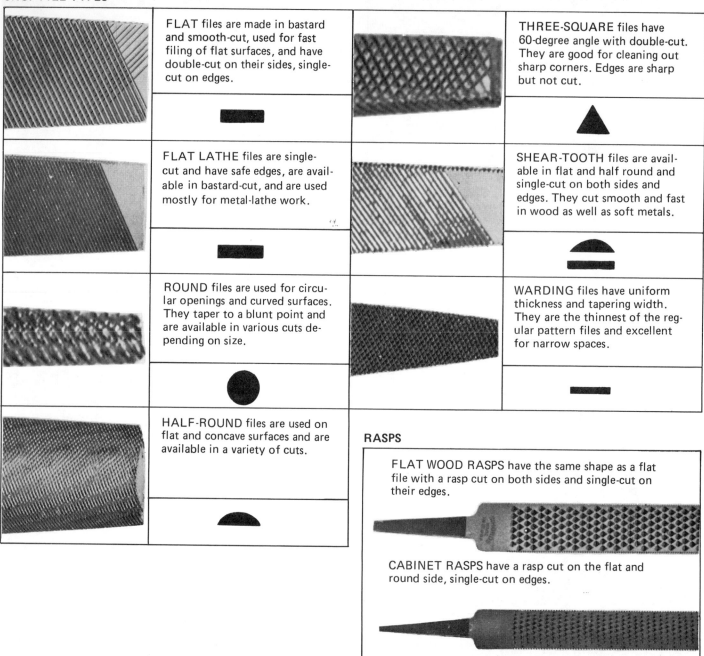

FLAT files are made in bastard and smooth-cut, used for fast filing of flat surfaces, and have double-cut on their sides, single-cut on edges.

THREE-SQUARE files have 60-degree angle with double-cut. They are good for cleaning out sharp corners. Edges are sharp but not cut.

FLAT LATHE files are single-cut and have safe edges, are available in bastard-cut, and are used mostly for metal-lathe work.

SHEAR-TOOTH files are available in flat and half round and single-cut on both sides and edges. They cut smooth and fast in wood as well as soft metals.

ROUND files are used for circular openings and curved surfaces. They taper to a blunt point and are available in various cuts depending on size.

WARDING files have uniform thickness and tapering width. They are the thinnest of the regular pattern files and excellent for narrow spaces.

HALF-ROUND files are used on flat and concave surfaces and are available in a variety of cuts.

RASPS

FLAT WOOD RASPS have the same shape as a flat file with a rasp cut on both sides and single-cut on their edges.

CABINET RASPS have a rasp cut on the flat and round side, single-cut on edges.

free hand for extra protection if you wish. Be sure it is not a floppy one. Any type of loose apparel that can snag is a hazard in *any* shop.

Clean files frequently, but not by rapping them on a hard surface as many do. Files are hard but brittle, and they can chip or break. It is best to use a soft wire brush and stroke across the teeth to remove waste. A special combination *file card and brush* made for this purpose is available. One side has a mat of soft-iron wire, the other is matted with a fiber material, so you are equipped for stubborn or easy waste removal. When some teeth are too clogged for the file card, you can pick out the waste with a length of stiff wire.

Don't use an awl or similar tool.

On occasion, I have cleaned wood-clogged files and rasps by soaking them for a few minutes in warm water and detergent—then working them with the file card. Be sure the file is completely dry before you store it.

A common technique—often used when working on soft or resinous material—is to stroke the file teeth lightly with a piece of chalk before filing. This prevents an adhesive bond from forming between the waste and the file teeth. At times I have dusted the tool with talcum powder. Both ideas work to minimize, if not eliminate, clogging.

SHOE RASP is a popular combination. Each side is half rasp and half double-cut. Its edges are flat and safe, but its ends are cut. One side is flat, the other oval.

NAME	APPROXIMATE SIZES OF RASPS (Inches)													
	LENGTH													
	6 inch		8 inch		9 inch		10 inch		12 inch		14 inch		16 inch	
	WIDTH	THICK.	WIDTH	THICK.	WIDTH	THICK.	WIDTH	THICK.	WIDTH	THICK.	WIDTH	THICK.	WIDTH	THICK.
CABINET RASP	11/16	3/16	29/32	1/4			1-1/8	9/32	1-11/32	11/32	1-9/16	3/8		
FLAT WOOD RASP			25/32	9/32			31/32	11/32	1-5/32	13/32	1-11/32	15/32		
HALF ROUND SHOE RASP	19/32	1/4	25/32	5/16			31/32	3/8	1-5/32	7/16	1-11/32	1/2	1-1/32	9/16
HALF ROUND WOOD RASP			7/8	9/32	31/32	5/16	1-1/16	11/32						

Use the rasp's flat side for outside curves. It cuts on the forward stroke, so a slight lift on the return is wise. It requires little pressure for cutting, especially with soft woods.

Use the round side for shaping convex forms. Rotate the tool as you stroke and use minimum pressure as you approach the final shape. Use sandpaper to complete the job.

FORMERS

You can't help but think of cheese graters when you look at these tools because the tooth design and action are similar. The resemblance ends there. These are most efficient cutters and probably one of the more ingenious ideas to emerge in the area of hand tools in quite some time.

Sometimes called *Surform®* tools, their blades are tool steel with hundreds of razor-sharp cutting edges. Each edge acts like an individual tool and has its own throat to lift and remove shavings from the work. Escape routes for waste are so generous it's almost impossible to clog these tools. In addition to forming and trimming wood, they can be used on plywood, composition materials, asphalt tile, hard rubber, plastics—even non-ferrous metals. Replaceable blades are available in regular or fine-cut grades. The latter are designed to take a finer bite and are best used for cutting metal and dense wood materials.

These tools can remove a lot of material or a little, and they can do it quickly or slowly. Much depends on feed pressure and the attitude of the tool in relation to the grain. In general, you work at an angle to the grain to do the basic forming and then gradually swing to an in-line stroke as you approach the shape you want. Be careful when shaving narrow surfaces because a cross-grain stroke can cause splintering and feathering on edges. Decrease feed pressure as you near the end of the job. Keep changing the position of the tool as you stroke so individual cuts made by the teeth will overlap.

How you grip the tool depends on its design. File types are held just as you would a conventional file or rasp. Pocket types are made for one-hand operation. Plane types are gripped pretty much as you would a regular plane.

Once you have become acquainted with these tools it's quite likely you will reach for one frequently instead of a file or a rasp or a plane. Remember they are *forming* tools—they do the bulk of the work before you finish up with sandpaper.

SCRAPERS

Scrapers are not as widely used today as they were once, simply because good sandpaper is so available. It's logical for this to happen, yet to eliminate scrapers completely can be a mistake. A recent, personal experience proves my point. An outside door had settled enough to bind on an oak threshold. To avoid removing the door so I could work on its bottom edge, I took a half-dozen swipes over the oak with a scraper, and the job was done. Sandpaper would have done the job, but not so easily or so quickly.

There are situations in the shop when it's wiser or better to use a scraper than sandpaper or another tool. Examples are removing old paint or varnish from furniture you want to refinish, smoothing ridges left by planing before you sand, and preliminary smoothing of boards that have been glued edge to edge, especially when hard glue is evident along the joint lines. There used to be many dedicated craftspeople, and still may be some, who preferred scraping hardwoods over sanding because it gave a surface gleam they could not duplicate with sandpaper.

Blade Scrapers—The simplest scraper is a spring-tempered, thin-steel tool available with either a straight or a curved blade. It's held firmly with both hands between thumb and fingers, and sprung to a slight curve by pressure of the thumbs. In use, it is held at an angle of about 75 degrees off horizontal and may either be pushed or pulled. Many experienced workers say that pushing is better, but I think the stroke direction depends on the job and the grain. One thing *is* sure—the scraper should produce shavings, not dust. Dust may indicate a dull edge.

Blade scrapers are available in different shapes. Some have both a concave and a convex edge, others resemble French curves. These special shapes are useful for making furniture.

Cabinet Scrapers—These have smaller blades mounted in a frame with integral handles. The handles are raised above the bottom of the tool so you don't scrape your hands while you are scraping the work. The blade is adjustable for projection and may be bowed to a correct arc by using a special thumb screw. The tool may be used for general work but is especially good on irregular grain and surfaces other tools can't conform to.

Double-Edge Scrapers—These have blades with a right-angle lip secured in a long or a short wooden handle. Longer handles let you apply more leverage and such tools are often used to scrape walls. In this type, blade widths run from about 1-1/2 to about 3 inches so the tools are very convenient for working in close quarters.

SCRAPING

Whenever possible, scrape so strokes are parallel to the grain of the wood. Cut with the grain rather than against it. Keep pressure constant on the tool throughout the stroke and bear down only as strongly as you must to keep the blade cutting. Follow the instructions in chapter 15 for maintaining the cutting edges. Edges that are not correctly sharpened can do more harm than good.

SANDING

You can spend a lot of time and do a good job fabricating a project and then ruin it by being

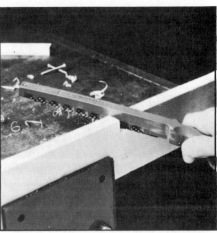

SURFORM® TOOLS cut like a horde of tiny planes, each cutting edge shaving and clearing its own path. Replacement blades are available for most designs. Work at an angle to remove stock quickly, then gradually bring the tool in line for finishing.

PLANE TYPE formers have handles like conventional planes. Start with oblique strokes. Keep the pressure even from heel to toe. Don't try to dig in.

MINI FILE formers are fine for slitting, notching and grooving. The blade is only 1/2-inch wide and functions well in tight places.

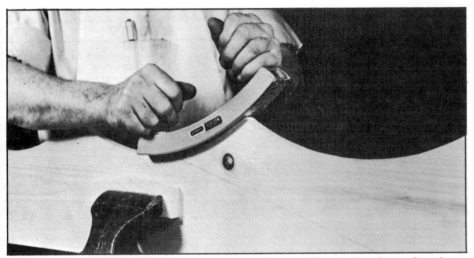

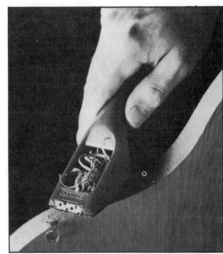

CONVEX FORMERS are good for gentle curves with a radius equal or larger than the tool's.

SHAVERS cut on the pull stroke and are designed for one-hand operation. When needed, it is all right to apply pressure on the toe with your free hand.

ROUND FILE formers can be used to enlarge holes and to shape or finish decorative cuts.

HAND SCRAPER is used for final smoothing before sandpapering. A good size is 3 by 5 inches of .035-gauge specially heat-treated steel.

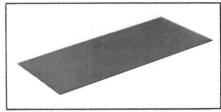

lax with final sanding. This is the step between the last tool job and the application of the finishing coats of stain, paint, varnish or whatever. It's an area that causes different reactions among workers. Some rush through a project so they can get to the finishing. Others do the opposite. Actually, there are no options here. How you sand will make the difference between a professional-looking project and one that screams "amateur."

Sanding does take some time, but it's not difficult to do. Its purpose is to remove any marks left by fabrication tools, and to smooth and equalize all surfaces so the full beauty of the wood and its grain will be brought out by the finishing coats. This may not apply so much to a project you intend to paint, but relying on a thick coating to hide goofs or laxity really isn't the way to go. Paint is not an infallible coverall.

Sandpaper is a cutting tool. It removes wood by various degrees in relation to the coarseness of the abrasive. The finer the abrasive, the less you can see or feel the ridge left by each piece of grit. In general, the correct procedure is to work through progressively finer grits of sandpaper until the wood feels satiny smooth. What grade you start with depends on the condition of the wood. It doesn't make sense to blindly follow the general rule if the condition of the wood is good enough that the optimum can be achieved by working with fine-grit paper only. Much of the wood we buy is in pretty fair shape, so examine it to see how you can get by with the *least* amount of work. The grades of sandpaper most commonly used in woodworking are 1-1/2, 1/2, 0 and 00.

The terms *open-coat* or *close-coat* tell you how much of the backing is covered with the abrasive grit. Close-coat paper has overall coverage—open-coat only 50 to 70%. Close-coat sandpaper will produce the smoothest finishes but it clogs more easily. That's why open-coat abrasives are selected for working on old wood and for removing old finishes. It is also a good choice for softwoods and resinous woods. Finer sandpaper

IDENTIFICATION OF ABRASIVE GRITS		Choose from these categories in relation to the condition of the wood. Some jobs can be done by working with the fine category only.	
NAME	GRIT NO.	GRADE NO.	GENERAL USAGE
VERY FINE	400	10/0	For polishing and smoothing between finishing coats and for smoothing the final coat. Use after applications of stain, shellac or sealers; also for super-fine finish on raw wood.
	360		
	320	9/0	
	280	8/0	
	240	7/0	
	220	6/0	
FINE	180	5/0	For the final smoothing before the application of stains or sealers.
	150	4/0	
	120	3/0	
MEDIUM	100	2/0	For intermediate smoothing to prepare the wood for the fine sanding and to remove any remaining roughness.
	80	1/0	
	60	1/2	
COARSE	50	1	For initial sanding when necessary and to prepare the wood for medium and fine work.
	40	1-1/2	
	36	2	
VERY COARSE	30	2-1/2	For very rough work only. May be used on unplaned wood and is often used in place of a file to round edges.
	24	3	
	20	3-1/2	
	16	4	

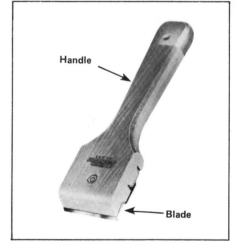

Handled SCRAPERS come with replaceable blades and are useful for removing paint and glue, as well as for wood scraping.

Hold scraper as shown and apply most of pressure with the hand over the blade. It is best to use a pulling stroke with this tool.

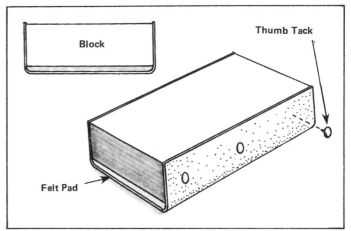

SANDING BLOCKS can be easily made by wrapping sandpaper around a palm-size block of wood and securing it with tape or tacks. A piece of felt placed under the paper makes a soft sander.

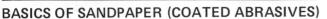

BASICS OF SANDPAPER (COATED ABRASIVES)

BACKING. May be cloth, paper or a special flex material.

ADHESIVE, or BOND. Various types are used, mostly hide glues, resins and waterproof synthetic resins.

GRAINS OF ABRASIVE. Most popular types are flint, garnet, aluminum oxide, and silicon carbide.

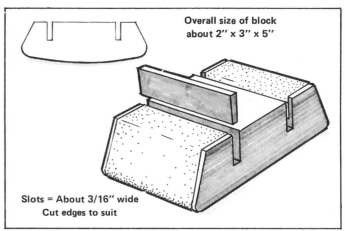

Overall size of block about 2″ x 3″ x 5″

Slots = About 3/16″ wide
Cut edges to suit

Another sanding block can be made as shown above. Sandpaper is held in place by wedges pushed in the slots. This type can be shaped to any curve. Be sure the paper is held taut.

BASIC FACTS ABOUT VARIOUS ABRASIVES											
	GRITS							GENERALLY AVAILABLE IN	USE ON		SUGGESTED APPLICATIONS
TYPE	Super Fine	Extra Fine	Very Fine	Fine	Medium	Coarse	Very Coarse		Wood	Metal	
FLINT PAPER			X	X	X	X	X	9″ x 10″ sheets 4½″ x 5″ packets	X		Rough work: finishing chores: lacks toughness and durability.
GARNET PAPER			220 A	120 C	80 D	50 D	30 D	9″ x 11″ sheets	X		Excellent general abrasive for all woodworking projects.
ALUMINUM OXIDE PAPER			220 A	120 C	80 D	50 D	30 D	9″ x 11″ sheets	X	X	Good for hardwoods, metals, plastics and other materials: long lasting.
ALUMINUM OXIDE CLOTH			120	80	50	30		in belt form for electric sanders	X	X	Cloth-backed belts are very strong and are a first choice for power-tool sanding.
SILICON CARBIDE WATERPROOF PAPER	400 A	320 A	220 A					9″ x 11″ sheets	X	X	Very good for wet sanding after primer coats and between finish coats: can be used with oil and similar lubricants or water.

NOTE: letter designation following the grit number indicates the degree of flexibility of the backing: A indicates a thin, soft backing; C and D indicate progressively stiffer and tougher backings.

Smooth rounded edges by using a strip of sandpaper like a shoe polish rag. Begin this way, but shift to stroke with the grain for finishing. You can support the paper with a piece of soft carpeting as well.

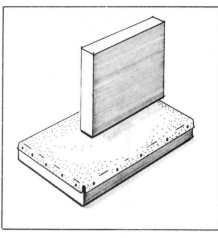

A stationary sanding block can be made for smoothing small pieces. The paper is taped or tacked to a large block which can be secured to a vise or with clamps to your bench.

Suit the back-up block to the work you are doing. Here sandpaper is used to widen a dado. Sandpaper can be wrapped around dowels for use in tight places as well.

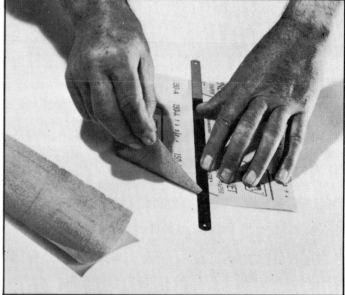

Standard sheets of sandpaper can easily be cut by holding a hacksaw blade firmly as you pull the paper against the serrated edge.

Place your fingers so the sandpaper mates with the contours of irregular shapes. Use the edge of the sanding pad to get into crevices and corners.

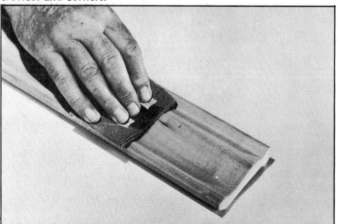

A piece of the molding you are working on can make a sanding block that fits exactly. Here the edges of the block have been sawed off so it will fit the major contours better.

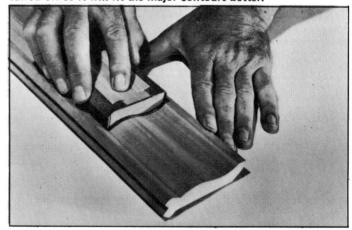

Commercially made sanding blocks are available in many different styles.

grades are always close-coat and they are the ones to use for polishing and for super finishes on hardwoods. In my shop I use the open-coat paper when I must—for rough sanding, for finish removal, for resinous wood. For super smoothness I do the last sanding steps with close-coat paper regardless of whether the wood is hard or soft.

Smooth and uniform finishes on flat surfaces are best obtained when the sandpaper is backed with a block of wood you can grip in your hand. Rigid backing provides a leveling action for the entire area and cuts down ridges and irregularities. It also allows more abrasive-to-work contact for faster sanding. The same block, or a second, special one, may be fitted with a soft pad for smoothing contours, or round surfaces. A soft backing lets the abrasive conform more readily to a curved shape. Soft-pad blocks can also be used with coarse papers for cross-grain sanding when you wish to remove a lot of material, and with fine paper for smoothest results when working with the grain. Whenever possible, work with the grain for the final steps.

When you are satisfied with the feel of the wood, dampen—don't wet—a lint-free cloth and wipe the sanded surface. When the wood is dry to the touch, do a final fine sanding. This will produce an especially fine surface.

Use a sanding stroke that is uniform in length, but don't overreach. Short, overlapping strokes are better because they let you maintain a uniform down pressure. Sand carefully when you near edges so you don't round off corners that should be square.

CONCEALING EDGES

One of the final steps in most projects is covering unattractive edges, particularly when you use plywood. Plywood panels are a boon to the woodworker, but they pose the problem of unattractive edges that can't always be concealed by joint design. Exposure occurs at the front edges of case goods and shelves, and at the perimeter of sections for table tops, trays and the like.

There are a number of ways to cover edges. Heavy strips of wood can be glued and nailed in place. Standard moldings are available that cover both single edges and corners. They come in various shapes and designs, and require a minimum of sanding.

Where it is appropriate, a raised lip can be used to conceal an edge. A straight strip is used for concealing the edge, and triangular strips or molding are used to blend the lip with the slab. Another way is to cut a rabbet in the strip used for covering the edges. This allows one piece to accomplish the work of two.

In construction, edges can be concealed by using solid stock inserted at the corners where pieces meet. This method requires pre-planning as the inserts take up space and can change a project's dimensions. Glue blocks placed behind these corners are useful for support.

WOOD TAPES

Another fine way to conceal edges is to work with wood-tape products. They may not be necessary if you plan to paint. A careful job of filling and sanding the edges before applying the finish-coats will probably do. But they should be used for any type of natural finish.

The wood tapes come in rolls and are actually flexible bands of veneer. More and more types have come on the market, so today you can find a match for just about any species of wood used as a surface veneer on plywood. The tapes are thin enough so you can cut them with a knife, yet strong enough so you don't have to worry about breaking them during application.

Different types are available. Some are self-adhesive, others are applied with glue or contact cement. If you work with a white glue, it is best to apply thin coatings to both surfaces and wait for the glue to become tacky before placing the tape. If you work with contact cement, read the instructions on the container. You must be sure the initial placement is correct because the cement bonds RIGHT NOW!

An exceptional product, so far as application is concerned, is simply called *woodtape®*. The veneer used is 1/48 inch thick and has a factory-applied thermo-setting adhesive. Don't let that term worry you because heat for the application is available from an ordinary electric household iron. Tapes come with a paper backing you peel off before use. They are sticky enough so the tape holds, but the bond will not be effective or permanent until you do the ironing job with the iron set at 400 degrees Fahrenheit (204°C.)—about the correct setting for COTTON.

Be sure the panel edges are square, smooth and free of sawdust no matter what tape you apply. It is not necessary to fill the edges but you should plug any large cavity that might cause a hollow to form in the tape.

Thermo-setting tape can be worked on as soon as it has cooled—contact-cement applications are ready to go right away—glue jobs require the correct amount of set time. Sand the tapes as you would any veneer—being aware of their thinness. All are quite smooth, so minimum sandpaper work is needed.

Incidentally, the tapes may be used as inlay strips and, because they cut so easily with a knife or shears, for marquetry and decorative overlays.

Standard moldings can be used to hide single edges, as stops, or as outside corner guards.

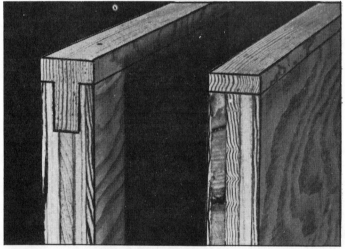

Both edges are concealed by wood strips. Example on left requires two rabbet cuts on the strip and a groove in the plywood.

THERMO-SETTING WOODTAPE® is pressed on with an ordinary household iron set at 400 degrees F. (204°C.). Remove the paper backing as you go—don't strip long pieces.

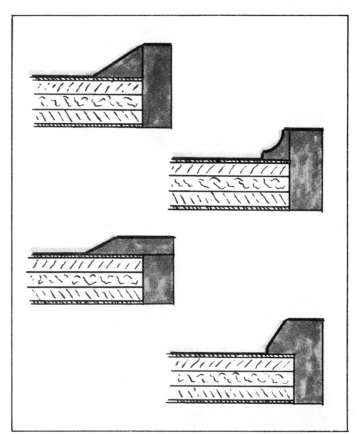

You can use solid-stock inserts to cover plywood edges at corners. They can be square, quarter-round, or triangular, and reinforced with glue blocks.

Raised lip can be made with a triangular strip, molding, two wood strips, or one piece with a rabbet.

Plans for edge-guide made with 1/4-inch plywood. The roller is cut from a 1-inch hardwood dowel and rides a nail axle.

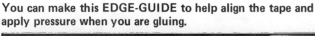

You can make this EDGE-GUIDE to help align the tape and apply pressure when you are gluing.

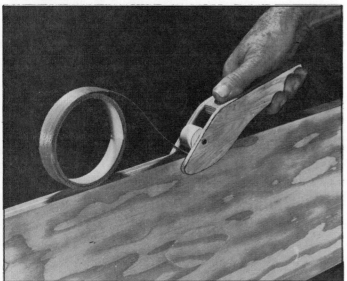

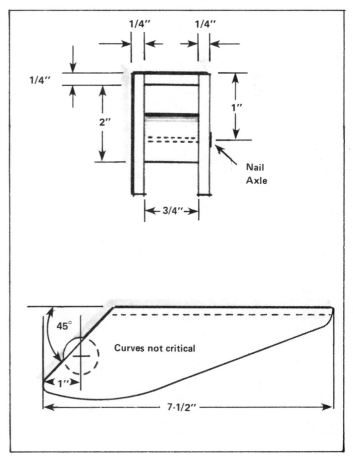

9

Vises & Clamps

VISES

The vise is a tool attached to a bench that will hold a piece of work steadily while you work on it. We commonly think of an iron *bench vise* which has solid metal jaws opened and closed by a screw bar. This kind of vise can be used for holding small pieces of work, but is primarily designed for working metal. Its jaws have rough inner edges and the surface of the work should be protected. Jaw covers can be made by bending small sheets of smooth metal at right angles and laying them over the jaws, or pieces of scrap can be placed between the jaws and the work. A bench vise with a 3 to 4-inch mouth is large enough for most work, but it is not essential in a woodshop. More useful for woodworkers is the wood vise.

Wood vises are mounted at the edge of the workbench with their jaws flush with the bench's top surface. This is done primarily to keep the work surface clear for any size project. Most often the vise is mounted at the left-front corner, but this is not an unbreakable rule. You can place a vise to suit yourself, but remember you want maximum clearance at the front and on each side. Many shops have two vises—one at the left-front, the other at the right-front edge, so the worker has a choice in relation to the size and shape of the wood and the job being done.

There are different-size vises and more expensive ones have special features like a retractable *dog* in the top edge of the forward jaw. This may be raised above the level of the bench to apply pressure to work backed up by a stop on the bench-top. It's a way of increasing the grip span beyond the maximum capacity of the vise itself, and it's handy for holding long or wide pieces for planing or even for clamping work edge to edge.

Another good feature you can look for on a vise is a half-thread on the screw bar. This makes it possible to slide the jaw forward against the work without having to do a lot of handle turning. A half-turn or so on the handle completes the tightening. It doesn't make you a better craftsperson but it is a convenience.

The design of the vise dictates how the tool must be attached. Fasteners may have to be installed from beneath or into the front edge of the bench, or both ways. Hardwood plates are screwed to the metal vise jaws. Screws for the back plate can be long enough to penetrate the edge of the workbench. The front plate can be attached with flathead screws and nuts, unless the design of the vise calls for another system. Plate-attachment screws must be countersunk enough so they can't mar the work. For maximum security, the fasteners attaching the vise to the bench should be heavy lag screws you turn with a wrench. Don't use common wood screws.

All woodworker's vises will accommodate at least a 2-inch-thick bench top. Some provide more leeway and, when secured from beneath, require a filler block between the vise flange and the bench. Be sure the thickness of the block is exactly right to position the top edges of the vise jaws flush with the surface of the bench.

Use a hardwood like maple or birch, 3/4-inch thick, for the wooden plates and, while you're at it, make an extra set you can store as replacement equipment. Don't replace the original ones unless it is really necessary. Slight scars can be removed by sanding or planing but be sure to recheck the countersinks for the attachment screws. Make them deeper, if necessary, after you have resurfaced the plates.

CLAMPS

The purpose of any clamp is to put the pressure on. In a sense, clamps supply extra hands with strength beyond your own. Most clamps are general-purpose: They can be used to secure glued joints, to hold together temporary assemblies, or to lock work to a bench top or sawhorse so you can apply other tools. Special-purpose clamps such as band or web clamps are designed for circular and irregular assemblies. Edge-clamp fixtures are used mostly in conjunction with bar clamps. Miter clamps are for frame work.

Clamps are a boon and a necessity. Some woodworkers claim you can't have too many, but you

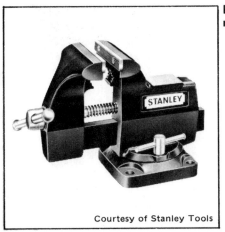

BENCH VISES are primarily for working metal and are not essential in a woodshop.

Courtesy of Stanley Tools

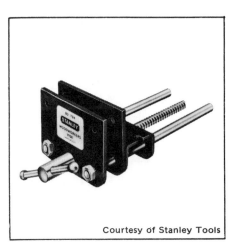

Courtesy of Stanley Tools

WOOD VISES require wood plates for their metal jaws. It is best to make the plates longer than the jaws. They should be held in place with countersunk screws or bolts. Some wood vises can be clamped to your workbench.

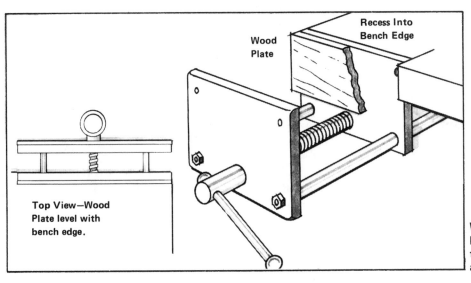

Wood Plate

Recess Into Bench Edge

Top View—Wood Plate level with bench edge.

WOOD VISES should be mounted so the back jaw and wood cover are recessed into the edge of the bench. There are models available which clamp to the bench.

A new concept in wood vises is called the ZYLISS vise, which is actually a kit that can be assembled to suit the job at hand. It clamps to the bench and holds work in either horizontal or vertical position.

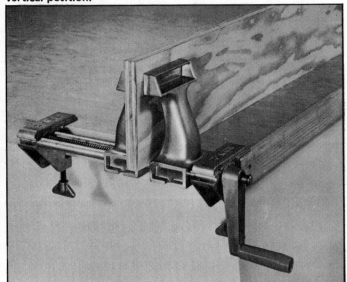

Grip handles this way and rotate your hands to open and close a HANDSCREW.

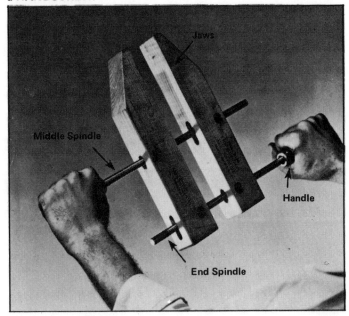

Jaws

Middle Spindle

Handle

End Spindle

SIZES OF HANDSCREWS		
OVERALL LENGTH OF JAWS inches	MAXIMUM OPENING BETWEEN JAWS inches	REACH – FROM MIDDLE SPINDLE TO END OF JAWS inches
4	2	2
5	2½	2½
6	3	3
7	3½	3½
8	4½	4
10	6	5
12	8½	6
14	10	7
16	12	8
18	14	9
20	14	10
24	17	12

should choose to fit the scope of your work. You may never need long bar or pipe clamps if you never become involved in gluing large slabs or assembling. furniture. On the other hand, a long edge-to-edge joint should have clamp pressure every 12 inches or so. The basic assembly of a chest of drawers will be easier if you don't have to skimp on clamps. If such work comes infrequently, there are ways to improvise shown later in this chapter.

Common general-purpose clamps are *handscrews*, *C-clamps*, and *clamp fixtures*.

USING CLAMPS

Clamps have a great mechanical advantage. If you apply a 20-pound twist on a 6-inch long handle and the jaw moves 1/8 inch per revolution you can get an effective pressure of over 1,500 pounds. You can see why it's easy to distort stock, or even crush softwoods. To prevent this kind of thing, don't play Tarzan with clamps. A visual check of the edges being brought together tells when pressure is sufficient. Most times it is wise to place blocks of wood between the clamp faces and the work. This accomplishes two things: it prevents the clamp from marring the work and it distributes the clamp pressure over a wider area. This is not necessary with handscrews because their design naturally distributes pressure over a wide area.

Long, glued joints tend to open more at the ends than at the center. Apply clamp pressure at the center to begin with. This will force excess glue and trapped air out to the edges. Tighten successive clamps as you approach the ends and use a little more pressure at those points. Because the wood will start to absorb glue, it is wise to see if the clamps can take a little more tightening after 5 minutes or so. Wipe off squeezed-out glue immediately with a damp—not wet—cloth.

Don't use clamps to compensate for poor-fitting joints. Using clamps to squeeze an oversize tenon into a mortise can split the work—it can even force the glue through the pores of the wood so it emerges on a surface. Don't use more glue than the job requires. It is assuring to see the glue squeeze out, but if the amount is excessive you are just wasting an expensive product. Always provide room for excess glue or for the glue to escape when you are doing closed joints such as mortise-and-tenon and dowel joints. Correct design of the assemblies and their components is shown in chapter 12.

Clamps are made for hand pressure so don't ever pound them with a mallet or use a length of pipe to increase leverage. You won't do the work any good and you may break or bend the clamp. Keep clamps clean by wiping off glue immediately. Use a soft brush to clean the screws; wipe them occasionally with a very small amount of light oil.

HANDSCREWS

Handscrews are favorites with woodworkers because they adjust easily to apply parallel pressures evenly over a broad area without marring the work. It takes a bit of practice, but you'll soon acquire the knack of adjusting the handscrew quickly by gripping the handles and rotating the jaws about the spindles. This should be done to bring the jaws approximately to the opening required. Then, situate the clamp so the center spindle is as close to the work edge as possible. Tighten the spindles lightly and alternately so you will be sure the jaws are parallel. Continue until you have the pressure you want. A common procedure is to tighten the end spindle first and then tighten the middle spindle.

The depth of a handscrew's throat is usually about half the length of the jaws. As you can see in the chart, there is quite a variety of sizes. A 12-inch size is a pretty fair choice for general work, at least to start with.

C-CLAMPS

C-clamps fall into large and small-size categories, but all are so named because of the physical shape. You might think of them as G-clamps as they do in England, but regardless, they are so useful in general shopwork they are usually included among the basic hand tools.

Clamps can be laminated steel, or of forged or cast, carefully heat-treated, high-quality iron or steel. Some have fixed or limited-action pads at the end of the screw. Others have a full swivel tip to conform to an irregularity or bear against a slanted surface. You should choose your clamps as you would any other tool. True, the amount of clamp pressure you require can affect a choice in structural quality, but generally, spending a little extra

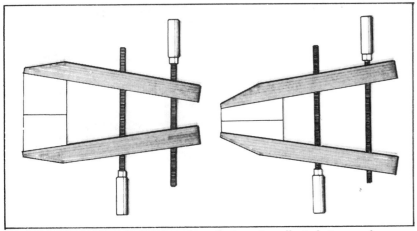

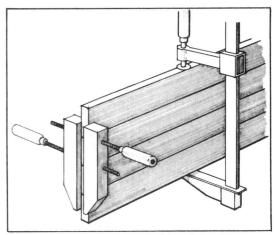

STANDARD HANDSCREWS have jaws that can be adjusted at an angle. Non-adjustable handscrews have jaws which always remain parallel.

Handscrews can be used to hold ends in alignment when joining pieces edge to edge.

If you cut accurate matching notches in the jaws of your handscrew, it will easily hold round or small square stock without interfering with the clamp's basic function.

HOW TO MAKE A MITER CLAMP

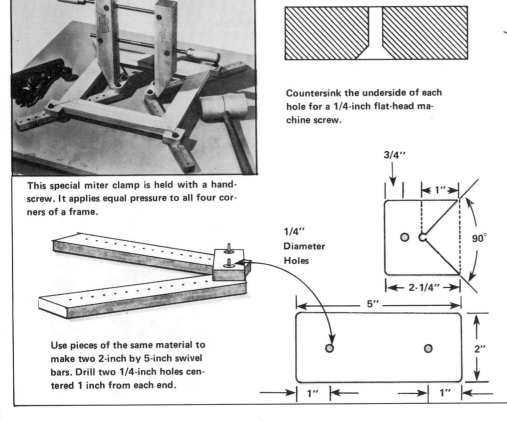

This special miter clamp is held with a handscrew. It applies equal pressure to all four corners of a frame.

Use pieces of the same material to make two 2-inch by 5-inch swivel bars. Drill two 1/4-inch holes centered 1 inch from each end.

Countersink the underside of each hole for a 1/4-inch flat-head machine screw.

Stack four strips of clear hardwood measuring 1 inch by 2 inches by 18 inches or longer, and drill 1/4-inch holes at 1-inch intervals.

1/4''
Diameter
Holes

3/4''

1''

90°

2-1/4''

5''

2''

1''

1''

Corner Block

Make four corner blocks by cutting 1-inch deep right-angle cuts into 2-1/4-inch square blocks. Drill a 1/4-inch hole 3/4 inch from the edge opposite your right angle. When cutting the notch, it is easiest to drill a relief hole first. The miter clamp is ready to assemble with eight 1/4 x 2-1/4-inch flat-head machine screws.

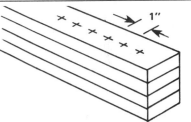

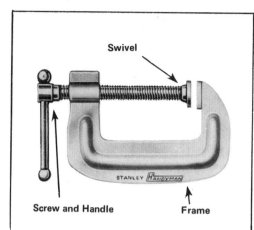

C-CLAMPS are widely used.

TYPES OF C-CLAMPS

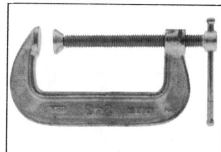

REGULAR THROAT

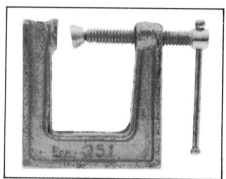

SQUARE FRAME

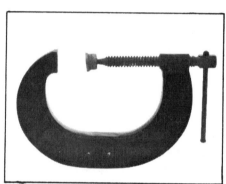

ROUND FRAME

BAR CLAMPS are used here with edge clamps to apply pressure downward on the work as well as against its sides.

C-CLAMPS are ideal for jobs like this. Blocks under the jaws protect the wood and spread the pressure over wider areas.

money now will amount to a saving in the long run.

When making a work choice, select the smallest C-clamp that will do the job—likewise, select the smallest throat depth the work permits. Never use a wrench or a piece of pipe to apply extra leverage to the handle.

BAR AND PIPE CLAMPS

These two types of clamps look very similar, but have one major difference. Bar clamps are permanently attached to their bars. Pipe clamps or fixtures may be attached to any length of pipe.

Bar clamps have wide mouths and close like a small vise. Maximum openings range from 6 inches to more than 30 feet. Some models have hinged tail stops for clamping slanted or irregular surfaces.

Pipe clamp fixtures can use any length of pipe. With half a dozen fixtures and an assortment of pipe lengths you can be ready for almost any job. You can also standardize the pipe lengths by locking the tail stop at any point on the pipe. In effect, you can have any size clamp within the limit imposed by the pipe length.

WEB OR BAND CLAMPS

Every shop should have a pair of these unique clamps because they enable you to hold difficult irregular assemblies. Sizes generally fall into light or heavy-duty categories. A typical light clamp has a 1-inch-wide, 12- or 15-foot-long nylon band. A heavy-duty clamp may have a 2-inch-wide pre-stretched canvas band that can be from 10- to 30-feet long. Clamps are also available with a 1-3/4-inch-wide steel band, but these are recommended for use on round shapes only.

The band on a small clamp is tightened through a ratchet mechanism actuated with a wrench or a screwdriver. A spring-loaded pawl affords a positive lock at any point along the band. The band on the larger model is tightened with a screw-handle arrangement. Self-locking cams guard against slipping.

In addition to woodworking applications, band clamps may be used for jobs like temporary baling of bundles, cartons, or luggage, and for securing loads on a wheelbarrow or pickup truck. When bands are used, there are no knots to tie or untie—or to slip.

MITER CLAMPS

Miter clamps are often called *corner clamps*. They work like a vise for holding miter joints rigid while the glue hardens. Because the joint is fully exposed, it can be nailed or screwed and removed immediately, if you wish.

A second kind of miter clamp is used with blind holes you bore into the back of the work. This clamp has the advantage of being able to pull together any angle miter joint.

HOLD-DOWN CLAMPS

Hold-down clamps are mounted on the work bench by drilling a hole for the bolt. The clamp slides over the head of the bolt and is held in place by tightening the lock nut.

SPRING CLAMPS

Spring clamps are like having extra hands with super-strong, never-tiring fingers. Jaw openings range from less than 1 inch to 4 inches. Overall length and reach increase in proportion to the gripping power of the tool. The spring on the larger sizes is so powerful you need two hands to open the jaws.

These clamps may be used anyplace where the spring pressure is adequate, but they are especially useful when fast application and removal is an advantage. Clamp pressure is always at the tip of the jaws, so you can localize the grip at any point within the tool's reach. You can use blocks to spread the grip over a wider area. Some are available with jaws shaped to grip round objects such as dowels, tubing, or pipe. Many types are on the market with jaws or handles, or both, covered with protective sleeves. This can provide handling comfort and protection for work surfaces.

UNIVERSAL CLAMP

This is actually a kit of parts including a clamp unit, a bench mount, miter attachments, and different size U-shaped jaws. The tool may be used like a light-weight bar clamp, as a holder for miter joints and even as a bench vise.

The secret of this clamp is the interchangeable jaws which can grip stock from 3/4- to 1-5/8-inches thick, and which can be inserted from either side of the clamp unit. One leg of the U-jaw is toothed so it can grip the wood. Because this can mar the stock, the clamp setup should be organized so any scar will be on the back side of the material, or you can use a protective wood guard under the jaw. One of the clamp's advantages is that it will do a bar-clamp's job without having to span the work. Thus, you can work from joint to joint as the job progresses.

HOMEMADE CLAMPS AND IMPROVISATIONS

There will be times when you find you do not have the right clamp for the job, or the clamp you need is in use elsewhere. Clamps can be improvised in many ways, a few of which are shown here. These examples only begin to examine the possibilities. Use your imagination.

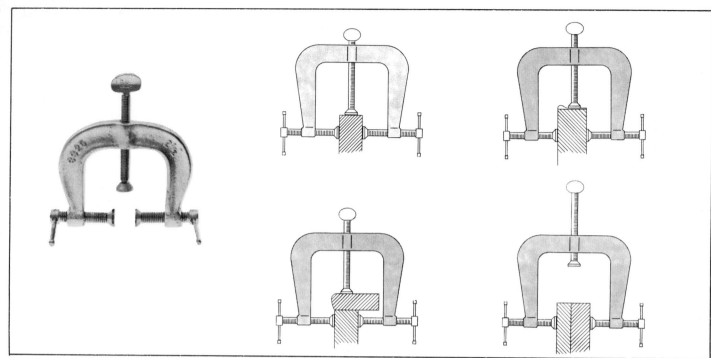

THE 3-WAY EDGING CLAMP can be used like a conventional C-clamp, but is designed for holding molding or other finishing pieces in place.

Some bar clamps are available with hinged tail stops for use with irregularly shaped work or for permanent attachment to a bench so they can be swung out of the way.

The double-bar design of these long PIPE CLAMPS exerts pressure on both sides of the work to prevent buckling. Smaller single-bar clamps are more common.

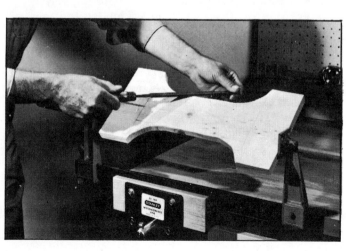

This unusual use of a bar clamp as a vise allows you to change the position of the work easily.

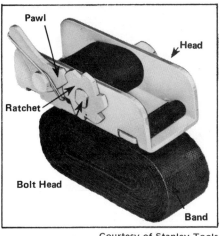

WEB CLAMPS can conform to any shape. Tightening is done by pulling the band through the head by hand, like a belt. Final pressure is applied by turning the bolt head with a wrench or screwdriver.

Courtesy of Stanley Tools

WEB CLAMPS are great for jobs like applying edge banding to a circular slab. There is little danger of marring finished work.

These MITER CLAMPS are set in holes drilled in back of work.

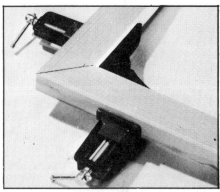

MITER CLAMPS hold a miter while the glue sets, or while you drill it to take a dowel.

You can make this MITER CLAMP yourself. It is designed to hold parts together tightly as you nail or glue them. See drawing at right.

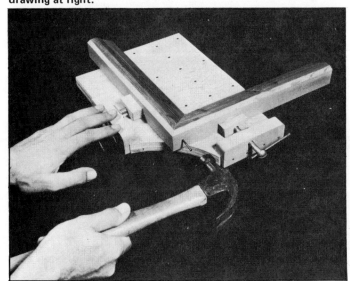

The overall dimensions of this miter clamp depend on your needs, but a base that is 3/4 inch by 12 by 12 inches is a versatile size. The size of the curve is not critical, but it should be enough to clear the work. A hole can be drilled through the bolt to hold a nail for turning, or you can use a screwdriver. Parts should be both glued and nailed together.

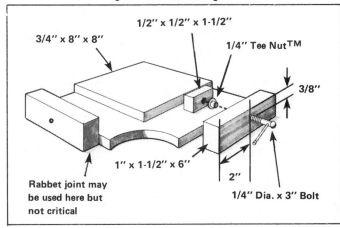

103

Courtesy of Stanley Tools

SPRING CLAMPS are versatile for fast application and removal.

To make this improvised clamp arrangement for an open frame, tack-nail or clamp right-angle stops and the straight stop to a flat surface. Use wedges to apply pressure.

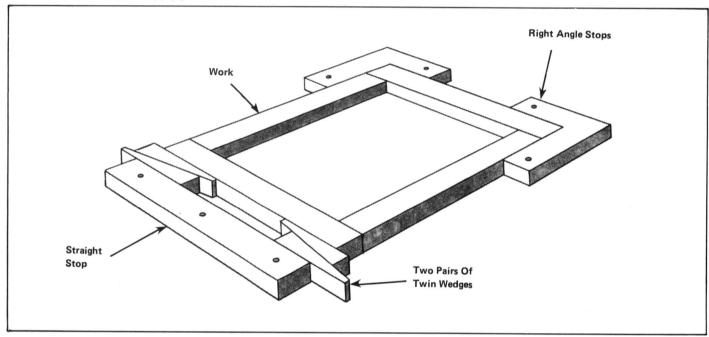

Right Angle Stops

Work

Straight Stop

Two Pairs Of Twin Wedges

UNIVERSAL CLAMPS pull parts together without spanning work. The clamp is seated on a slide unit on bench and can easily be removed.

The miter attachment hooks over serrations in the clamp unit and can suit almost any size right-angle miter.

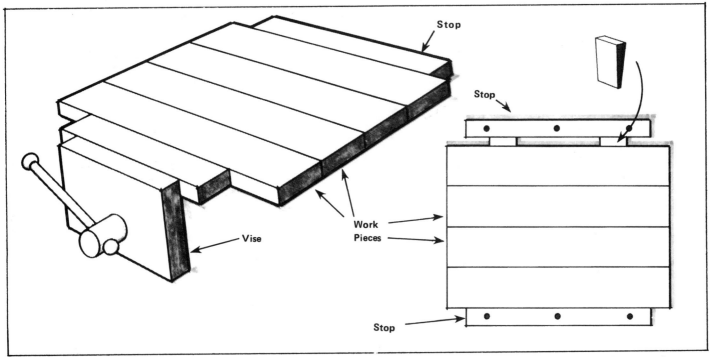

Improvised clamps for edge-to-edge joints can be made either by laying the work on the table and using your wood vise to apply pressure, as on the left, or by using two stops with small wedges. Stops need only be tacked or clamped in place.

A web or band clamp can be improvised using sash cord and a block clamp. Avoid clothesline because it stretches. Pieces of cardboard should be placed between the work and the cord where it might damage the wood. Cord can be knotted to suit the size of the project. Final tightening is done with the block clamp or with a dowel which is twisted in the cord until it is tight, like a tourniquet.

Circular work can be clamped with bar clamps either before the stock is cut, as at bottom, or cut pieces can be secured with cleats held by C-clamps and then joined with bar clamps.

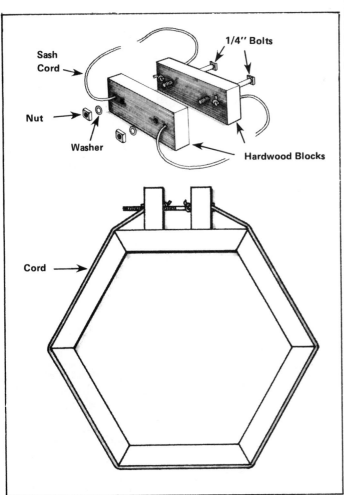

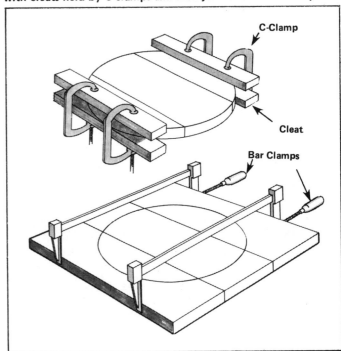

10

Special Tools

There are a number of tools which are only occasionally used in woodworking, but are used so often on household repair jobs they should be included in your tool kit.

PLIERS

There are many types of pliers but not all are useful in a woodshop. The handiest ones are the *slip-joint, water-pump* or *channel-type* varieties. Pliers are essentially a gripping tool. Too often they are used as wrenches, prys, rippers, and nail pullers. If you must use pliers to turn a nut, select the water-pump or channel-type because you can adjust these to keep the jaws parallel and grip the nut firmly with less chance of slippage. Slip-joint pliers, especially short ones on which you can't apply much leverage, can chew up a nut or bolt head to the point where you might not be able to use a wrench on it later.

Some examples of the use of pliers in a woodshop include: use as a hand-pressured vise or clamp to grip small pieces, cutting wire, pulling brads or small nails when the head projects enough for a good grip and you can pull straight out, bending small pieces of metal, straightening a hinge or similar piece of hardware, and holding a nail or a screw when it is too awkward to work in normal fashion.

A special use I found is indenting a dowel to be used in a joint. The plier's serrated teeth form short grooves to make room for excess glue. Rotate the dowel and move it longitudinally as you open and close the pliers to form the dents.

WRENCHES

Wrenches are long, steel fingers you can use to grip nuts and bolts securely. They supply leverage you can't get any other way. Like pliers, there is a large assortment to choose from. You can use a good variety if you are involved in general mechanics, house maintenance, plumbing, and the like, but if your interests are pretty much in woodworking, you'll do well with an adjustable wrench and a selection of open-end wrenches. You can buy beyond these basics as your needs increase.

A primary rule of good practice with all wrenches is to choose the size to suit the work. With fixed wrenches it is a matter of selection—with an adjustable wrench it is a matter of setting the jaws snug enough to obtain a good parallel fit. Never use a section of pipe or any other device to lengthen the tool's handle for more leverage. This is a tempting procedure, especially when the nut—or whatever—is frozen. It is better—for both the work and the tool—to choose a larger wrench. Or, try to loosen the stubborn thing by applying a penetrating oil or special liquid and allowing time for the fluid to sink in before you apply the wrench. Pull on a wrench, don't push it. This can prevent some skinned knuckles should your hand slip. Don't overdo with any wrench. Once a fastener is tight, let it alone. That extra turn we love to take is wasted effort. It can put a needless strain on the fastener and it can damage the work.

NUT DRIVERS

Nut drivers look and work something like screwdrivers but instead of a blade, they end in hexagonal sockets that fit over hex nuts and bolt heads. They are very handy for light and medium-duty fastening, especially when the work area is too cramped to use a conventional wrench. Shanks on some models are hollow so the tool can follow a nut over an extending threaded shaft.

These tools are very popular with electricians, electronic workers, and appliance men for quick tightening or removing of hex-head nuts or sheet-metal screws. Be sure you use the correct-size driver for the nut or screw. Don't overdo the torque, especially when driving sheet-metal screws—it is far too easy to strip the threads in the work.

SNIPS

Chances are you will need a tool to cut thin sheet metal. You don't want to be over-equipped in this area so your best bet, at least to start, is to

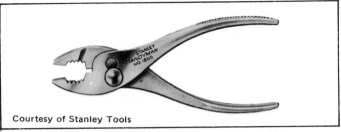

Courtesy of Stanley Tools

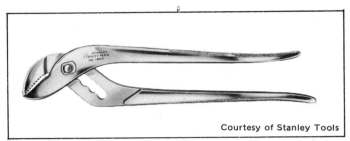

Courtesy of Stanley Tools

SLIP-JOINT pliers often have areas near the joint which can be used to do a limited amount of wire cutting. The joint can be adjusted for two jaw positions.

WATER-PUMP Pliers are adjustable to any of several indented positions.

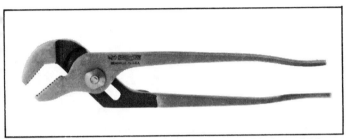

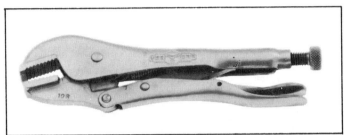

CHANNEL-TYPE pliers are adjusted by a movable jaw which fits into any of several grooves or channels.

LEVER WRENCH appears under several names and is a hybrid between pliers and a wrench. Its jaws can be locked in place, and it is adjustable.

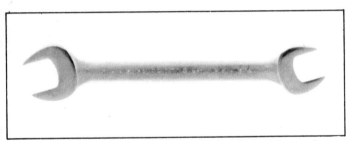

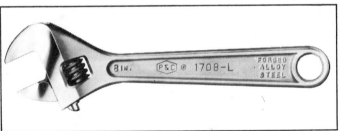

OPEN-END WRENCH has different size heads at either end for fitting bolt heads and nuts. Available in either inch or metric sizes.

ADJUSTABLE OPEN-END WRENCH has a jaw which is opened or closed by turning a screw in its head.

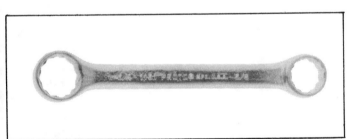

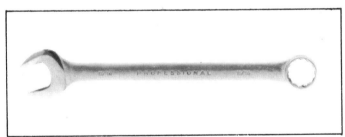

BOX WRENCH has different size closed heads at each end designed to fit over the top of a bolt head or nut. Available in inch or metric sizes.

COMBINATION OPEN-END-BOX WRENCH has an open end and a box end. They are both the same size and the tool can be reversed to suit your need. Available in inch or metric sizes.

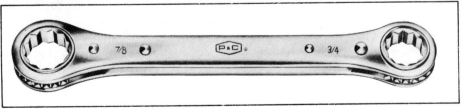

FLAT RATCHET WRENCH is available in both inch and metric sizes.

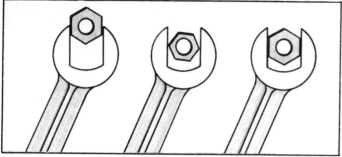

The jaws of either an adjustable or fixed-head wrench should fit snugly against the sides of the fastener. A partial grip or the wrong size wrench can damage both the fastener and the wrench.

Courtesy of Stanley Tools

DUCKBILL SNIPS have a variety of uses in the shop.

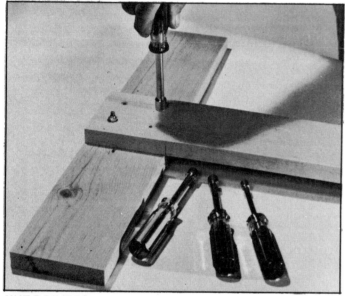

NUT DRIVERS are available in sets. A common one contains sizes for 3/16 to 1/2 inch. Some are color-coded so you can tell size without having to measure or test.

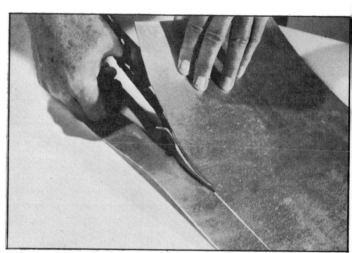

In making straight cuts, let the work bear against the side of the blade and keep one handle on the bench top. This helps you to guide and gives you more leverage.

When a curve is too small for the snips to move around, make relief cuts which allow the waste to drop off as you go. This allows more room for the blade, but watch out for sharp edges!

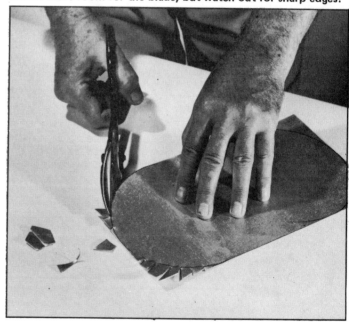

PUTTY KNIVES are useful for smoothing or scraping.

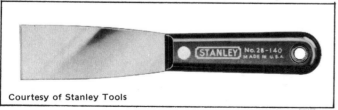

Courtesy of Stanley Tools

choose a tool that will cut both straight *and* curved lines. *Straight-pattern snips* will do this so long as the curve is gentle, but the *duckbill pattern* seems to come closer to being all-purpose. These have blades that follow a taper from pivot to point. The blades are beveled so moving to the left or the right as you cut is a bit easier.

Duckbills come in lengths from about 7 to 13 inches with cutting edges running from 2 to 3 inches. The longer the tool, the more leverage you can apply. The greatest cutting force is closest to the pivot point—cutting near the throat of the blades is always easier. Most experienced workers don't take full-blade cuts for two reasons. One is the leverage factor—the closer you get to the tips, the harder it is to cut. The other is the slight imperfection in the work caused by the tip of the blades when they close. Keep the length of each cut to about 3/4 the length of the blades.

Sheet-metal cutting produces sharp edges, points and corners, so you must work carefully to avoid damage to your hands. It is a good idea to wear gloves, especially when you have a lot of cutting to do.

PUTTY KNIVES

Putty knives are designed for spreading dough-like materials such as putty, spackling compound, or wood dough. In woodworking, putty knives are used for filling and concealing holes such as countersinks, and as scrapers for removing such things as excess glue before it hardens. Some putty knives have wide blades and are called *scrapers.* These are often recommended for removing wall-paper. Another type is called a *joint knife* and is used for smoothing the joints between sections of Sheetrock™

WOOD-THREADING TOOLS

Imagine doing and showing a project held together with nuts and bolts made of wood! Think of the strength a dowel will have if it is threaded and used like a screw or bolt. Few of us think of working wood this way, yet it can be fun and the technique has many practical applications. Once you get involved you will become more and more intrigued.

Wood-threading and tapping would be pretty difficult if the how-to methods had to be improvised, but they don't. Special tools make the work pretty easy. Tool sets include a *die* for male threads and a *tap* to cut matching female threads. The most common tool sizes run from 1/2 to 1 inch in diameter—prices range from $30 to $50 for a set including both the tap and the die.

You'll find threading easiest when the wood has a fine grain—maple, birch, beech, cherry and similar species are good candidates. If the wood has some moisture content, so much the better. Technically, 20% moisture is about ideal but you don't have to be that persnickety about the whole thing. Make a test cut. If you find the wood is too dry and tends to crumble or tear, rub it with a candle or a very light oil. Another, probably better way to improve your cut is to soak the wood in warm water for a half-minute or so.

I found readymade dowels good for screw-post material. Be sure the dowel is not so oversize you must force it into the die. The spindle you are going to thread should be an easy slip fit in the die's entrance hole. A little sanding will reduce a dowel enough for a good fit. It also helps to sand or file a slight chamfer at the starting end.

The job is simple to do and goes fast when the die has a sharp cutter. You just turn the die about the spindle to produce a V-shaped chip which curls out and falls off. A fairly long chip will usually indicate the die's cutter is sharp enough. Crumbling can also happen when you are cutting open-grain woods like oak and ash. Such woods can be cut with the die—you just won't get as clean a thread.

Tapping—making internal threads in a hole—works best when you enter from the flat-grain side of the stock. It's okay to come in from an edge when you must, but should you try to tap into end grain, you'll usually end up with a rough, unusable hole. In any case, the thread cut with the tap will not be as good as the thread you form with a die. It is not so critical because it is an appearance factor only, and tapped threads are always hidden.

Some tearing will occur where the tap enters the hole and where it breaks out. You can't avoid this but you can eliminate the imperfections by working with oversize stock and then planing or sanding after the threads are cut.

Another solution is to use a countersink—if you have one large enough—at each end of the hole before doing the tapping. Drill deeper than necessary if you are going to tap a blind hole, and retract the tap frequently to clear away waste. If you allow wood chips to pile up they will interfere with the cutting and cause broken threads.

To judge the size of the tap hole you need, just measure the outside diameter of the pilot which is at the starting end of the tap. Be sure the pilot can turn freely in the hole. Be especially careful when you start the tap to keep it square to the surface of the work. Make a quarter turn counter-clockwise for every half turn or so you make clockwise. The tap can be turned with a regular tap wrench. If you lack one, use a small C-clamp as a handle.

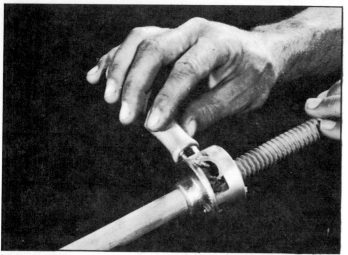

Male thread is cut by the die as you turn it about the spindle. A long, curling chip indicates a good rate of cutting and a sharp cutter.

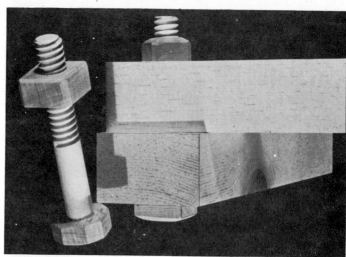

Nuts and bolts made of wood can be used for practical or novel applications. With well-formed threads they can be tightened enough to make a good glue joint.

You can make these marking gauges. The post on the left rides a drilled hole and is locked in place by a wood screw. The screw on the center bears against a flat cut on the post. The gauge on the right has a threaded post and a tapped hole.

Drawer handles can be attached with threaded dowels. They will make your project stronger.

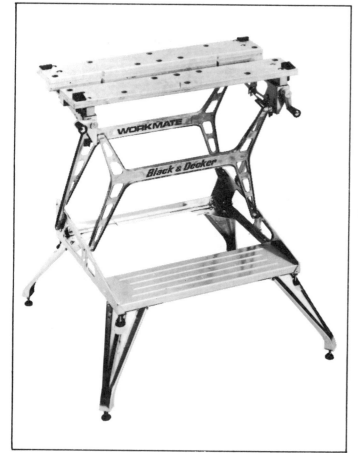

Workmate™ is a versatile addition to any shop.

WORKMATE™

This combination portable vise, workbench and sawhorse is manufactured by Black & Decker®. It can be folded and stored or carried to any job. It is so versatile, it can do almost any job a full-size workbench with a wood vise can do. In addition, a number of accessories are available, including special clamps and guides for power saws and routers. Even if you have an adequate home workshop, this tool can be useful. In homes where space is at a premium, Workmate™ deserves special consideration.

11

Materials

LUMBER

Wood is called *hard* or *soft*, but the terms don't mean much in a literal sense. Actually, they are botanical catagories—hardwoods come from broad-leafed deciduous trees; softwoods from cone-bearing or evergreen trees. If you have ever worked with fir, you know it is hardly *soft* in a workable sense, yet it is classified as a softwood. Walnut and mahogany are hardwoods which cut easily.

The cellular structure of wood dictates whether it is *open-grain* or *close-grain*. This characteristic affects procedures when you are ready for finishing. An open-grain wood like oak or ash requires a filler to pack the pores and smooth the surface. Close-grained woods like maple or birch do not require that extra step because sanding alone produces a suitable surface for final coats.

A tree adds an outer layer of wood for each year of its growth. That's why you can tell the age of a tree by counting the rings in a log cross section. These growth rings, and how the log is cut up into boards, determine the grain pattern. You could learn to recognize any species from its grain even though there is some variation from tree to tree in the same species. Variations also occur in the same species in relation to geographical location.

If you slice a log lengthwise, you can get maximum width with a prominent grain pattern. This is an economical way to cut and most yard lumber is produced this way. Another way to mill a log is to quarter it lengthwise first and then slice off boards from the broad face of each quarter-round section. This results in an even and attractive grain pattern, but the procedure is relatively expensive. It is used mostly to get boards from the more exotic hardwoods.

A third common way to cut a log is to mount it in a giant lathe and turn it against a knife to slice off long, thin sheets of veneer. Called *rotary cutting*, this produces layers for common plywoods as well as veneer sheets.

Fresh-cut lumber contains a considerable amount of moisture. Drying is done to minimize the moisture content before the lumber is used. A lot of distortion would result if drying were to occur *after* fabrication. A common procedure is to place the green wood in large sheds where the atmosphere can be controlled. Sometimes steam is introduced first to make the moisture content as uniform as possible before the final drying takes place. Another method is to stack the boards with spacers between them and just let them sit in the open air.

Lumber doesn't stop "breathing" until it is finally sealed and coated. Even wood milled and dried correctly can become distorted, so be sure to coat all exposed edges and surfaces when you finish a project, *including those that can't be seen!*

Lumber isn't cheap, so it makes sense to buy the most economical grade that is acceptable for the project you have in mind. Sometimes you can save money by buying low-grade material and culling out the good sections. For example, there is usually a lot of clear material in a long knotty-pine board.

Buy only as much lumber as you need for the project on hand. This will cut down on the amount of storage space you need and you won't have to worry about distortion that might occur before you use the material.

PLYWOOD

You know how much easier it is to split a board than it is to crack it at right angles to its grain. Plywood has strength in both directions. It is a sandwich of wood veneers glued together with the grain of each ply running at right angles to the adjacent plies.

There are two types of plywood, each having several different grades. *Exterior-type* plywood is bonded with 100% waterproof glue while *interior type* uses a highly moisture-resistant glue. The veneers used on the inner plies of interior-type plywood may be lower grade than those used in exterior type. Be careful when you select your plywood. Exterior type should be used on any project that is likely to face dampness or high humidity over long periods.

Plywood is graded according to the appearance of the outside plies. Grade is indicated by a letter code stamped on the panel. Plywood is also classified by group. More than 30 species of trees are used to make plywood and they are divided into four groups according to strength. Each panel carries a stamp which gives you all this information.

Aside from strength, plywood has several advantages over solid lumber. You can get large slabs without having to glue several boards edge to edge. Stresses are so equalized that warping and similar distortions are nearly eliminated. Plywood is also less expensive than most solid lumber and it conserves rare woods because the inner plies can be made of more available wood, yet it can still have a rare wood on the outside.

The most obvious disadvantage of plywood is that the ply lines are visible on all edges. These are not pretty when left exposed—so, when they are not hidden by joint design, they must be covered with a material matching the surface veneers. This can be done with thin or thick strips of solid material or with veneer-like strips of wood tape. Wood tapes are available in many species and may be applied in various ways. These are discussed in chapter 8 on shaping and finishing.

HARDBOARDS

Hardboards are made from small chips of wood specially processed to be reduced to individual fibers. Fibers are bonded with *lignin*—nature's wood-binding substance—then subjected to tremendous heat and pressure. The result is a dense, uniform, smooth-surfaced panel. This material can be worked with any woodworking tool and is an excellent base for painting because it is hard and smooth.

There was a time when hardboard was used mostly for drawer bottoms and cabinet backs, but innovations in sizes, textures and finishes have made it acceptable for broader uses. Wall paneling is an area where hardboard has really come into its own. Woodgrained panels that simulate species like teak, oak and cherry are available. You can get embossed or textured panels with the feel and look of materials such as marble, leather, or even tapestry-filigreed panels. Of course, the best-known is the perforated variety, called *pegboard,* used with ready-made metal or plastic fixtures for hanging tools, garden equipment, kitchen accessories, and so on.

Example uses for plain or fancy hardboards are accent panels on furniture or walls, dividers and screens, grills, louvered inserts or doors, and veneer-type coverings for furniture.

PARTICLE BOARD

Particle board, like hardboard, is a manufactured wood product. It is made from whole chips or particles of wood instead of fibers. A lot of waste material from mills is utilized to make particle board. The finished panel has no grain and is practically warp-free. Various densities are available for specific purposes, but the most common type found in lumber yards is of medium density in thicknesses of 1/8 to 3/4 inch in 4- by 8-foot panels. A good many suppliers are carrying pieces cut to size for use as shelves.

Particle board is a low-cost, high-strength material you can utilize in many ways. Its nail-holding strength is not very great, especially when you drive into edges. I recommend that you use glue-joint connections for strength. Use sheetmetal screws instead of wood screws to attach hardware.

The wood material in partical board is bonded with a very abrasive resin-type adhesive. While the material may be worked with regular woodworking tools, it will dull them quickly.

Particle board takes paint well, but requires filling first, especially on exposed edges. Use a thick putty material as a filler. Sand it after it has dried and paint over the smooth surface.

TYPES OF WOOD		
HARDWOODS		**SOFTWOODS**
ash	gum	cedar
beech	hickory	cypress
birch	mahogany	Douglas fir
cherry	maple	fir
chestnut	oak	hemlock
elm	tulip (whitewood)	pine
		redwood
		spruce

COMMON LUMBER TERMS

DIMENSION LUMBER: Material at least 2-inches thick and at least 4-inches wide.

STRIPS: Material less than 2-inches thick and 4-inches wide.

TIMBERS: Material greater than 4-inches thick by 4-inches wide.

BOARDS: Material less than 2-inches thick but with a width greater than 4 inches; often called *yard boards.*

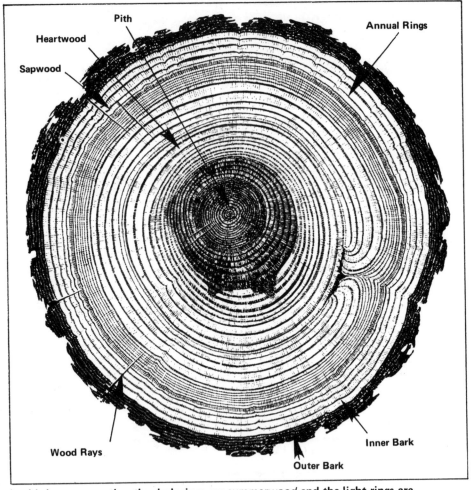

Heartwood
Pith
Sapwood
Annual Rings
Wood Rays
Outer Bark
Inner Bark

In this log cross section the dark rings are *summerwood* and the light rings are *springwood*. These are sometimes called *earlywood* and *latewood*.

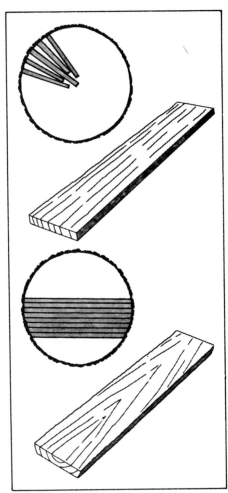

Boards are usually cut from logs in two ways. QUARTER-SAWED boards are cut parallel to the wood rays which produces an edge grain board as shown at the top. PLAIN-SAWED boards have a flat grain as on the bottom.

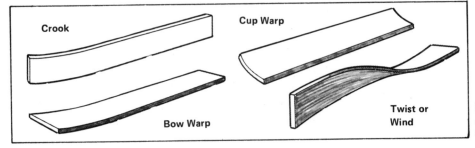

Crook
Cup Warp
Bow Warp
Twist or Wind

Depending on the way a piece of wood is cut from the log, drying can cause it to warp in a number of different ways.

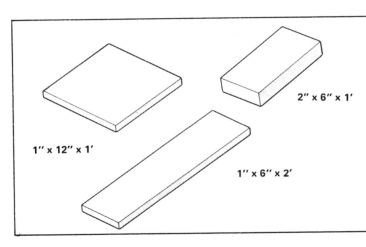

1" x 12" x 1'
2" x 6" x 1'
1" x 6" x 2'

WHAT IS A BOARD FOOT?

All three pieces shown here equal one board foot. This formula can be used to find the number of board feet in any piece of lumber —

$$\frac{T'' \times W'' \times L'}{12} = \text{board feet}$$

T" = thickness in inches
W" = width in inches
L' = length in feet

EXAMPLE — A piece that measures 4 inches by 24 inches by 12 feet

$$\frac{4 \times 24 \times 12}{12} = 96 \text{ board feet}$$

113

RELATIVE CHARACTERISTICS OF SOME POPULAR WOODS

WOOD	HARDNESS	WEIGHT	STRENGTH	GRAIN	GLUING QUALITY	NAILING QUALITY
ASH	high	high	medium	open	medium	medium
BASSWOOD	low	low	low	medium	high	high
BEECH	high	high	medium	medium	low	low
BIRCH	high	high	high	closed	medium	low
CHERRY	high	medium	medium	medium	high	medium
GUM	medium	medium	medium	medium	high	high
HICKORY	high	high	high	open	high	low
MAHOGANY	medium	high	medium	open	high	medium
MAPLE	high	high	high	closed	medium	low
OAK	high	high	high	open	high	high
PINE	low	low	low	closed	high	high
POPLAR	low	low	low	open	high	high
REDWOOD	low	low	medium	medium	high	medium
WALNUT	high	medium	medium	medium	high	medium

NOMINAL AND ACTUAL SIZES OF LUMBER
All dimensions given in inches

NOMINAL SIZE (what you order)	ACTUAL SIZE (what you get)	NOMINAL SIZE (what you order)	ACTUAL SIZE (what you get)
1 X 2	3/4 X 1-1/2	2 X 4	1-1/2 X 3-1/2
1 X 3	3/4 X 2-1/2	2 X 6	1-1/2 X 5-1/2
1 X 4	3/4 X 3-1/2	2 X 8	1-1/2 X 7-1/4
1 X 5	3/4 X 4-1/2	2 X 10	1-1/2 X 9-1/4
1 X 6	3/4 X 5-1/2	2 X 12	1-1/2 X 11-1/4
1 X 8	3/4 X 7-1/4	3 X 4	2-1/2 X 3-1/2
1 X 10	3/4 X 9-1/4	4 X 4	3-1/2 X 3-1/2
1 X 12	3/4 X 11-1/4	4 X 6	3-1/2 X 5-1/2
2 X 2	1-1/2 X 1-1/2	6 X 6	5-1/2 X 5-1/2
2 X 3	1-1/2 X 2-1/2	8 X 8	7-1/2 X 7-1/2

CLASSIFICATION OF SPECIES BY STIFFNESS:
Group 1 contains the strongest woods

Group 1	Group 2	Group 3	Group 4
Douglas Fir 1	California Red Fir	Western Hemlock	Alaska Yellow Pine	Engelmann Spruce
Larch	Douglas Fir 2	Western White Pine	Alder	Incense Cedar
Southern Loblolly Pine	Grand Fir	White Fir	Lodgepole Pine	Subalpine Fir
Southern Longleaf Pine	Noble Fir	White Lauan	Ponderosa Pine	Sugar Pine
Southern Shortleaf Pine	Pacific Silver Fir		Red Cedar	Western Poplar
Southern Slash Pine	Port Orford Cedar		Redwood	Western Red Cedar
Tanoak	Red Lauan			
Western Pine	Sitka Spruce			

Douglas Fir 1 — California, Idaho, Montana, Oregon, Washington, Wyoming, Alberta and British Columbia.
Douglas Fir 2 — Arizona, Colorado, Nevada, New Mexico, Utah

Copyright 1966 American Plywood Association.

MOST COMMON LUMBER CLASSIFICATIONS—GRADES

COMMON		SELECT	
Grade	Description	Grade	Description
1	Small knots permissible so long as they are they are sound—good choice for paint jobs—may be used with a minimum of waste.	1 (clear)	Top grade material—good choice for fine cabinetwork and natural finishes—generally clear of any defects—often graded as "B and Better."
2	Generally considered a utility grade—more and larger knots are permissible—makes acceptable knotty paneling.	2 (clear)	
3	Expect some waste areas—greater number of more pronounced blemishes permissible.	C (select)	Small number of minor blemishes permissible—still a good material to work with.
4	Lowest usable grade—many defects—contains good areas that may be culled out and used as a higher grade material.	D (select)	Contains more minor defects and blemishes—considered the lowest finishing grade, but very good for painting.
5	Used mostly for very rough work such as forming for concrete and for making crates—lowest quality.		

CONVERSION CHART FOR LUMBER
(changing linear feet to board feet)

.333=1/3 .666=2/3
.167=1/6 .833=5/6
.500=1/2

THICK. inches	WIDTH inches	LENGTH (feet)							
		10	12	14	16	18	20	22	24
1	2	1.666	2	2.333	2.666	3	3.333	3.666	4
1	3	2.5	3	3.5	4	4.5	5	5.5	6
1	4	3.333	4	4.666	5.333	6	6.666	7.333	8
1	5	4.167	5	5.833	6.666	7.5	8.333	9.167	10
1	6	5	6	7	8	9	10	11	12
1	7	5.833	7	8.167	9.333	10.5	11.666	12.833	14
1	8	6.666	8	9.333	10.666	12	13.333	14.666	16
1	9	7.5	9	10.5	12	13.5	15	16.5	18
1	10	8.333	10	11.666	13.333	15	16.666	18.333	20
1	12	10	12	14	16	18	20	22	24
1	14	11.666	14	16.333	18.666	21	23.333	25.666	28
1	16	13.333	16	18.666	21.333	24	26.666	29.333	32
2	2	3.333	4	4.666	5.333	6	6.666	7.333	8
2	3	5	6	7	8	9	10	11	12
2	4	6.666	8	9.333	10.666	12	13.333	14.666	16
2	6	10	12	14	16	18	20	22	24
2	8	13.333	16	18.666	21.333	24	26.666	29.333	32
2	9	15	18	21	24	27	30	33	36
2	10	16.666	20	23.333	26.666	30	33.333	36.666	40
2	12	20	24	28	32	36	40	44	48

LETTER SYMBOLS FOR GRADING VENEERS IN PLYWOOD

N
Special order "natural finish" veneer. Selected all heartwood or all sapwood. Free of open defects. Allows some repairs.

A
Smooth and paintable. Neatly made repairs permissable. Also used for natural finish in less demanding applications.

B
Solid surface veneer. Circular repair plugs and tight knots permitted. Can be painted.

C
Minimum veneer permitted in Exterior type plywood. Knotholes to 1 inch. Occasional knotholes 1/2 inch larger permitted providing total width of all knots and knotholes within a specified section does not exceed certain limits. Limited splits permitted.

C plugged
Improved C veneer with splits limited to 1/8 inch in width and knotholes and borer holes limited to 1/4 inch by 1/2 inch.

D
Used only in Interior type for inner plies and backs. Permits knots and knotholes to 2-1/2 inches in maximum dimension and 1/2 inch larger under certain specified limits. Limited splits permitted.

Courtesy
American Plywood Association

GRADE-USE GUIDE FOR APPEARANCE GRADES OF PLYWOOD　　Courtesy American Plywood Association

	Symbol	Description and Most Common Uses	Veneer Grade			Most Common Thickness (inch)						
						1/4	5/16	3/8	1/2	5/8	3/4	1
INTERIOR TYPE	N-N, N-A, N-B, N-D INT-DFPA	Natural-finish cabinet quality. Select all-heartwood or all-sapwood veneer on both sides. For furniture having a natural finish, cabinet doors, built-ins. Use N-D for natural-finish paneling.	N	N,A B or D	C or D	•					•	
	A-A INT-DFPA	For interior applications where both sides will be seen. Faces are smooth and suitable for painting.	A	A	D	•		•	•	•	•	•
	A-B INT-DFPA	For uses similar to Interior A-A, but where the appearance of one side is less important and two smooth, solid surfaces are necessary.	A	B	D	•		•	•	•	•	•
	A-D INT-DFPA	For interior uses where the appearance of only one side is important. Paneling, built-ins, shelving, partitions and flow racks.	A	D	D	•		•	•	•	•	•
	B-B INT-DFPA	Interior utility panel used where two smooth sides are desired. Permits circular plugs. Paintable.	B	B	D	•		•	•	•	•	•
	B-D INT-DFPA	Interior utility panel for use where one smooth side is required. Good for backing sides or built-ins.	B	D	D	•		•	•	•	•	•
	DECORATIVE PANELS	Rough-sawn, brushed, grooved or striated faces. Good for interior walls, built-ins, counter facing, displays and exhibits.	B or btr.	D	D		•	•	•			
	PLYRON INT-DFPA	Hardboard faces on both sides may be tempered, untempered, smooth or screened. For counter tops or shelving.			C & D				•	•	•	
EXTERIOR TYPE	A-A EXT-DFPA(4)	Use where appearance of both sides is important. Fences, built-ins, signs, boats, cabinets, and tote boxes.	A	A	C	•		•	•	•	•	•
	A-B EXT-DFPA(4)	Use like A-A EXT where appearance is less important.	A	B	C	•		•	•	•	•	•
	A-C EXT-DFPA(4)	Use where appearance of only one side is important. Siding, fences and structural uses.	A	C	C	•		•	•	•	•	•
	B-C EXT-DFPA(4)	An outdoor utility panel for farm service and work buildings.	B	C	C	•		•	•	•	•	•
	B-B EXT-DFPA(4)	An outdoor utility panel with solid paintable faces for uses where higher quality is not necessary.	B	B	C	•		•	•	•	•	•
	HDO EXT-DFPA(4)	High-Density Overlay plywood with hard, semi-opaque resin-fiber overlay. Abrasion resistant. Painting not ordinarily required. For signs, cabinets and counter tops.	A or B	A or B	C Plugged			•	•	•	•	•
	MDO EXT-DFPA(4)	Medium-Density Overlay with smooth, opaque resin-fiber overlay heat-fused to one or both panel faces. Ideal base for paint. Highly recommended for siding and other outdoor applications. Also good for built-ins, signs and displays.	B	B or C	C			•	•	•	•	•
	303 SPECIAL SIDING EXT-DFPA	Grade designation covers proprietary plywood products for exterior siding and fencing with special surface treatment such as V-groove, channel groove, striated, brushed, rough sawn.	B or btr.	C	C				•	•	•	
	T 1-11 EXT-DFPA	Exterior type, sanded or unsanded. For siding and accent paneling.	C or btr.	C	C					•		
	PLYRON EXT-DFPA	Exterior panel surfaced on both sides with hardboard. Faces are tempered, smooth or screened.			C				•	•	•	
	MARINE EXT-DFPA	Made with Douglas fir or Western larch only. Special solid-jointed core construction. Subject to special limitations on core gaps and number of face repairs. Ideal for boat hulls. Also available with overlaid faces.	A or B	A or B	B	•		•	•	•	•	•
	SPECIAL EXTERIOR	Premium exterior panel similar to Marine grade.	A or B	A or B	B	•		•	•	•	•	•

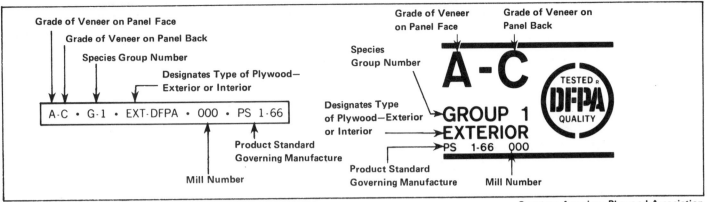

Grade of Veneer on Panel Face
Grade of Veneer on Panel Back
Species Group Number
Designates Type of Plywood—
Exterior or Interior

A-C • G-1 • EXT-DFPA • 000 • PS 1-66

Product Standard
Governing Manufacture

Mill Number

Grade of Veneer on Panel Face
Grade of Veneer on Panel Back
Species Group Number

A-C
GROUP 1
EXTERIOR
PS 1-66 000

TESTED R
DFPA
QUALITY

Designates Type of Plywood—Exterior or Interior

Product Standard Governing Manufacture
Mill Number

Courtesy American Plywood Association

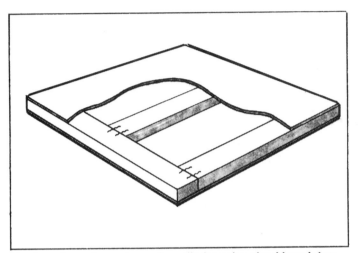

Hardwood panels can be made easily by using glued butt joints and corrugated nails to make a frame, and then covering it with 1/8-inch hardboard.

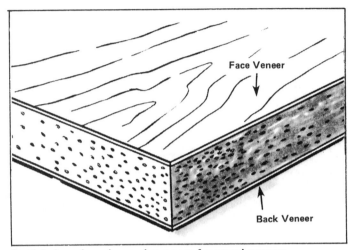

Face Veneer

Back Veneer

Particle board can be used as a core for wood veneers, hardboard, sheet plastic and laminates. Both front and back covers should be similar material to avoid unequal stresses and warping.

This coffee table is made entirely of particleboard. The table was painted after the surfaces and edges were filled with a water-based wood dough.

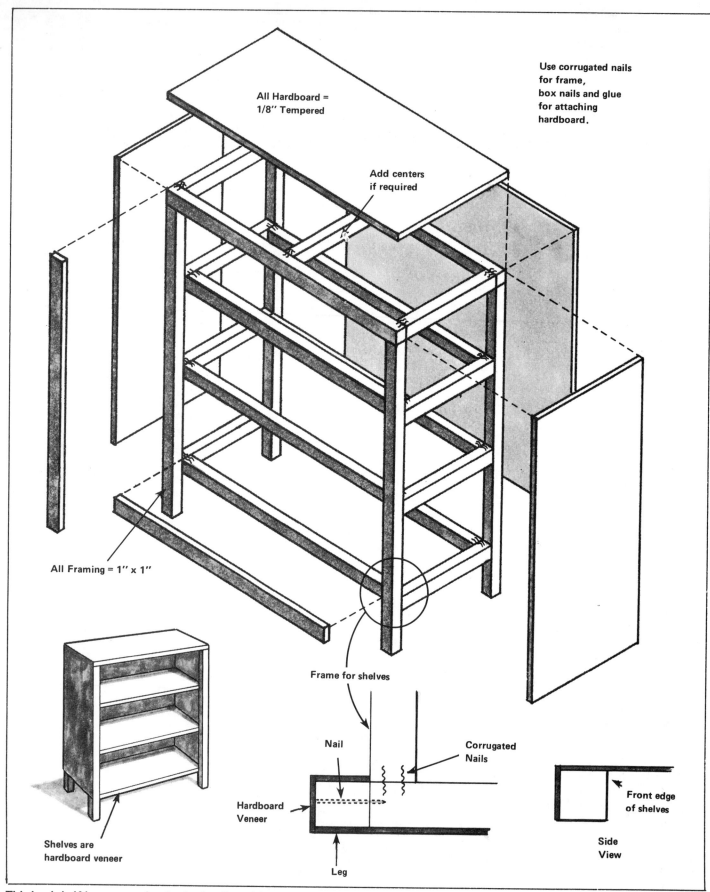

All Hardboard =
1/8″ Tempered

Use corrugated nails
for frame,
box nails and glue
for attaching
hardboard.

Add centers
if required

All Framing = 1″ x 1″

Frame for shelves

Nail

Corrugated
Nails

Hardboard
Veneer

Front edge
of shelves

Leg

Side
View

Shelves are
hardboard veneer

This bookshelf is an example of using hardboard for quick and easy building.

Putting Pieces Together

You are now ready to put things together. If you have followed the directions in the previous chapters, you have probably discovered that you are better with handtools than you supposed. There is nothing secret or terribly difficult about woodworking. Once you develop the right work habits, good work should follow naturally.

Joints, glues and fasteners are the key to binding pieces together. Properly planned and used, they can make an ordinary project something to be proud of.

JOINTS

Many projects depend on joints for looks and durability, but the two factors are relative. The shelves you construct in a garage to hold gardening equipment do not have to be as pretty as the bookshelves you design for a den or family room. The drawer intended to hold stamps and pencils does not require the strength of a shop drawer meant to hold tools.

Some people love to do joints—others don't. If you are one of the former, you'll do mortise-tenons and dovetails no matter what. If you belong to the latter group, you'll seek less time-consuming designs. Both approaches are fine. A good general rule is to use the easiest-to-make joint adequate for the project. This makes even more sense because of the many super adhesives available. Glue from a bottle can make a bond stronger than the material being joined.

Appearance has to do with how many joint lines can be seen and whether end grain is visible after the parts are joined. A miter hides end grain and the unattractive cores of plywood, yet it has only a little more strength than a butt joint. The slanting cut provides a bit more glue area.

Joints must tolerate stress and strain, so view the potential failure points and design to prevent breakdowns. Joint failure in a drawer, for example, is most likely to occur where the front of the drawer connects to the sides. The heavier the contents, the greater the strain each time you pull the drawer out. This is one of the reasons why the

dovetail is used so often in drawer construction. The joint will hold together even if the glue fails. The dovetail has always been a symbol of dedicated craftwork which is why a visible one is not considered objectionable.

Accuracy is critical regardless of the joint you decide to use. Even a simple butt joint will not hold as it should unless the mating edges are true to each other. Too large a tenon can split a mortise. On the other hand, you can't rely on glue to compensate for sloppy fits. A dowel must be a nice slip fit in its hole and the same is true for the inserted part of any joint.

Don't rely on clamps to force parts together. You should be able to mate components with hand pressure. Clamps are designed to hold the parts together until the glue dries. Wood putty and fillers are a boon. They can be used to fill hair-line cracks and joint lines, and to conceal nails and screws. However, they were not invented for use as cover-ups for indifferent work.

Butt Joints—The butt joint is the simplest joint. It is made by placing the end of one piece of wood against the side of another and fastening them firmly to each other. If appearance is important, you should know that the end grain of one piece will be exposed when a butt joint is used to make a corner. The butt end should be square and the side smooth to ensure a tight fit.

If nails are used as fasteners, they are driven diagonally through both pieces. This is known as *toenailing.* Dowels or other fasteners can be used as well.

A butt joint is not a very strong joint, but it can be strengthened in a number of ways I'll tell you about. However, simply pounding more nails into the joint will not work and may actually produce a weaker joint.

Miters—Miters, or *mitres,* are butt joints with the angle of the joint shared equally between the two pieces being joined. Most often the two pieces are cut at a 45-degree angle and joined to form a 90-degree or right-angle miter. With any miter the two

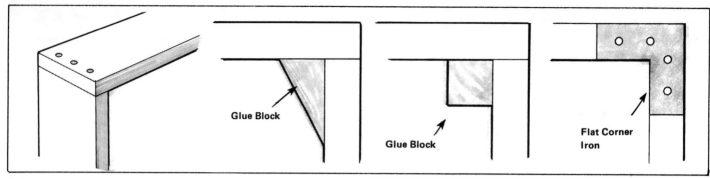

BUTT JOINTS set at right angles leave the end grain visible. They may be reinforced with glue blocks or corner irons.

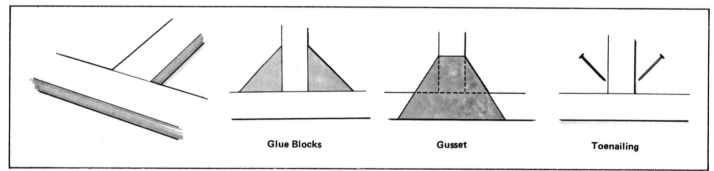

The end grain is still visible on a **FLAT CORNER.** Corrugated nails, dowels or metal corner braces can be used as support.

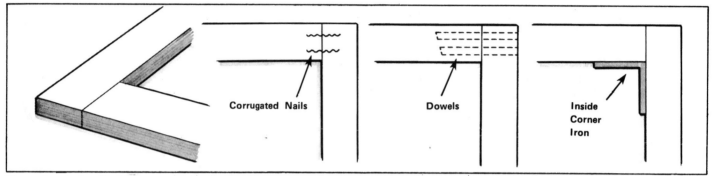

A projecting butt joint does not have the problem of exposed end grain. It may be reinforced with glue blocks, gussets, or by toe-nailing. The use of dowels for support is discussed with dowel joints.

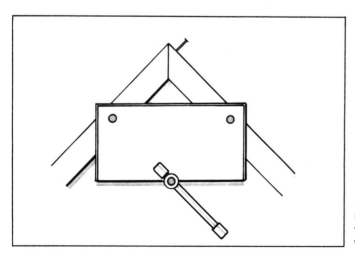

Nails or screws can be used to secure a miter, but grip the parts securely so they won't slip out of alignment when you are adding fasteners.

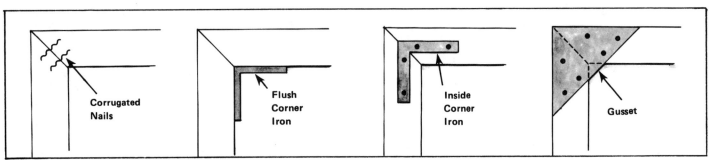

RIGHT ANGLE and FLAT MITERS can be reinforced with corrugated nails, corner irons or gussets made with plywood.

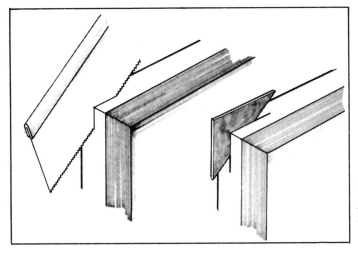

In cases where appearance is important, you might consider a FEATHERED MITER. A saw cut is made in both pieces of the miter and a piece of veneer is glued into the kerf. The feather is trimmed to fit after the glue dries.

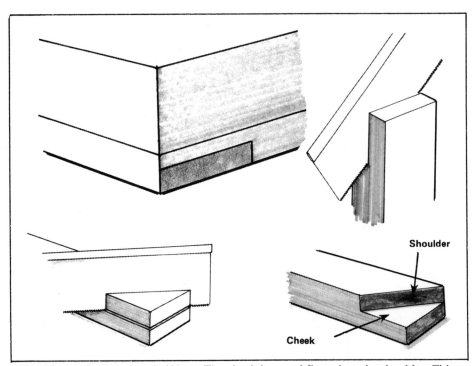

MITERS can also be cut as half laps. The cheek is sawed first, then the shoulder. This produces a triangular face. The resulting joint has a very neat appearance.

pieces should be cut at the same angle. Angle dividers can be used to determine the correct angle to cut.

A right-angle miter can be drawn by squaring a line across the face of the piece, then measuring along one side to a point equal to the width of the piece, and connecting this point with the other end of the squared line.

Miters are usually cut in miter boxes like the one shown in chapter 3. A back saw or other fine-toothed saw is used because a tight fit is important. Miters are usually nailed or nailed and glued. For this it is best to use a miter clamp as shown in chapter 9.

Lap Joints—There are many joints where two boards cross. These are called *lap joints*. An overlap is simply one board laid across another and fastened. A full lap requires cutting a U-shaped notch in one board to accommodate another board. A half lap requires cutting notches in both pieces.

The notch is made by laying the boards in position and marking shoulder lines the width of one on the other with a knife or pencil. A marking gauge is used to mark the depth of the notch. Then the shoulder lines are cut with a backsaw or other fine-toothed saw.

For a half lap, both pieces are marked with a gauge, but one is cut to the top of the depth line and the other to the bottom of the depth line. Several parallel cuts can be made between the shoulder cuts and the waste can be cleaned out with a chisel or by paring with a knife. Chisel from both sides toward the center. Slant the chisel slightly outward to avoid breaking the grain.

The notch for a corner or end lap joint is gauged across the end of the stock. The cheek cut is made first, then the shoulder cut.

Rabbets—A rabbet is an L-shaped cut in the edge of a piece of wood. The square edge of another piece of wood slipped into the L-shaped cut, or two rabbets fitted together, form a rabbet joint.

To cut a rabbet in the end of a piece of wood, mark a line the width of the joining piece across the face and down the edges. Then mark the depth of the rabbet on the end and sides with a gauge, and cut out the waste with a backsaw. A chisel or a rabbet plane can be used for the final cleaning. Rabbet planes have a spur for cutting across the grain. A rabbet can also be cut in the side of a piece of wood with a rabbet plane. The depth gauge and the fence control the depth and width of the cut.

Dadoes—In woodworking, a *groove* is a narrow channel cut *with* the grain of a piece of wood. A *dado* is a narrow channel cut *across* the grain and is usually used for holding shelves. A dado that

OVERLAP

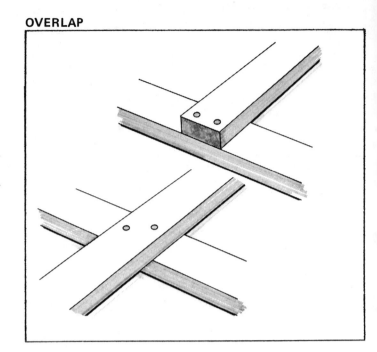

FULL LAP

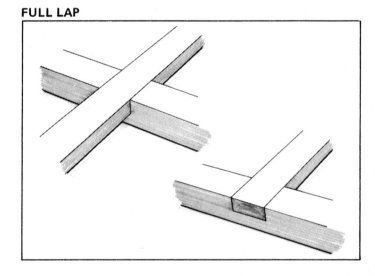

HALF LAP

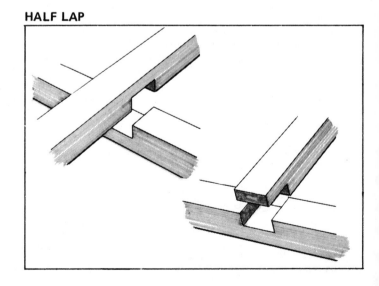

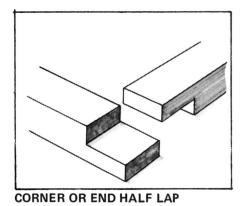

CORNER OR END HALF LAP

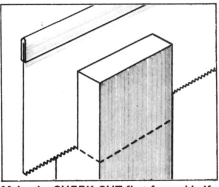

Make the CHEEK CUT first for end half laps.

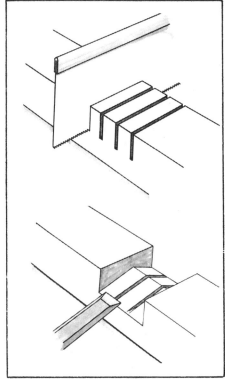

The U-shaped cut for a LAP JOINT can be made by cutting the shoulders first and then making a series of parallel saw cuts in the waste area. Use a chisel to clear the waste. Chisel toward the center from both sides.

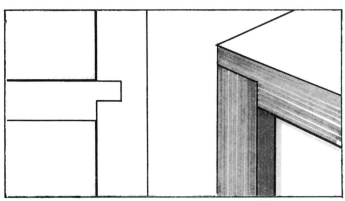

RABBETS are L-shaped. They are often used with dadoes in shelving.

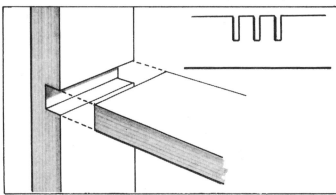

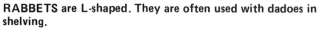

You can make a THROUGH DADO with a saw by making the shoulder cuts first and then parallel saw cuts between. The waste is cleaned out with a chisel or a plane.

A pocket is made first at the end of a STOPPED DADO, then the dado is finished with a saw and chisel or a plane. Two saw cuts make the notch for the inserted piece.

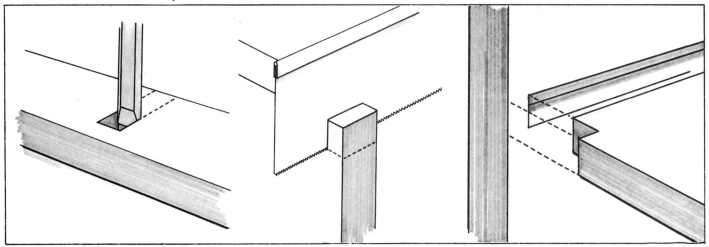

holds the entire end of the second piece is sometimes called a *housed joint.* If the end of the second piece is visible on both sides of the dado, it is called a *through dado.* If the dado does not extend across the entire width of the board, and the end of the second piece is concealed, it is called a *stopped* or *blind dado.*

A through dado can be cut with a saw and cleaned out with a chisel, or it can be cut with a plane. For a stopped dado it is best to cut a pocket at the stopped end with a chisel, and then use a plane or a saw to finish the cutting.

Dado joints can be glued, nailed or held with screws. Dadoes add strength to shelves, and their ends can easily be covered with strips of wood or wood tape.

Dowels—These round wooden pegs can be purchased in most hardware and home supply stores. They are usually made of maple or birch and come in 3-foot lengths with diameters ranging from 1/8 to 1 inch. Dowels can be used to support and strengthen almost any kind of joint. They are especially useful for butt and edge-to-edge joints. They can be used as a substitute for mortises and tenons, or for dovetails in making furniture.

To make a dowel joint, matching holes must be drilled in each of the pieces to be joined. It is usually easiest to clamp the parts in position and then drill through one piece into the other. If this is impossible, measure and drill through one piece very carefully and use it for marking the other piece. Test the holes with a dowel before fastening. If the fit is wrong, glue a dowel into the hole, sand it off flat, and drill again.

Blind dowel holes can be laid out in several ways. The two pieces can be clamped together with their butting surfaces in position next to each other. A square is then used to draw lines across both faces at the desired locations. Then the two pieces are separated and each is marked with a gauge across the squared lines to locate the centers for the dowel holes. Use an awl to mark center holes.

Another way to match centers is to mark your points on the end of one piece with a square and gauge, and use those to make matching marks on the second piece. A third way is to make a template. Nails driven through a block, or holes drilled in a block through which you can mark with an awl can be used. In either case, the marks on both pieces will match. The dowel centers shown in the picture can also be used.

The holes should be drilled with an auger bit. A depth gauge is used to regulate the depth of the holes. Make sure your drill is square to the surface of the work. A tool called a *doweling jig* is available. It works on either the end or edge of a piece

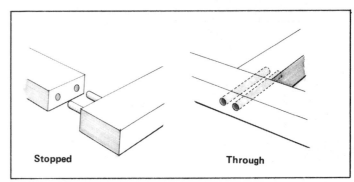

Stopped   **Through**

DOWEL JOINTS can be either through or stopped. Through joints are simpler because both pieces can be drilled at once.

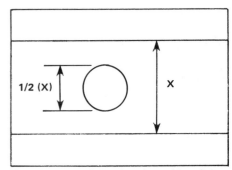

1/2 (X)   X

The diameter of the dowel used in a joint should be about half the thickness of the stock.

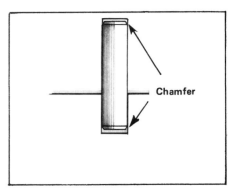

Chamfer

The dowel should be chamfered at each end and should be 1/32- to 1/16-inch shorter than the *combined* depth of the holes.

The dowel should be spiraled or grooved to allow glue to spread.

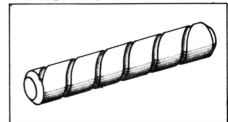

DOWEL CENTERS are used to match hole locations for mating pieces. The dowel centers are placed in holes drilled in one piece and pressed against the matching piece. The points on the centers mark the locations of the holes required in the second piece.

The holding power of screws driven into end-grain can be greatly strengthened by placing a dowel for the screws to penetrate and grip. The end of the dowel should be sawed flush.

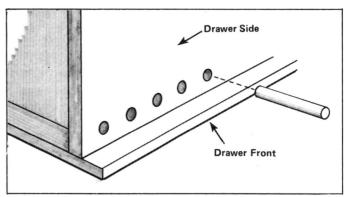

Dowels can be used in place of a dovetail to hold the sides of a drawer to the front. Hold pieces together to drill. Use long dowels and trim flush after glue dries.

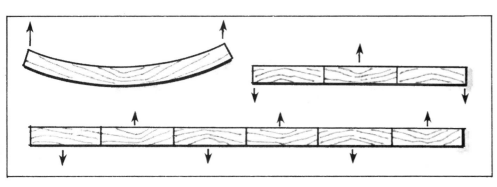

To prevent warping, a large board should be ripped into equal parts and glued together with the middle piece inverted. With large assemblies of pre-cut boards, invert alternate ones to avoid warping.

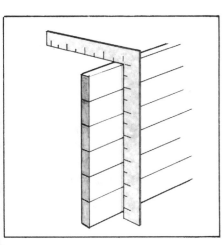

Pieces for an EDGE-TO-EDGE JOINT must be checked for fit at all points, and for squareness.

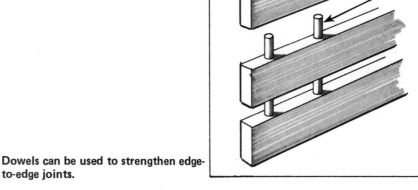

Dowels can be used to strengthen edge-to-edge joints.

125

Mark the position for dowel holes on one piece, then line up pieces with the joining faces up and use a straight edge to carry the lines across the other pieces.

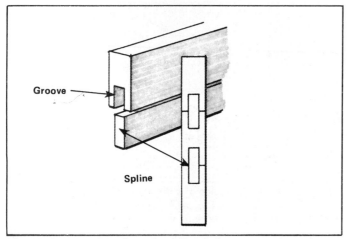

SPLINES made of hardwood or plywood can strengthen edge-to-edge joints.

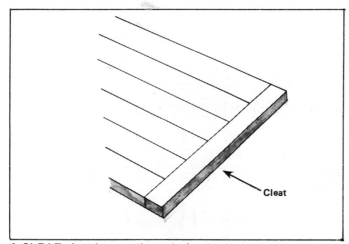

A CLEAT placed across the end of a glued edge-to-edge joint provides stability.

The CLEAT can be shaped to form a lip.

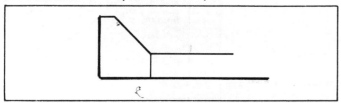

of wood and will handle material up to 3-inches thick.

Dowel pins should be slightly shorter than the combined depth of the two holes—say 1/32 or 1/16 inch. Both ends of the pin should be slightly chamfered with a knife or sandpaper to ensure a smooth fit. Either a spiral notch or a groove should be cut along the entire length of the pin to permit the escape of excess glue and trapped air when the dowel is put in place. This groove will also help prevent splitting the pieces holding the dowel. **Edge-To-Edge Joints**–There will be occasions when you will want to cover very large surface areas. Sometimes you can use plywood for this, but for bench tops or butcher boards you will have to join pieces edge to edge. Even if you can obtain a piece of lumber large enough to cover the area, large pieces warp easily. It is best to rip the piece into equal thirds and glue them together with the middle piece inverted. When gluing several precut boards together, it is best to invert alternate ones. This equalizes the stresses and prevents warping.

Edge-to-edge joints can be strengthened in several ways. Dowels can be used effectively to make a strong joint. Grooves can be cut in adjoining edges to hold other strips of wood, called *splines,* for added support. Plywood is good material for splines. Hardwoods can be used, but be sure you cut so the grain direction is across the strip rather than along it. Finally, boards glued edge to edge can be strengthened by adding cleats at either one or both ends. The cleat can use dowel joints for extra strength as well.

When joining boards edge to edge, try to match the grain of the boards. Use heartwood or sapwood, which have the boldest grain patterns, because they tend to warp less as they dry. Try to match heartwood to heartwood or sapwood to sapwood for the best fit. Be sure to remove all excess glue because glue will not absorb stain or other finishes.

Mortise and Tenon Joints–These joints look more difficult to make than they are. A *mortise* is a rectangular cavity cut into a piece of wood into which another piece, the *tenon,* is fitted. A simple way to cut a mortise is to remove most of the waste wood with an auger bit, and trim and smooth it with a chisel. Or you can cut a mortise with a chisel alone.

A mortise that goes through the board is called a *through mortise.* A *blind* or *stopped mortise* extends only part way through the board and can be drilled by using a depth gauge to control the bit. A scrap of wood can be used to control the depth of your chisel cuts. The tenon for a blind mortise should be cut 1/16-inch shorter in length than the mortise to allow for the glue.

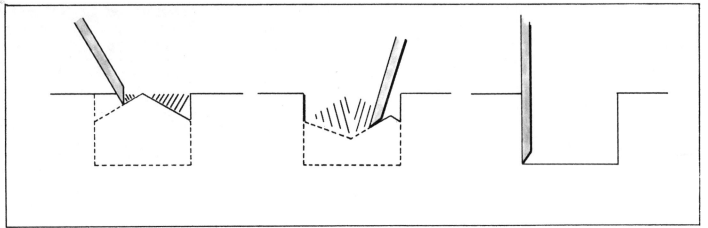

To cut a deep mortise with a chisel, work from both ends with a series of angle cuts, moving the waste toward the center. Clear out the last bit of waste from the shoulders with vertical shearing cuts.

TENONS

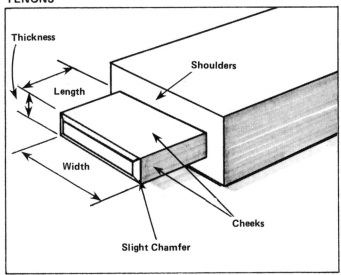

The thickness of the TENON should equal 1/3 to 1/2 the thickness of the stock. The end should be slightly chamfered to leave room for glue.

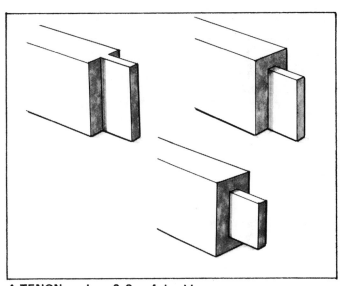

A TENON can have 2, 3 or 4 shoulders.

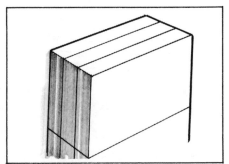

TO CUT A TENON: Mark the cheek lines with a marking gauge and the shoulder lines with a square.

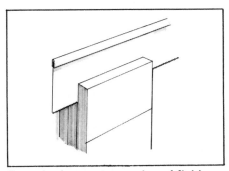

Start cheek cuts at an angle and finish straight across.

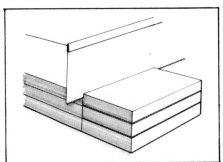

Place the work flat and make the shoulder cuts. A block clamped to the sawblade can be used to control the depth of cut.

The tenon is marked with a square and marking gauge. The cheek cuts are made first. Then the work is laid flat and the shoulder cuts are made. Make sure that your blade is cutting on the waste side of your guidelines. Otherwise your tenon will be too small. A block of wood clamped to the saw blade can be used as a depth control. If necessary, finish the tenon with a chisel.

You can *pin* a mortise and tenon joint by boring a hole through both parts with an auger bit and inserting a dowel. It is best to bore the mortise first, insert the tenon, and mark the center of the hole on it with an awl. Then drill the matching hole slightly closer to the shoulder of the tenon. This will help to draw the shoulders in tight when the pin is driven through, and will give the joint extra strength.

The edges of the tenon can be sloped for wedged mortise and tenon joints. This leaves space for the wedges which are driven in after the tenon is in place. One variation of this involves sloping the edges of the mortise away from the side holding the shoulders. The tenon is cut square and wedges with glue are used to fill the space left by the slope when the tenon is in place. A variation of this is to make two saw cuts in the tenon and drive the wedges into the kerfs.

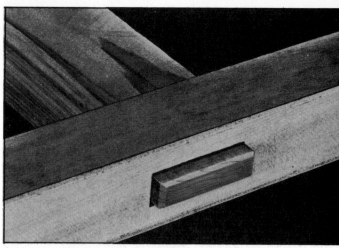

A MORTISE AND TENON JOINT should fit tightly. A through mortise is shown.

A MORTISE can be either through or blind.

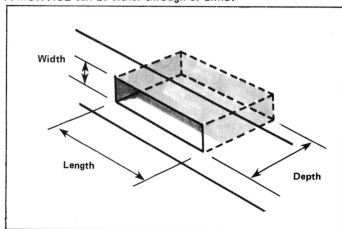

MAKING A MORTISE THE EASY WAY

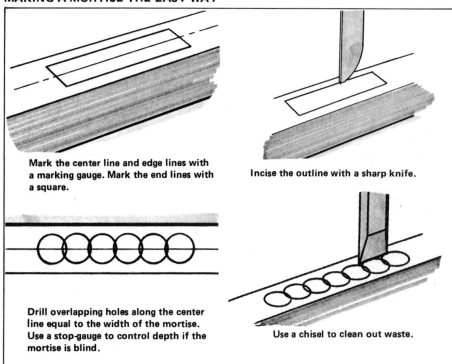

Mark the center line and edge lines with a marking gauge. Mark the end lines with a square.

Drill overlapping holes along the center line equal to the width of the mortise. Use a stop-gauge to control depth if the mortise is blind.

Incise the outline with a sharp knife.

Use a chisel to clean out waste.

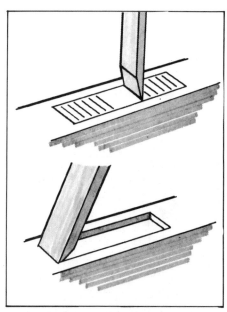

To form a shallow mortise with a chisel, make a series of vertical cuts from both ends and clean out waste with the bevel down. Repeat until finished. Clean with vertical shearing cuts.

WAYS TO PIN A MORTISE-TENON JOINT

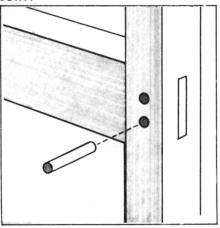

A mortise and tenon can be pinned with dowels through the sides . . .

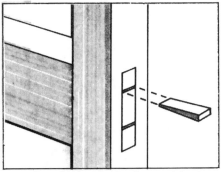

or wedges driven into kerfs sawed in the tenon . . .

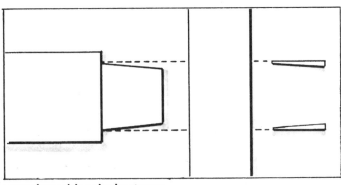

or wedges with a sloping tenon . . .

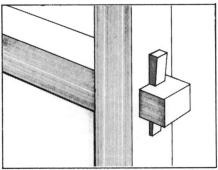

or with a wedge or dowel locking through the assembly.

A *finger lap* joint, often called a *lock* or *pin joint,* is a series of open mortise and tenon joints in a line which lock together to form a corner. This joint is commonly used in constructing boxes, but has less strength than a dovetail.

Dovetails—This joint is *the* mark of a craftsman. Making dovetails requires time and care, but their added strength is worth the effort. The projections at the *end* of a board are called *pins:* the spaces between them are *sockets.* The projections on the *face* of the joining board are called *dovetails.* The spaces between them are also called *sockets.* Dovetails are usually wider than their matching pins, but they should not be more than four times wider because the stress could break the pins.

To make a single dovetail, lay out the socket with a bevel. Make the side cuts first and clear the waste with a chisel. Place the socket at the desired position on the mating piece and mark its outline with a knife. Then cut out the pin with a saw and chisel. This process can be reversed. The pin can be made first and used as a guide for marking the socket. In either case you should work for a good fit. When several single dovetails are to be made, it is a good idea to make a template.

In making multiple dovetails, the choice between making the pins or sockets first is again up to you. In both cases the shoulder lines are marked first, using the thickness of the joining piece as a guide. The stock is then divided into as many equal parts as there are to be dovetails. Count the two half-pins at each outer edge as one. The dividing lines are the centerlines of each pin or dovetail. The narrow width of the pin, usually about 1/8-inch is then marked on either side of the center lines, and a bevel is used to mark the proper angles. These lines are then squared over the edge. Mark the waste wood to avoid mistakes. The side cuts are made first and the waste wood is removed with a chisel. The resulting piece is then used as a template for marking its mate. If the work is done carefully, the two pieces will fit snugly.

Coped Joints—These joints are used for matching pieces of coping or molding by following the contour of the mating piece. The simplest method requires you to make a simple 45-degree miter cut in the coping first. Then place the molding on its back and cut along the line of the miter cut with a coping saw. This will automatically produce the correct contour. It works with the most irregular molding.

The second method is shown on page 15. Put the moldings together at a right angle and

VARIATIONS OF MORTISE-TENON JOINTS

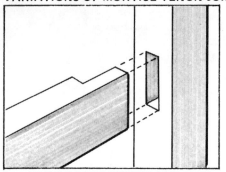

In a BARE-FACED TENON AND MORTISE the tenon is shaped like a rabbet.

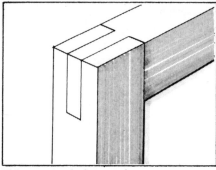

This open variation used to turn a corner is sometimes called a SLIP JOINT.

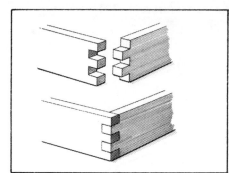

A FINGER LAP or a LOCK or PIN JOINT is often used for boxes.

DOVETAIL JOINTS

A well-made DOVETAIL JOINT is usually not concealed because it is considered the mark of excellent craftpersonship.

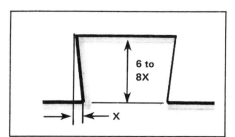

The angle of the pin should be 1/6 to 1/8 the length of the peg. A greater angle is required for softwood than for hardwood.

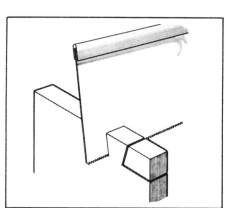

You can cut the pin first for a dovetail. Do the cheek cuts, then the shoulders.

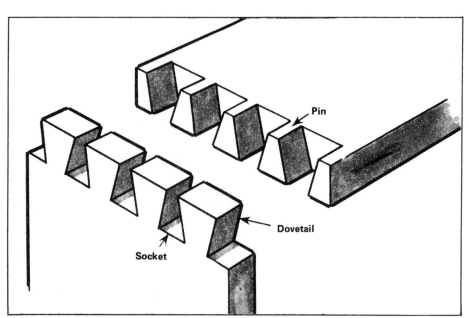

The two joining pieces are cut so they fit precisely. A DOVETAIL JOINT should hold even if the glue fails.

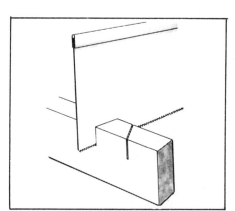

Use the pin as a pattern for the socket and cut with a saw. Clean with a chisel.

You can also start by making the socket and using it as a pattern for the pin.

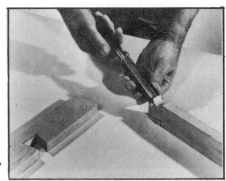

Make the shoulder cuts on the pin first, then cut the cheeks with a chisel.

MULTIPLE DOVETAILS: Divide the stock into equal spaces. Use these marks as centerlines and lay out slant lines with a bevel. Depth should equal the thickness of the stock.

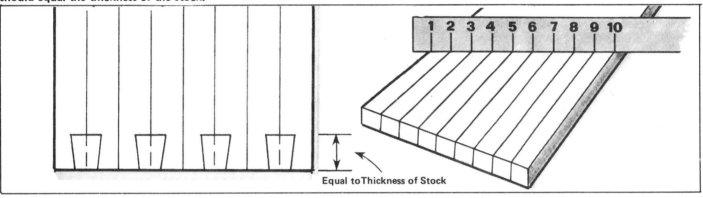

Equal to Thickness of Stock

Use a template for marking end cuts when many dovetails are required.

Use a block of wood to make a guide for cheek cuts. Note how the waste is marked with X's.

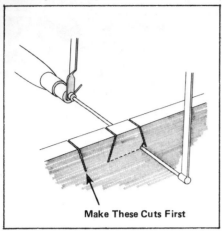

Make These Cuts First

A coping saw can be used to remove the bulk of the waste. It is best not to cut clear to the bottom line.

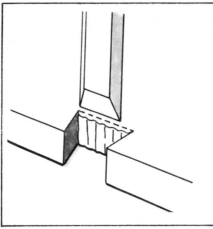

Use a chisel for final clearing. Work from both sides.

Use the completed part for marking its mate.

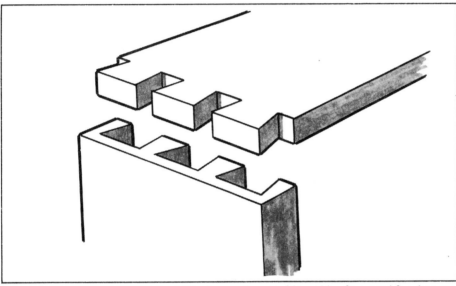

A HALF-BLIND DOVETAIL is visible from only one side and is often used for drawers. The blind sockets should be between 2/3 and 3/4 the thickness of the stock. They are shaped with chisels.

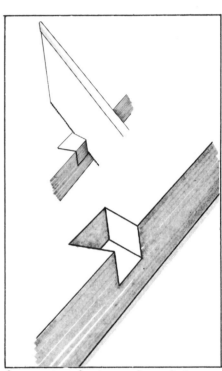

A saw cut made at an angle can help get the job started.

A COPE CUT follows the contour of its mating piece. Place the molding on its base and make a 45-degree miter cut. Then place it on its back and follow the line of the miter cut with a coping saw.

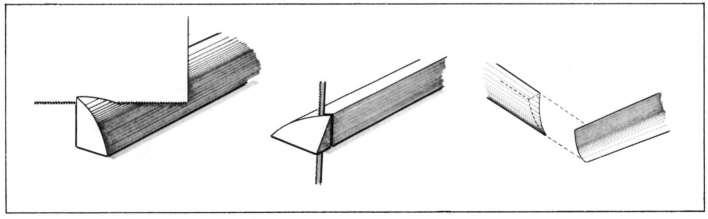

use your compass to trace the contour of one piece onto the other. A coping saw is used to make the cut.

SPLICES

A splice connects pieces end to end along the same line. There are splices designed to hold weight or resist tension, but the most common use for woodworking is simply to gain additional length. A well-made splice will be as strong as the wood itself.

Several simple splices can be used in woodworking. An *end butt* is simply a glued butt joint laid end to end. It can be strengthened with dowels or straight plates. A *plain scarf* involves cutting angles that coincide in the two ends and joining them. A *finger splice* is similar to a finger lap joint laid flat. A *face dovetail* can also serve as a splice.

GLUES

A properly glued joint can be stronger than the wood around it, but that requires proper selection and application of the glue. Generally, softwoods are easier to glue than hardwoods, and sapwood is easier than heartwood. Many glues are currently on the market. New ones seem to arrive everyday. The most commonly used glues for woodworking are listed on page 134, along with their characteristics. Study that chart and make the choice most suited to your needs. Also, read the manufacturer's instructions carefully before using the glue.

NAILS, BRADS AND TACKS

Selecting nails for a particular job sounds simple, but should be done with care. There are many kinds of nails available, each designed to do a specific task better than any other nail. The holding power of a nail depends on the pressure of the wood fibers in contact with its surface. Wood fibers are pushed aside and compressed when a nail is driven through. Their tendency to spring back to their original position causes them to press against and hold the nail. Holding power can vary according to the nail's size, shape and surface treatment. As a rule, hardwoods hold better than softwoods.

Holding power can be increased by altering the shape of the nail's point. The most important thing you need to know about points is that long, sharp points have greater holding power, but tend to cause splitting. *Blunt points are less likely to split the work.* Hardwoods split more easily than softwoods, but you should be careful with softwoods such as Douglas fir and white cedar. When there is a chance of splitting, it is best to blunt the point of the nail with a hammer. Boring a pilot hole with an awl or a smaller blunt nail, or rubbing the nail with soap, wax or grease can also reduce the chances of splitting.

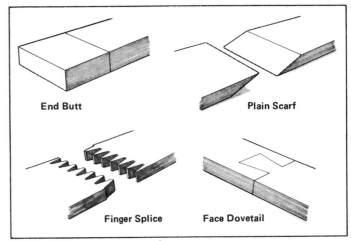

End Butt · **Plain Scarf** · **Finger Splice** · **Face Dovetail**

SPLICES

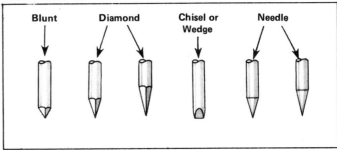

POINT SHAPES

Blunt · Diamond · Chisel or Wedge · Needle

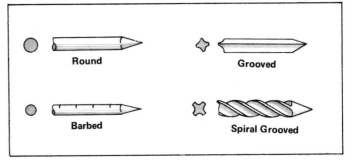

SHANKS

Round · Grooved · Barbed · Spiral Grooved

MOST COMMON WOOD GLUES

Type	Preparation	Clamping Time		Best Temperature Fahrenheit	Moisture Resistance	Waterproof	Remarks
		Softwood	Hardwood				
Animal Liquid Hide	Ready to use.	3 to 4 hours	2 hours	70 degrees or over. Warm the glue if the room is cold.	Good	No	Good choice for general furniture work but not for outdoor projects. Provides some strength even when joints are poorly fitted, will resist heat and is easy to use.
Powdered Casein	Mix with water.	3 to 4 hours	2 hours	Must be above freezing. Works best at warmer temperature.	Good	No	Especially good for oily woods like yew, teak, lemon, but it will stain woods like redwood. Works fairly well as a joint filler. Okay for general woodworking but do not use on outdoor projects.
Polyvinyl White Glue	Ready to use.	1-1/2 to 2 hours	1 hour	60 degree minimum	Good	No	This is a very good all-around glue. It's quick-setting, easy to use and does not require maximum clamping. Do not use on outdoor projects.
Plastic Powdered Resin	Mix with water.	16 hours	16 hours	70 degree minimum	High	No	Best for wood projects that will be exposed to considerable moisture and joints that are close fitting and clamped tightly. Not good for oily woods.
Resorcinol	2-part mix, follow directions on container.	16 hours	16 hours	70 degree minimum	Very High	Yes	This is the glue to use for outdoor projects, boats, wooden water containers. It is also excellent for joints that are poorly fitted, but do not use when temperature is below 70°F.
Urea Resin	2-part mix, follow directions on container.	Seconds with commercial heating equipment.		70 degree minimum	High	No	This is not a typical home workshop ashesive. It works best when moisture content of wood is minimal.
Contact Cement	Ready to use.	Bonds on contact. No clamping required.		70 degree minimum	High	No	Not used for general woodworking. Use for bonding thin materials such as veneers, laminates, plastics and so forth, but remember that parts can't be shifted after contact is made. Read directions carefully.
Epoxy Cement	2-part mix.	Amount of clamping depends on product but will set faster with heat. Some require none: read directions on the package.			Very High	Yes	This is not a general woodworking adhesive, but it is good for bonding dissimilar materials. Some types can be used to fill holes. Use carefully: read the directions on the package.

Nails vary in the design of their shanks. The nails you are most likely to use will have round shanks, but oval, square and triangular nails are also available. Barbed nails have small barbs in their shanks, either along their full length or near the head. Barbs increase holding power and allow a short nail to do the work of a longer one. Grooved nails, either spiral or longitudinal, are grooved along their full length. As you drive the nail, the wood fibers are compressed into the grooves which gives the nail more holding power. Coated nails hold better because of the adhesive power of the coating. The coating also helps prevent rust.

Nail heads are designed for specific jobs. The shape you choose should depend on the hardness of the wood and the likelihood of the nail working through. In general, nails with broad heads hold better.

Nail Size—The size of most nails is designated by the penny system. Originally this system was based on the price per hundred nails, and it still uses the abbreviation "d" for penny from the name of the ancient Roman coin, *denarius.* Today, penny, or d, indicates the length of a nail. A 2d nail is one-inch long. For each additional penny, 1/4 inch is added to the length until it reaches 3 inches. Then the system becomes less regular. Nails smaller than 1 inch or larger than 6 inches are measured in fractions of inches. Nails over 4 inches are usually called *spikes.* Brads and tacks are measured in fractions of inches.

The diameter of a nail is determined by the gauge of the wire it is cut from. It is expressed in terms of *Steel Wire Gauge.*

Types of Nails—The most commonly used nails in woodworking are wire nails. They are cut from various gauges of wire and have round shanks without a taper. They come in a wide variety of types.

Common Nails have flat heads and are used for most rough work, for framing, and to secure siding, sheathing and subflooring.

Box Nails are similar to common nails except they are more slender. They can be used where a common nail might cause splitting. They are sometimes barbed or coated for better holding.

Finishing Nails are lighter gauge than common nails and have tulip-shaped heads. They can easily be driven below the surface of the work with a nail set. Then they can be concealed with putty.

Wire Brads have almost no heads at all and may be considered special finishing nails. Length in inches is used to distinguish size. Special nail setting tools for brads are available.

Casing Nails are similar to finishing nails except the gauge is larger and their heads are tapered. They can be set and concealed. They are used for exterior trim.

Flooring Brads are similar to casing nails but have larger, tapered heads. They can also be set and are used for floors.

Double-Headed Nails, sometimes called *duplex, scaffold* or *staging nails,* are for work that is to be taken apart later. The nail is driven in up to the first head, leaving the second head exposed for easy extraction.

Tacks can be used for small nailing jobs. Some come with decorative heads. A number system is used to indicate size. Use a piece of cardboard or a straw to hold tacks for driving. Push the tack through the cardboard and hold the cardboard rather than the tack.

NAIL SUBSTITUTES

Corrguated-steel fasteners, sometimes called *wiggle nails,* are simply pieces of corrugated steel sharpened on one edge. They are good for strengthening glued joints, particularly miter or butt joints. They are widely used by manufacturers of boxes and furniture because they are inexpensive, quick, and require little skill to use. They are available in 1/4, 1/2 and 1-inch sizes and have as few as two, or as many as seven corrugations. They are made with plain edges for hardwood and with saw edges for softwood. Some have parallel ridges while others have ridges that slant slightly toward each other at the top. This tends to pull the wood together. There are special fastener sets available for each size. There are also circular corrugated fasteners available for joining more than two edges.

When using a corrugated fastener, place it away from the edges of the assembly and diagonal to the grain to avoid splitting. Use light hammer blows distributed evenly across the edge of the fastener to drive it in.

GAUGE EQUIVALENTS FOR NAIL SIZES	
GAUGE	**INCHES**
2	.2625
3	.2437
4	.2253
5	.2070
6	.1920
7	.1770
8	.1620
9	.1483
10	.1350
11	.1205
12	.0985
13	.0915
14	.0800
15	.0673

CASING NAILS

	Size (d)	Length in Inches	Gauge	Approximate Number Per Pound
	3	1-1/4	14-1/2	630
	4	1-1/2	14	490
	6	2	12-1/2	245
	8	2-1/2	11-1/2	149
	10	3	10-1/2	94
	16	3-1/2	10	75

TACKS

Number	Length in Inches
2	1/4
2-1/2	5/16
3	3/8
4	7/16
6	1/2
8	9/16
10	5/8
12	11/16
14	3/4
16	13/16
18	7/8
22	1

WIRE BRADS

	Length in Inches	Gauge
	3/16	20 to 24
	1/4	19 to 24
	3/8	18 to 24
	1/2	14 to 23
	5/8	13 to 22
	3/4	13 to 21
	7/8	13 to 20

FINISHING NAILS

	Size (d)	Length in Inches	Gauge	Approximate Number Per Pound
	2	1	16-1/2	1350
	3	1-1/4	15-1/2	880
	4	1-1/2	15	630
	6	2	13	290
	8	2-1/2	12-1/2	196
	10	3	11-1/2	125

COMMON AND BOX NAIL SIZES

Size d	2	3	4	5	6	7	8	9	10	12	16	20	30	40	50	60
Length In Inches	1	1-1/4	1-1/2	1-3/4	2	2-1/4	2-1/2	2-3/4	3	3-1/4	3-1/2	4	4-1/2	5	5-1/2	6
COMMON NAILS																
Gauge	15	14	12-1/2	12-1/2	11-1/2	11-1/2	10-1/4	10-1/4	9	9	8	6	5	4	3	2
Approximate # Per Pound	845	540	290	250	165	150	100	90	65	60	45	30	20	17	13	10
BOX NAILS																
Gauge	15-1/2	14-1/2	14	14	12-1/2	12-1/2	11-1/2	11-1/2	10-1/2	10-1/2	10	9	9	8	—	—
Approximate # Per Pound	1010	635	473	406	236	210	145	132	94	88	71	52	46	35	—	—

2 3 4 5 6 7 8 9 10 12 16 20 30 40 50 60

Common Nails are shown. Box Nails are slimmer, but come in the same lengths.

The *Scotch*™ *fastener* is also used for supporting glued joints. It can be applied in two steps and is less likely to cause splitting than a corrugated fastener.

SCREWS

This type of fastener offers several advantages over nails for the woodworker. Screws have greater holding power than nails and they can be withdrawn without damaging the work. They are neater looking than nails and can be tightened to draw pieces together. However, they are more expensive than nails and require more time to drive.

Wood Screws—These are made of either unhardened steel, stainless steel, aluminum, copper or brass. The steel may be bright finished, blued or plated with chrome, zinc or cadmium. Wood screws are threaded from their point for approximately two-thirds their length. They are commonly found with either of three shapes of head: flat, round or oval. Another type head, less often seen, is called a *fillister*. Screw heads usually have either a single slot or a crossed slot called a *Phillips head.*

The single slot on a *drive screw* does not extend to the edge of the head because this screw is driven part way with a hammer and then finished with a screwdriver. If the slots were extended to the edge, the blows from the hammer might break the head.

Two other screw types are seen only infrequently. A *Freason head* is similar to Phillips head. A *Pozidriv®* screw has even more slots for greater driving power. Each of these heads requires a different type of screwdriver. For woodworking, the single slot and Phillips head will do almost any job.

The size of a screw is designated by its length and diameter. The length of a screw is measured from the point of the screw to the point where the surface of the wood should be when the screw has been driven. Length tells you the depth the screws will reach. Screws range from 1/4 inch to 6 inches. Up to 1 inch, sizes increase by 1/8 inch. From 1 to 3 inches, sizes increase by 1/4 inch. From 3 to 6 inches, sizes increase by 1/2 inch.

The diameter of a screw is given as a gauge number signifying the outside diameter of the screw's unthreaded shank. These numbers range from 0 to 24, but numbers 2 through 18 are most commonly used in woodworking. Different length screws are usually available in several different gauges.

Selecting Screws—To obtain maximum holding power, the screw selected should be long enough so 2/3 of its length will enter the lower board. Bright-finished screws hold best because their threads are sharp. Plating screw threads rounds the edges and sometimes clogs them.

Flat-Head Screws are used where the head must be flat with the surface of the work. The screw hole must be countersunk or counterbored to make room for the head. This is the most commonly used screw.

Round-Head Screws protrude above the surface of the work. They can be ornamental, but are best used when the wedging action of a flat head might cause splitting. Both flat- and round-head screws can be concealed by counterboring and plugging the hole.

Oval-Head Screws protrude slightly and are sometimes used in place of flat heads because of the greater strength of their heads.

Fillister-Head Screws are chosen for strength and because their flat-bottomed heads do not produce the wedging action of an oval or flat head. They can easily be seated in a counterbored hole.

Special Screws—Several types of screws are made for special purposes.

Dowel Screws have threads on both ends. They are often used in joints. Starter holes are drilled in both pieces. The screw is twisted into one piece and the mating piece is twisted on.

Special Shaped Woodscrews include a variety of hooks and eyes. The threaded portion is anchored in the wood and their heads are used for attaching articles. Only a starter hole is needed for these screws because the shank protrudes. Turn the screw clockwise with your thumb and fingers to seat it. Use an open-end adjustable wrench to drive the screw home. A screwdriver placed through a screw eye can also be used to tighten it. A square screw hook can be driven by placing a small piece of pipe over the hook and turning it clockwise.

WASHERS: Different washers are available for different screwheads. Flat washers are for round-head screws. Raised countersunk and flush countersunk washers are for oval and flat-head screws.

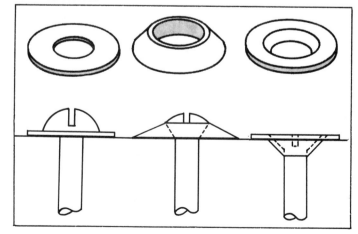

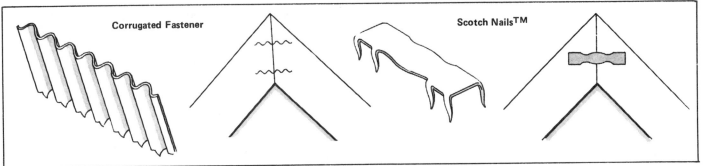

Corrugated Fastener   Scotch Nails™

Nail substitutes such as CORRUGATED FASTENERS and SCOTCH NAILS™ are useful where nails might split the work or for spanning two pieces as in a miter joint.

WOOD SCREWS

SCREW NUMBER	18	16	14	12	10	9	8	7	6	5	4	3	2
DIAMETER IN INCHES	.294	.268	.242	.216	.190	.177	.164	.151	.138	.125	.112	.099	.086
LEAD HOLE Twist Drill Diameter In Inches	5/32	9/64	1/8	7/64	7/64	3/32	3/32	5/64	5/64	5/64	5/64	1/16	3/64
Drill Size	23	28	31	36	36	41	41	48	48	48	48	53	56
Auger Bit Number	4	3	3										
BODY HOLE Twist Drill Diameter In Inches	19/64	17/64	1/4	7/32	3/16	3/16	11/64	5/32	9/64	1/8	7/64	7/64	3/32
Drill Size	M	G	D	3	13	13	18	23	28	31	36	36	41
Auger Bit Number	5	5	4	4	3	3	3	3					
COUNTERSINK Auger Bit Number	10	9	8	7	6	6	6	5	5	4	4	4	3

| 18 | 16 | 14 | 12 | 10 | 9 | 8 | 7 | 6 | 5 | 4 | 3 | 2 |

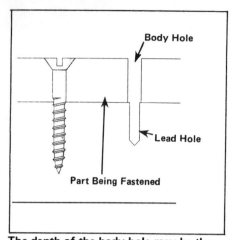

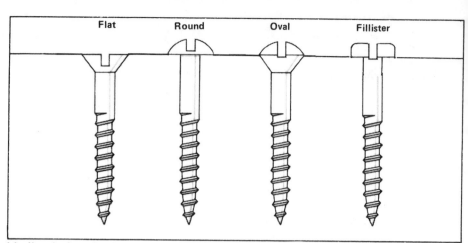

The depth of the body hole may be the full thickness of the part being fastened. The depth of the lead hole should be about 1/2 the length of the threaded portion of the screw.

Ideally, the length of a screw should be about 1/8th inch less than the total thickness of the parts being put together. In practice, choose the longest suitable screw. A flat-head screw rests at or below the surface of the work. A round-head screw rests above the surface unless the hole is counterbored. An oval-head screw requires a partial countersink. A fillister-head screw rests above the surface unless the hole is counterbored.

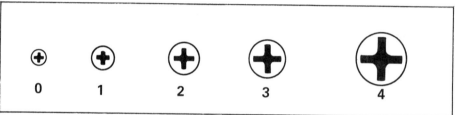

Actual sizes of PHILLIPS-HEAD SCREWS.

SCREWS ARE AVAILABLE IN THESE LENGTHS

LENGTH (Inches)	NUMBER OF SCREW																	
	0	1	2	3	4	5	6	7	8	9	10	11	12	14	16	18	20	24
1/4	X	X	X	X														
3/8			X	X	X	X	X	X										
1/2			X	X	X	X	X	X	X									
5/8				X	X	X	X	X	X	X	X							
3/4					X	X	X	X	X	X	X	X						
7/8							X	X	X	X	X	X	X					
1							X	X	X	X	X	X	X	X				
1-1/4							X	X	X	X	X	X	X	X	X			
1-1/2							X	X	X	X	X	X	X	X	X	X		
1-3/4									X	X	X	X	X	X	X	X	X	
2									X	X	X	X	X	X	X	X	X	
2-1/4										X	X	X	X	X	X	X	X	
2-1/2													X	X	X	X	X	
2-3/4														X	X	X	X	
3															X	X	X	
3-1/2																X	X	X
4																X	X	X

Lag Screws are very large screws with unslotted square or hexagonal heads. They are used for fastening heavy wood or metal parts to wooden surfaces or masonry in which expansion shields have been placed. They are driven with a wrench. Size is designated by both diameter and length.

Hanger Bolts have woodscrew threads on one end and machine-screw threads on the other. A square or hexagonal nut fits the machine-screw threads and is designed to be removed without dislodging the bolt. Hanger bolts are used where the article attached to the wood must be unfastened occasionally. Like lag screws, size is designated by diameter and length.

To drive a hanger bolt, lock two nuts together on the machine screw threads *short of the shoulder of the thread.* This will prevent the nuts from jamming the thread. Drill a starter hole and drive the bolt with a wrench applied to the top nut. When the bolt is set, the nuts can be removed.

Sheet-Metal Screws are useful with plywood or particle board. They hold well and tap their own holes. Lengths run from 1/8 inch to 2 inches in various gauges.

Too Tight—Too Loose?—You can loosen a screw that fits too tightly by soaking it in hydrogen peroxide. If you withdraw and redrive a screw in the same hole, it may fit loosely. If the fit is not too loose, dipping the screw in glue or paint might be enough to make it tight. If the hole is too large, a wooden match or toothpick can be inserted as a plug, and then the screw can be driven.

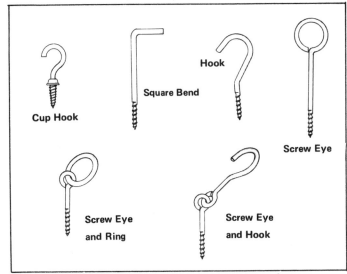

SPECIAL SCREWS are available in a wide variety of types.

DIAMETER IN INCHES	LENGTH IN INCHES
1/4 5/16	1 to 12
3/8 7/16 1/2	1 to 12
5/8 3/4	1-1/2 to 16
7/8 1	2 to 16

LAG SCREWS, often called *lag bolts*, have square or hex heads and are used for heavy-duty fastening.

DOWEL SCREWS are used for joining pieces edge to edge.

HANGER BOLTS are used to attach items to wood that must be unfastened occasionally.

SHEET METAL SCREWS

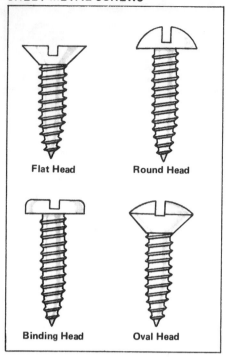

Flat Head Round Head

Binding Head Oval Head

CORNER IRONS

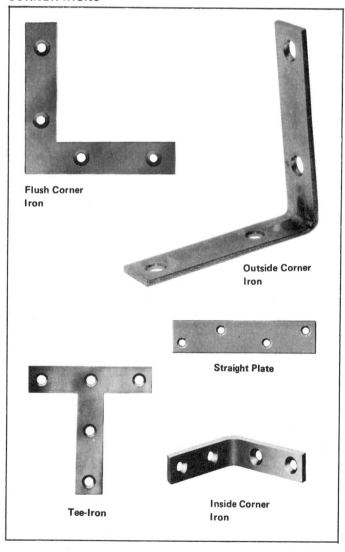

Flush Corner
Iron

Outside Corner
Iron

Straight Plate

Tee-Iron

Inside Corner
Iron

CORNER IRONS

Metal plates drilled and countersunk to accommodate screws are available for strengthening joints. They are about 1/16-inch thick and 1/2-inch wide. Most common types are *straight plates*, right-angle *corner irons*, T-shaped *Tee-irons*, and *flush corner irons* which are L-shaped. They are attached with flat-head screws.

BOLTS, NUTS AND WASHERS

Bolts—These are used in heavy construction because they have greater strength than screws. They are not meant to be threaded into the wood and holes must be drilled so they can pass through. A nut is used to secure a bolt. Both the bolt and the nut are specified by length and the diameter of the thread.

Selecting Bolts—Bolt lengths range from 3/4 inch to 20 inches. Lengths are measured the same way as in screws. Diameters vary from 3/16 to 3/4 inch.

Machine Bolts have square or hexagonal heads. The head is held with a wrench while the nut is tightened. Threads are either fine or coarse.

Carriage Bolts are used only with wood. They have round heads with a square shoulder underneath. When the bolt is drawn into the wood, the shoulder prevents the bolt from turning as the nut is tightened.

Stove Bolts were originally used in making metal stoves. They are available in smaller sizes than other bolts and have slotted heads.

Nuts—Several types of nuts are available. Square and hexagonal nuts are tightened with a wrench. Castellated nuts are used with cotter pins, drilled bolts or capscrews. Cap nuts are used when appearance is important or when the end of a bolt protrudes and is a hazard. Wingnuts are used where changes or adjustments are to be made. Knurled nuts can be used in place of wingnuts.

Oil applied to the threads of a nut before it is placed on a bolt will help prevent corrosion from "freezing" the nut to the bolt.

Washers—These are used to distribute pressure over a wide area and to prevent the nut from cutting the wood as it is tightened. Lock washers are used to prevent the nut from working loose.

WALL FASTENERS

Several fasteners are designed for anchoring screws in walls made of masonry.

Lead Shields, Expansion Plugs and **Fiber Anchors** are hollow tubes made of soft materials used in solid masonry walls. They are placed in a drilled pilot hole and a screw is driven into their unthreaded center. The threads of the screw cut threads in the plug and force it to expand to fill the hole and anchor the screw. They are available in an assortment of lengths with diameters ranging from 5/32 to 3/4 inch.

MACHINE BOLTS

DIAMETER IN INCHES	LENGTH IN INCHES
1/4	1/2 to 8
5/16	1/2 to 10
3/8	3/4 to 12
7/16	1 to 12
1/2	1 to 25

Hex Head

Countersunk Head

Oval or Button Head

CARRIAGE BOLTS

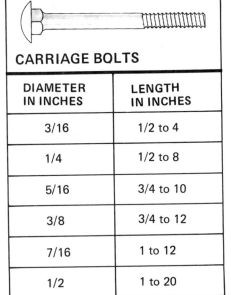

DIAMETER IN INCHES	LENGTH IN INCHES
3/16	1/2 to 4
1/4	1/2 to 8
5/16	3/4 to 10
3/8	3/4 to 12
7/16	1 to 12
1/2	1 to 20

NUTS

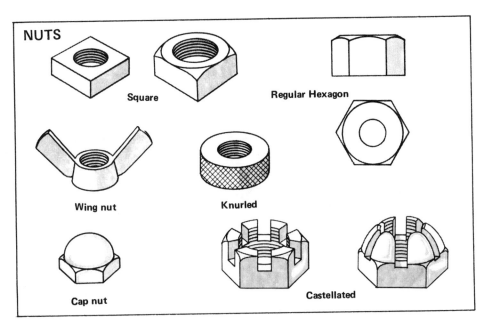

Square

Regular Hexagon

Wing nut

Knurled

Cap nut

Castellated

WASHERS

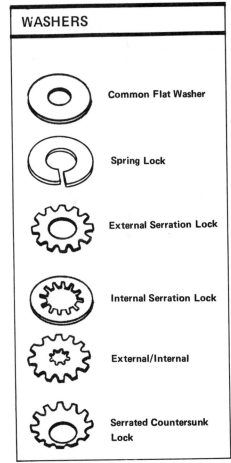

Common Flat Washer

Spring Lock

External Serration Lock

Internal Serration Lock

External/Internal

Serrated Countersunk Lock

STOVE BOLTS

DIAMETER IN INCHES	LENGTH IN INCHES
1/8 5/32	3/8 to 2
3/16	3/8 to 6
1/4	1/2 to 6
5/16 3/8	3/4 to 6
1/2	1 to 4

Button Head

Truss Head

Countersunk Head

Jack Nuts are placed in a hole and the threads of the screw draw its parts together to form a shield around the hole. They should be used on thin, hollow walls or hollow-core doors.

Molly® Bolts or Expansion Anchors are used with composition wallboard. They are inserted in a drilled hole. As the screw is turned, prongs are forced outward to form a broad shield that anchors the screw. About ten turns of the screwdriver completes the spreading. The screw is then removed, inserted through the fixture to be attached, and redriven.

Toggle Bolts are used to fasten woodwork to hollow tile walls or concrete block. After the bolt is inserted, the wings on the nut spread open as the screw is tightened. Unlike the Molly® bolt, the screw cannot be withdrawn without losing the nut.

TEE NUTS™

These are so named because of their shape. They provide a way to put steel threads in wood. The nut is set on one side of a through hole and acts as an anchor for the screw driven from the other side. Tee Nuts™ come in various sizes.

STORING FASTENERS

Loose nails and screws are a safety hazard. They should be kept in boxes or cans. A sample can be taped on the outside of the container for easy identification. There are a number of plastic containers available. Some people prefer using glass jars so they can see the contents. There is a danger of breaking the jars, but that is minor. One common method of storage is to tack or screw the jar tops to the bottom of a board or shelf at eye level. The jars hang from their tops and can be seen and opened easily.

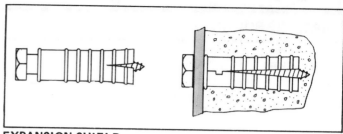

EXPANSION SHIELD

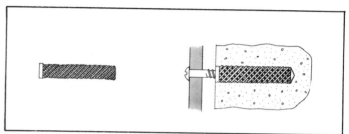

FIBER ANCHOR

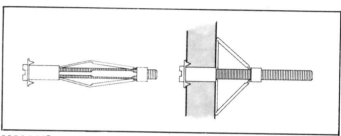

MOLLY® BOLT

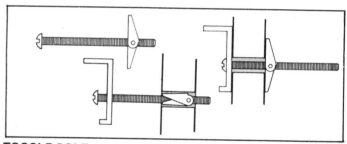

TOGGLE BOLT

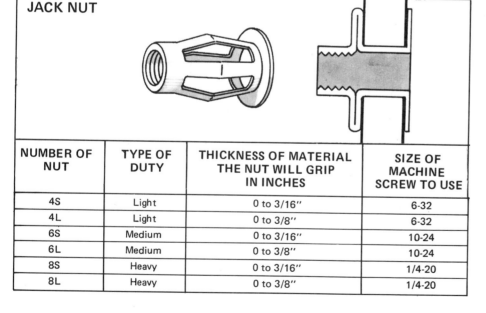

JACK NUT

NUMBER OF NUT	TYPE OF DUTY	THICKNESS OF MATERIAL THE NUT WILL GRIP IN INCHES	SIZE OF MACHINE SCREW TO USE
4S	Light	0 to 3/16"	6-32
4L	Light	0 to 3/8"	6-32
6S	Medium	0 to 3/16"	10-24
6L	Medium	0 to 3/8"	10-24
8S	Heavy	0 to 3/16"	1/4-20
8L	Heavy	0 to 3/8"	1/4-20

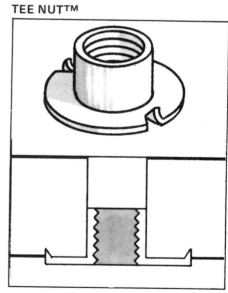

TEE NUT™

Tools You Can Make

Although I have now talked about most of the tools you are likely to buy for woodworking, there are several other tools which you will probably need. These you can make yourself. Working carefully with the following directions, you should be able to produce two useful tools and your first real piece of furniture, your workbench.

Begin with the sawhorses first. This will give you practice with your tools and the horses can be used in making your workbench. These projects should be fun. You should enjoy yourself. Work slowly—don't rush. Properly made, these projects will serve you for a long time.

SAWHORSES

Sawhorses are like portable workbenches you can use in or out of the shop. In the shop, they make it more convenient to make preliminary sizing cuts on large panels and long boards, and they are useful when you are gluing with bar clamps. Outside the shop, they can become a workbench when you straddle them with a few boards or a sheet of plywood, or they can be used as low scaffolding.

Sawhorses can be basic or elaborate. Basic does not mean weak. They should be made sturdily, without wobble, whether you design from scratch or work with one of the sets of ready-made sawhorse hardware. Add braces across the legs and a shelf between them. These additions provide rigidity and the shelf has practical uses.

There are several sawhorse designs shown here. All should be made between 24 and 30-inches high. This puts you above the work and gives you a clear line of sight. Length can vary. Cut one leg and use it as a pattern for the others.

TOTE BOXES

The tote box is a means of carrying some essential tools when you are doing on-location work. Like the sawhorse, it can be basic or fancy, but it should definitely be sturdy. Tote boxes are usually subjected to a lot of abuse so take as much time as you need to make it right to begin with. You will save time and effort in the long run.

This basic SAWHORSE is put together with metal brackets which set the correct leg angles. Bevels on the ends of the legs are not essential so assembly requires little time. Bracing the legs and adding the shelf strengthens the horse and makes it more useful.

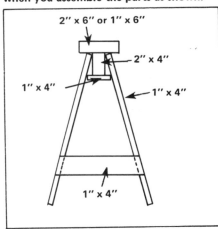

This design lets you avoid cutting a bevel. Leg angle is automatically established when you assemble the parts as shown.

2" x 6" or 1" x 6"

2" x 4"

1" x 4"

1" x 4"

1" x 4"

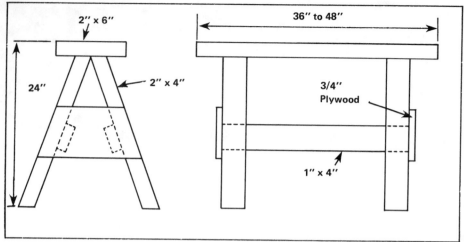

This BASIC SAWHORSE is easy to make. Legs should be beveled at the top and bottom 15 to 20 degrees.

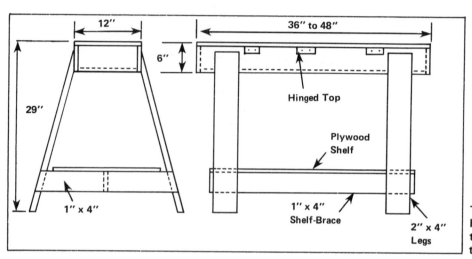

The top of this DOUBLE-DUTY SAW HORSE serves as a tool box. Assemble the top as a unit then add the legs. Use three hinges on the top.

Basic TOTE BOX is made of 3/4-inch plywood or lumber. Bottom of metal lath or hardware cloth attached with fence staples keeps interior clean. Box can be as large as you need.

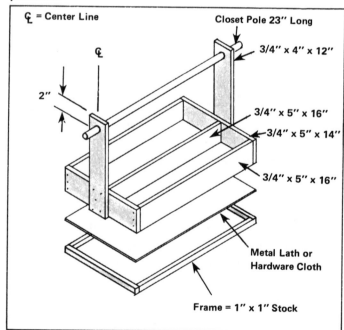

"TOUGHIE" SAWHORSE made from fir lumber. Use lag screws and wood screws for assembly throughout.

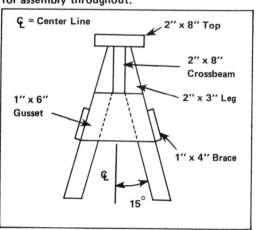

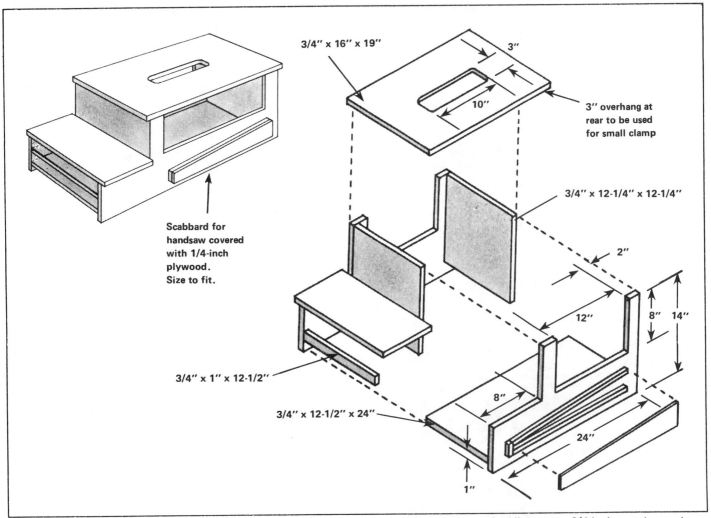

3/4" x 16" x 19"

3"

10"

3" overhang at rear to be used for small clamp

3/4" x 12-1/4" x 12-1/4"

2"

12"

8"

14"

Scabbard for handsaw covered with 1/4-inch plywood. Size to fit.

3/4" x 1" x 12-1/2"

3/4" x 12-1/2" x 24"

8"

24"

1"

This COMBINATION STOOL-TOTE BOX is useful for remodeling and other on-location work. All parts are 3/4-inch exterior grade fir plywood. Assemble with waterproof glue and 6d nails.

Extra space for tools can be made by installing a perforated hardboard divider between the verticals of your tote box. Frame the hardboard before installing. Tools can be hung on standard brackets.

This tote box is mounted on casters and is actually a portable shop. Overal dimensions should be 14-inches wide by 30-inches high by 36-inches long. Use 3/4-inch plywood throughout.

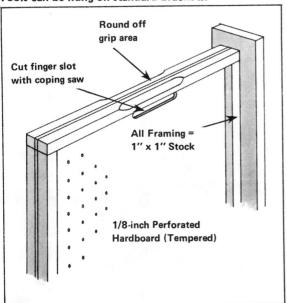

Round off grip area

Cut finger slot with coping saw

All Framing = 1" x 1" Stock

1/8-inch Perforated Hardboard (Tempered)

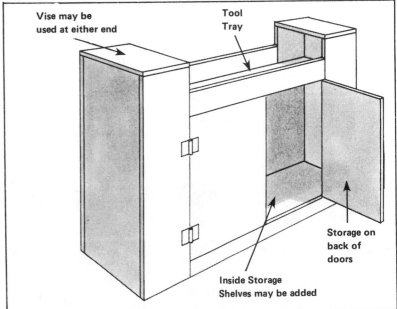

Vise may be used at either end

Tool Tray

Storage on back of doors

Inside Storage Shelves may be added

WORKBENCH

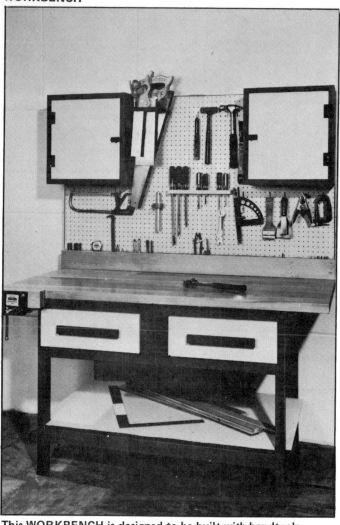

This WORKBENCH is designed to be built with handtools.

Right drawer is organized to hold all drilling tools. Keep tools used infrequently in their original cartons for protection.

Left drawer holds chisels, shaping tools and miscellaneous tools like tapes and knives. The partitioned sliding tray keeps chisels apart.

Left cabinet holds planes. Small blocks are installed on the shelves to elevate the planes and protect their cutting edges.

Right cabinet stores miscellaneous fastening materials.

BUILD A WORK BENCH

The workbench is the key to a pleasant, efficient shop. Many times it starts as a quickie solution and grows haphazardly. Then it becomes an eyesore and an irritant. It can be unsafe and isn't likely to inspire quality, or production. It's okay to build in stages, but each step should be aimed toward providing good working conditions and adequate storage for the tools you own and those you will add.

This workbench is compact—it requires about 2-1/2 by 5 feet of floor space—but it has generous work surface and plenty of storage space. Even though the bench is well equipped with tools, you'll note there is still more room in the cabinets and drawers. Each drawer has a sliding tray to increase capacity and is partitioned to protect individual tools.

Joints used in this design are not fancy, but they are adequate and strong. The assembly is a bit unusual because I've avoided nuts and bolts, but it's been tested on many projects and has proved to be strong and durable. This speeds up construction and lets you move right along without waiting for glued joints to set and dry. You can save more time—and a lot of effort—if you have many of the parts cut to size at the local lumber yard. This will increase cost, but it will get the project done faster. Use the dimensions from the bill of materials which includes the exact size of all parts.

Study the frame drawing and detail A before you start construction. The detail shows the procedure followed throughout the basic frame assembly. Use a gutter spike when you are driving through the *width* of a piece. Use 20d common or box nails when you are fastening through the *thickness* of the part. In either case, be sure to drill a 1/8-inch hole through the part being fastened. If you find this isn't sufficient help when driving the fastener, extend the hole farther into the mating part—don't enlarge the hole. Coat mating surfaces with a thin layer of white glue and drive the fasteners home slowly. Many light strokes are better than a few heavy ones. Don't try to see how fast you can sink the nails. Be sure to provide the nail spacing shown in the drawing.

Start assembly by putting together the back legs and rails and the top rail. The notch in the top rail needed to accommodate the legs is shown in detail B. Attach the top rail to the legs with glue and 12d nails.

Put the front legs and rails and the divider together. Be sure the divider measures exactly 6 x 6 inches and is centered between the legs. Secure the divider by coating its ends with glue and then driving two 20d nails through the top rail. Secure it at

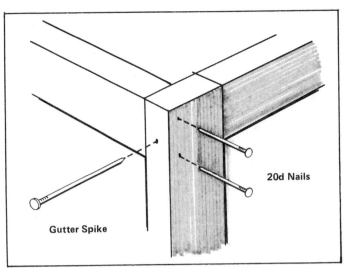

DETAIL A: Nailing procedure for the basic frame. Use a gutter spike for driving through the width of the piece. Use 20d common or box nails for driving through the thickness. Before driving nails, be sure to drill 1/8-inch pilot holes through the part being fastened.

DETAIL B: Notches in the top rail are needed to accommodate the back legs.

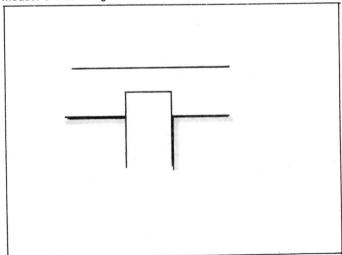

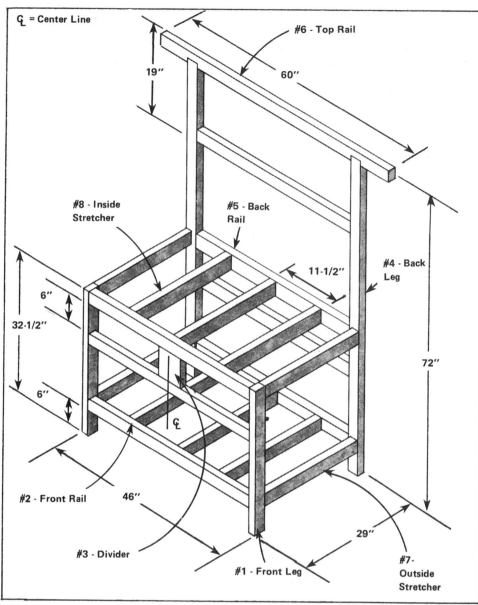

ℂ = Center Line

#6 - Top Rail

19"

60"

#8 - Inside
Stretcher

#5 - Back
Rail

11-1/2"

#4 - Back
Leg

6"

32-1/2"

72"

6"

#2 - Front Rail

46"

29"

#3 - Divider

#1 - Front Leg

#7 -
Outside
Stretcher

ℂ

BASIC WORKBENCH PLANS.

Center the divider, part #3, exactly between the two front legs.

the bottom by toenailing with 6d finishing nails.

Put the two assemblies together by connecting them with the stretchers. This is a good time to use bar clamps if you have some. They can hold the parts together as you do the nailing. Otherwise, set the stretchers on end as you attach the front and rear leg assemblies.

It's a good idea to add the drawer supports and guides while the bench frame is still open. Pre-assemble the drawer supports, but remember one part is longer than the other because of the way the front legs are situated. Attach the supports by using glue and toenailing with 4d finishing nails. The top surface of each support base must be flush with the top edge of both the front and rear rails.

Make the rabbet cuts at each end of the drawer guides and center them exactly in the opening formed by the front legs and the divider. Use glue and two 4d nails at each end of the guides.

Make the drawers by assembling sides and ends like an open box and then adding the bottom. Add the slides—after coating them with glue—by driving 4d finishing nails through them and the drawer bottom into the sides. Be sure to set the nails. It isn't necessary to fill the holes. Add the drawer front with glue and 3d nails driven from the inside of the drawer. Add the pull by using four 6d nails through the front or by using wood screws from the inside. Screws take a little more time, but they do provide more strength.

Drawer guides are 1/2-inch plywood strips positioned to straddle the guides already in place in the bench frame. It might be wise to place the drawers and to mark the location for the guides from beneath. Don't place them so tightly you will have difficulty sliding the drawer.

ANGLE BRACES, part #9, are not shown in the drawing, but are easy to add and give extra strength. Make 45-degree cuts at each end so the braces mate exactly with rails and stretchers. Use one at each corner.

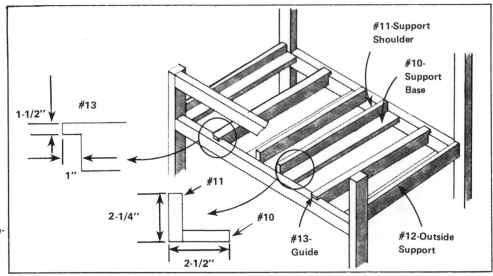

DRAWER GUIDES, part #13, have rabbet cuts at each end and are centered exactly between the inside surface of the front legs and the divider.

DRAWER GUIDES and SUPPORTS should look like this after installation.

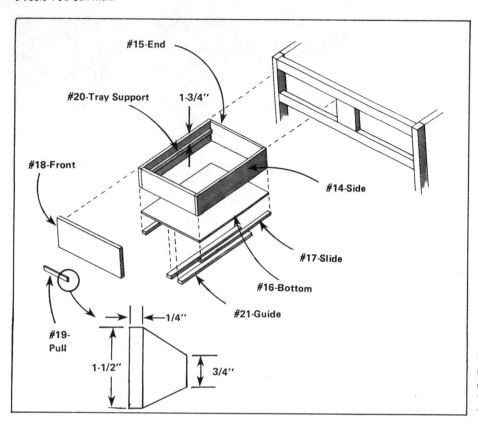

#15-End
#20-Tray Support
1-3/4"
#18-Front
#14-Side
#17-Slide
#16-Bottom
#21-Guide
#19-Pull
1/4"
1-1/2"
3/4"

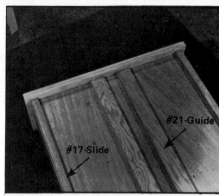

Attach guides to the bottom of the drawer with glue and nails at each end and at the mid-point.

DRAWER SIDES should be joined first, then attach the bottom. Materials list gives dimensions. Drawer guides straddle the guides already in place on the frame. Detail C shows plans for sliding trays.

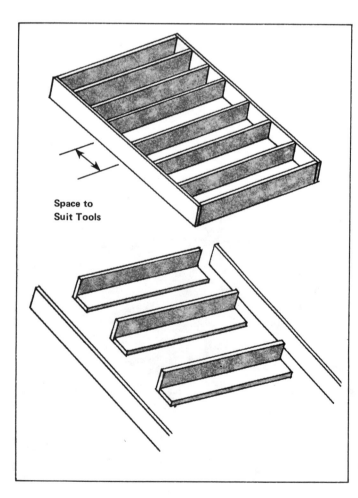

Space to Suit Tools

The partitioned sliding trays are pre-assembled L-shaped pieces held together with side strips. This design allows you to do the job without having to cut dadoes for partition strips. Make the width of the L-shaped pieces to suit the tools you will store.

Begin the bench top by first attaching the stop to the back legs. Add the remaining boards one at a time by driving two 16d nails into each stretcher. You can use clamps to hold each board in place as you do the nailing. You can notch for a woodworker's vise now if you have one on hand. If you don't, you can always cut the notch later.

The bottom shelf must be installed in two pieces. It can be a one-piece affair if you install it during the assembly of the basic frame. Be aware the front and back notches are not similar.

Add the tool-board back-up pieces (parts #25, 26 and 27) and then attach the perforated hardboard with #6 x 3/4-inch round-head screws spaced about 12-inches apart along the perimeter.

DETAIL C shows trays made from 1/4-inch plywood. Assemble with glue and #19 x 3/4-inch brads. Make L-shapes and space to suit tools. Butt together with strips. Overall dimensions of trays are 1-5/8-inches by 11-1/4 inches by 16-1/2 inches.

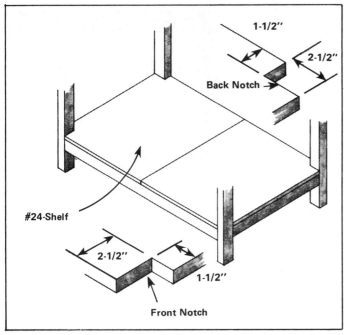

The two parts of the bottom shelf are notched and attached to the frame with 6d nails. Note the difference between the front and back notches.

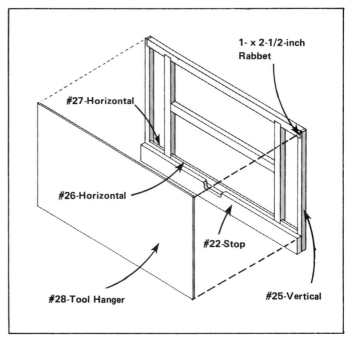

Frame for perforated hardboard is made by attaching parts #26 and #27 with 5d nails. Part #25 is then attached with 5d nails at the top, and 9d nails at the bottom. Board is attached to the frame with #6 x 3/4-inch round-head wood screws.

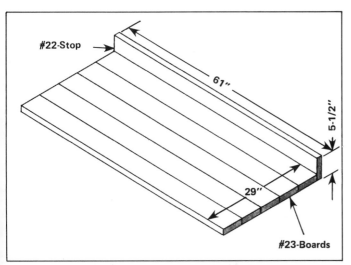

BENCH TOP begins by attaching stop to back legs with 9d nails. Boards for top should be attached to the frame with 16d nails.

Cabinets, like the drawers, are assembled like open boxes. Remember to install the shelves and the hanger block before you add any framing. Hang the cabinets with two 1/4 x 2-inch lag screws. These pass through the hangar block and the pegboard and into the top rail of the bench frame.

Attach the frame pieces to the front of the cabinets and then cut the doors to fit. Allow for a 1/16-inch clearance on all edges except the hinge side. I used a slide bolt to hold the doors shut, but you can substitute magnetic catches if you wish. If so, you must add a door pull or drill a hole so you can pull the door open. Or, you could create a notch in the lower board to allow pulling the edge of the door.

Many types of ready-made hangers are sold for use with perforated hardboard so you can be selective. Buy hangers designed for the tools you wish to hang in the open. Drawings on the following page show examples of tool holders you can make yourself.

The project bench was painted in gay colors—mostly reds and yellows. You might prefer to leave everything in natural tones. In any case, the bench top, the stop, and the vise jaws should be left natural. An application of a good resin sealer, followed by a sanding, is a wise way to start whether the next step will be paint or varnish.

153

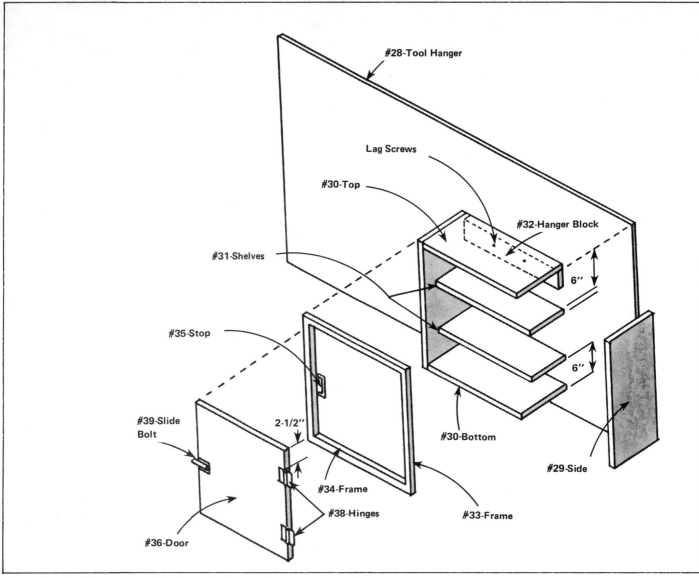

Assemble all cabinet parts with glue and 6d nails. Set all nails and conceal with wood putty. Dimensions of all cabinet parts are found on the materials list.

You can make a number of different tool holders easily and quickly. Design them to fit your tools.

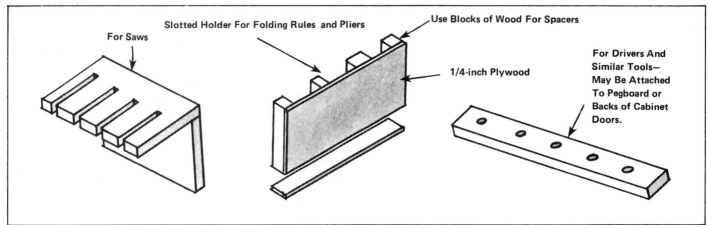

MATERIALS LIST FOR WORK BENCH

NUMBER ON PLANS	NAME	PIECES REQUIRED	SIZE	MATERIAL
BASIC FRAME				
1	Front Legs	2	1-1/2″ x 2-1/2″ x 32-1/2″	Fir
2	Front Rails	3	1-1/2″ x 2-1/2″ x 43″	Fir
3	Divider	1	1-1/2″ x 6″ x 6″	Fir
4	Back Legs	2	1-1/2″ x 2-1/2″ x 70-3/4″	Fir
5	Back Rails	4	1-1/2″ x 2-1/2″ x 41″	Fir
6	Top Rail	1	1-1/2″ x 2-1/2″ x 60″	Fir
7	Outside Stretchers	4	1-1/2″ x 2-1/2″ x 25″	Fir
8	Inside Stretchers	6	1-1/2″ x 2-1/2″ x 26″	Fir
9	Optional Braces	4	1-1/2″ x 2-1/2″ x 8″	Fir
DRAWER SUPPORTS AND GUIDES				
10	Drawer Base Support	4	3/4″ x 2-1/2″ x 26″	Plywood
11	Drawer Support Inside Shoulder	2	3/4″ x 2-1/2″ x 26″	Plywood
12	Drawer Support Outside Shoulder	2	3/4″ x 2-1/2″ x 25″	Plywood
13	Drawer Guides	2	1-1/2″ x 2-1/2″ x 31″	Fir
DRAWERS				
14	Sides	4	3/4″ x 5-1/8″ x 24″	Plywood
15	Ends	4	3/4″ x 5-1/8″ x 16-3/4″	Plywood
16	Bottom	2	1/4″ x 18-1/4″ x 24″	Plywood
17	Slides	4	1/2″ x 1″ x 24″	Fir
18	Front	2	3/4″ x 6-3/4″ x 19-1/4″	Plywood
19	Pull	2	1″ x 1-1/2″ x 12″	Fir
20	Sliding Tray Support	4	3/4″ x 1″ x 22-1/2″	Fir
21	Guides	4	1/2″ x 1-1/2″ x 24″	Plywood
BENCH TOP				
22	Stop	1	1-1/2″ x 5-1/2″ x 61″	Fir
23	Boards	5	1-1/2″ x 5-1/2″ x 61″	Fir
BOTTOM SHELF				
24	Shelf	2	3/4″ x 23″ x 29″	Particleboard
PEGBOARD AND BACKUP				
25	Verticals	2	1-1/2″ x 1-1/2″ x 39-1/2″	Fir
26	Horizontal	1	3/4″ x 2″ x 41″	Plywood
27	Horizontal	2	3/4″ x 2″ x 6″	Plywood
28	Tool Hanger	1	1/8″ x 34″ x 61″	Perforated Hardboard (tempered)
CABINETS				
29	Sides	4	3/4″ x 8-1/4″ x 19″	Plywood
30	Top and Bottom	4	3/4″ x 8-1/4″ x 16-1/2″	Plywood
31	Shelves	4	3/4″ x 6″ x 16-1/2″	Plywood
32	Hanger Block	2	3/4″ x 2-1/2″ x 16-1/2″	Fir
33	Frame	4	3/4″ x 1″ x 19″	Fir
34	Frame	4	3/4″ x 1″ x 16-1/2″	Fir
35	Stop	2	1/2″ x 3/4″ x 3″	Fir
36	Door	2	3/4″ x 16″ x 17″	Plywood
38	Hinges	2 pair	2-1/2″ butt	Brass
39	Slide Bolt	2	2″	Brass

FASTENERS

NAME	QUANTITY	NAME	QUANTITY
3d Finishing Nails	1 lb.	20d Common or Box Nails	2 lb.
4d Finishing Nails	1 lb.	#19 3/4-inch Brads	1 Box
6d Finishing Nails	1 lb.	Gutter Spikes	1 doz.
12d Nails	1 lb.	#6 x 3/4-inch Round-Head Screws	1 doz.
16d Nails	2 lb.		
1/4″ x 2″ Lag Screws	4 lb.		

14

Projects

Five Board Bench

MATERIALS

Part No.	Pieces Needed	Size
1	2	3/4" x 8" x 8"
2	2	3/4" x 2" x 16"
3	1	1-1/2" x 9" x 18"

Use knotty pine lumber throughout.

INSTRUCTIONS

Cut parts 1 to overall size. Form hole with brace and expansion bit or coping saw. Make slanted cuts to the hole and then shape notches for parts 2.

Size parts 2 and attach to parts 1 with glue and finishing nails.

Size part 3 and attach to understructure with glue and finishing nails driven through the top.

Round all edges and "distress" all surfaces by drilling tiny holes at random and by hitting gently with a length of small chain. You can also form small dents by tapping with a hammer. The intent is to make the project look old and used.

Apply coat of walnut or dark-maple stain. Let stain set for 10 to 15 minutes and wipe off excess with a cloth. Let stain remain darkest at joint lines and in corners. Apply matte-finish varnish when the stain is dry.

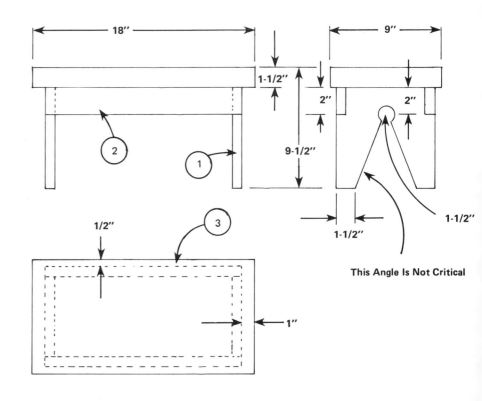

This Angle Is Not Critical

Coffee Cup Tree

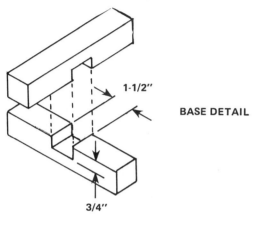

1-1/2"

BASE DETAIL

3/4"

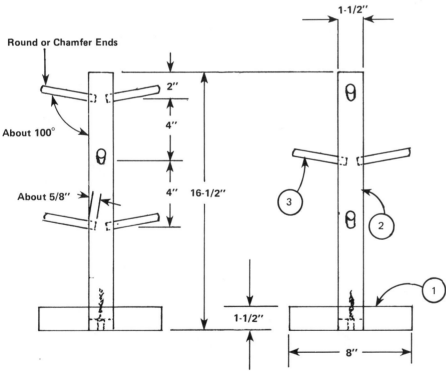

Round or Chamfer Ends

About 100°

About 5/8"

1-1/2"

2"

4"

4"

16-1/2"

1-1/2"

8"

MATERIALS

Part No.	Pieces Needed	Size
1	2	1-1/2" x 1-1/2" x 8"
2	1	1-1/2" x 1-1/2" x 15"
3	6	1/2" dia. x 3-5/8" dowel

INSTRUCTIONS

Cut parts 1 to size and form crosslap joint as shown in base detail. Put pieces together with glue and hold under clamp pressure.

Cut part 2 to size and lay out location points for dowels. Make a guide block so you can bore holes accurately with a brace and bit. Depth of the holes is not critical, but stay close to 5/8 inch.

Cut dowels to length and glue in holes.

Counterbore hole in base using a 5/8-inch bit. Attach part 2 by applying glue and driving a 2-inch flat-head or round-head screw.

Round all edges slightly with sandpaper and finish to suit. You can attach a piece of felt to the base with glue if you wish.

Laminated Cutting Board

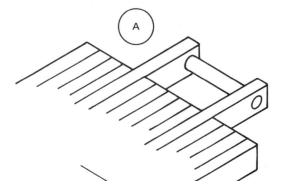

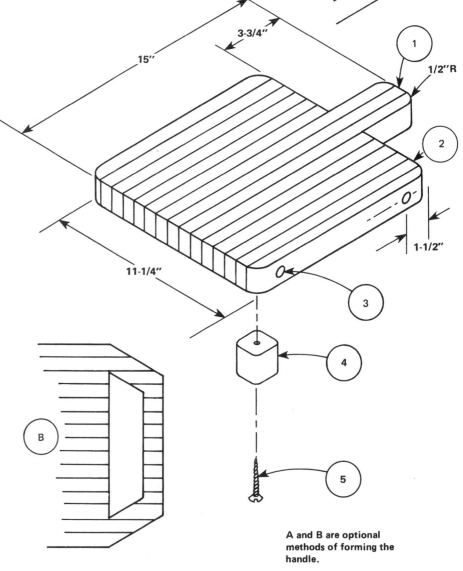

MATERIALS

Part No.	Pieces Needed	Size
1	3	3/4'' x 1-1/4'' x 15''
2	12	3/4'' x 1-1/4'' x 11-1/4''
3	4	3/4'' dia. x 5-1/4'' dowel
4	4	1-1/2'' x 1-1/2'' x 1-1/2''
5	4	2-1/2'' flat-head woodscrew

Maple or birch are good woods for this type project. Pine will work, but cutting surface will mar quickly.

INSTRUCTIONS

Cut parts 1 and 2 to size. If you wish, you can work with a 2-inch stock (net equals about 1-1/2-inches). This will make a thicker board, but will reduce the amount of ripping needed.

Laminate pieces using glue with clamps, or by using glue and nailing successive pieces together. If you use the latter method, space the nails so they will not be in the way of the dowel holes you must drill. Wipe off all excess glue with a damp cloth.

Bore holes for the dowels after glue is dry. Coat dowels with glue and tap them into place. In this case, 3/4-inch dowels are used.

Cut feet to size and form a shank hole and countersink for the screw. Position the feet so they are 1-1/2-inches from the edges of the board. Attach with glue and the screw.

Drill a 1/2-inch hole through the handle if you wish to hang board when it is not in use.

Corners can be rounded with a rasp. All surfaces should be sanded thoroughly. Finally, rub the board with salad oil. The oil treatment can be repeated as the board requires it.

A and B are optional methods of forming the handle.

Modern Bench

DETAIL A

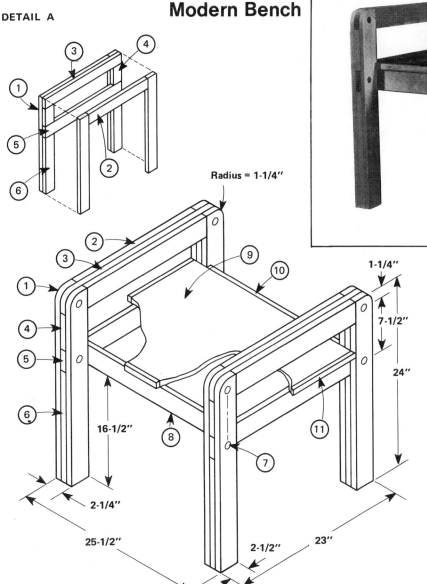

Radius = 1-1/4"

MATERIALS

Part No.	Pieces Needed	Size
1	8	3/4" x 2-1/2" x 24"
2	4	3/4" x 2-1/2" x 18"
3	2	3/4" x 2-1/2" x 23"
4	4	3/4" x 2-1/2" x 5"
5	2	3/4" x 2-1/2" x 23"
6	4	3/4" x 2-1/2" x 14"
7	8	3/4" dia. x 2-1/4" dowel
8	2	3/4" x 2-1/2" x 22-1/2"
9	1	3/4" x 18" x 24-1/2" plywood
10	2	1/2" x 3/4" x 21"
11	2	1/2" x 3/4" x 18"

All parts are pine except the seat, part 9, and the dowels, part 7. These should contrast in color. A material like walnut or mahogany is recommended.

INSTRUCTIONS

Study the drawing before starting work, especially detail "A" which shows how pieces are assembled to form legs.

Cut all parts for leg assemblies to size and join part 3 to two pieces of part 1. Add one of part 2, part 4, part 5, and part 6. Final step is to add two of part 1 and the other part 2. Assembly can go quickly if you work with glue and finishing nails that you set and hide with matching wood dough, or you can work with only glue and clamps.

Bore the holes and glue in dowels. Cut dowels a bit long as you can sand them flush after the glue dries.

Form radius at the top of each leg and sand all surfaces thoroughly.

Join two leg assemblies by installing part 8 with glue and finishing nails. Be sure the top edges of parts 8 are flush with the top edges of parts 5.

Cut part 9 to size and attach to parts 8 and 5 with glue and finishing nails. If you wish to avoid nailing through part 9, attach it from

underneath with small glue-blocks and screws.

Final step is to attach edge pieces—parts 10 and 11—with glue and finishing nails. These pieces hide edges of the plywood.

Be sure all visible nails are set and concealed, and all surfaces are smooth.

This project is designed for natural finish. A coat of sealer followed by a light sanding and one or two coats of matte-finish varnish will complete the work.

Magazine Stand

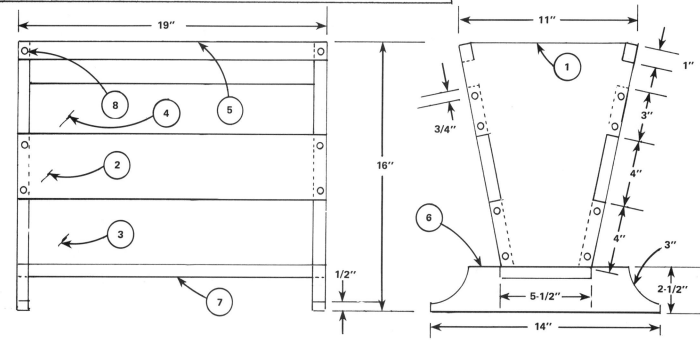

MATERIALS

Use knotty pine throughout.

Part No.	Pieces Needed	Size
1	2	3/4" x 11" x 13-1/2"
2	2	3/4" x 4" x 19"
3	2	3/4" x 4" x 17-1/2"
4	2	3/4" x 3" x 17-1/2"
5	2	3/4" x 1" x 19"
6	2	3/4" x 21-1/2" x 14"
7	1	3/4" x 5-1/2" x 19"
8	28	3/8" dia. x 1-1/2" dowel

INSTRUCTIONS

Shape parts 1. Lay out and cut the notches for parts 2 and 5 very carefully. Note that parts 3 and 4 are butted against the inside surface of Part 1.

Cut parts 2, 3, 4 and 5. Assemble with glue and two finishing nails at each joint. Locate the nails so they will not interfere with the dowel holes you will drill later. Use a plane to shave off the bottom edge of part 3 so it will conform with the bottom edge of part 1.

Cut part 7 and shape parts 6. Cut notch so part 7 will fit exactly. Form radii with coping saw.

Sand all surfaces. Join the two assemblies with glue. Nail through the bottom of part 7.

Dowels are optional and are only used with part 2 in photo. To add, mark off locations of holes and bore them to a depth of 1-1/4-inch. Coat dowels with glue and tap into place. Wipe off excess glue and saw dowels almost flush. Sand after glue dries. If you wish, you can allow the dowels to project. Exposed ends should be rounded off with sandpaper before the dowels are glued in place.

The project may be left natural or distressed and toned with maple or walnut stain.

Planter With Pot Shelf

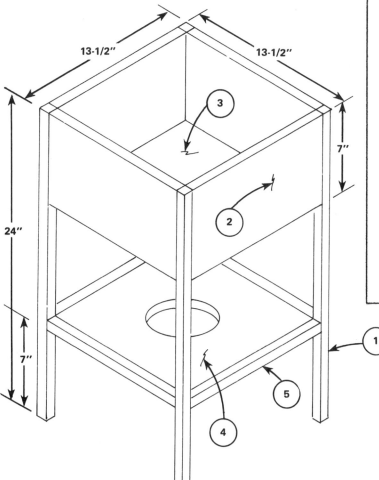

13-1/2" 13-1/2"

7"

24"

7"

MATERIALS

Part No.	Pieces Needed	Size
1	4	3/4" x 3/4" x 24"
2	4	3/4" x 7" x 12"
3	1	3/4" x 12" x 12" plywood
4	1	3/4" x 12" x 12" plywood
5	4	3/4" x 3/4" x 12"

INSTRUCTIONS

Cut parts 1 and 2 to size. Coat mating edges with glue and assemble by driving finishing nails through part 1 into the end of part 2. Space nails to avoid interference when attaching adjacent pieces. Be sure all surfaces are flush with each other.

Cut part 3 to size and install with glue and nails.

Cut part 4 to size and lay out the center for the hole. Make the hole large enough to hold a plastic container in which you will place a clay pot. Mark the hole with a compass or dividers and cut it out with a coping saw.

Add parts 5 to part 4 with glue and nails. Each corner must form a close-fitting notch for the legs. Coat the surfaces of the notches with glue and install by nailing from the outside edges of parts 1.

Set all exposed nail heads and fill holes with wood dough.

Thoroughly sand and apply a coat of sealer. The project may be left natural, stained or painted.

Line the inside surfaces of the upper box with plastic sheeting, cemented or stapled in place.

Place a 1-inch thick layer of small stones in the bottom of the box before you fill with soil.

161

Butcher Block End Table

MATERIALS

Part No.	Pieces Needed	Size
1	20	3/4" x 2" x 18"
2	4	3/4" x 2" x 14"
3	8	3/4" x 2" x 18"
or	4	1-1/2" x 2" x 18"
4	4	5/8" dia. x 5-1/4" dowel

INSTRUCTIONS

Saw parts 1 to size but leave a little extra so you can plane edges smooth. Do the same with parts 2. You can make the top with 3-inch stock, which equals about 2-1/2-inches, if you wish. This makes the slab a bit thicker, but saves the time and effort required to do rip cuts.

Coat mating surfaces with a light film of white glue and assemble with clamps. Alternate method is to nail and glue pieces consecutively. Wipe off excess glue with a damp cloth and set aside until glue hardens.

Make legs by laminating two pieces of 3/4-inch stock or by using a single piece of 1-1/2-inch material. Be sure dimensions equal the size of the corner notches in the slab.

Attach legs to slab with glue and by using bar clamps or band clamp, or by improvising with rope. Bore holes for dowels after glue has set and clamps are removed. Cut dowel a bit longer than necessary, coat it lightly with glue and tap into place. Sand it flush with adjacent surfaces after the glue has set.

Sand all surfaces smooth. Round all edges just enough to break the sharp corners.

Projects like this look fine when protected with an application of sealer and finished with one or two coats of matte-finish varnish.

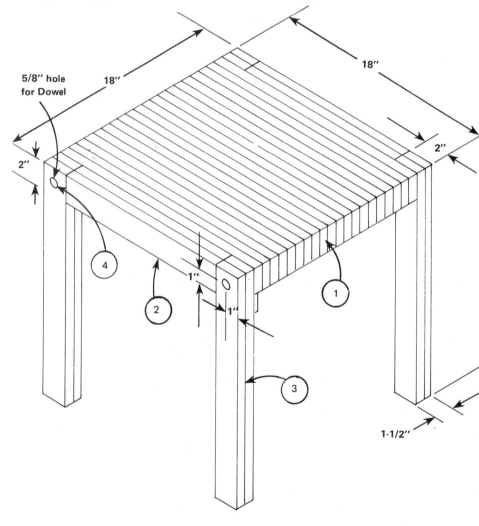

5/8" hole for Dowel

18"

18"

2"

2"

1"

1"

1-1/2"

1

2

3

4

Bird Feeder

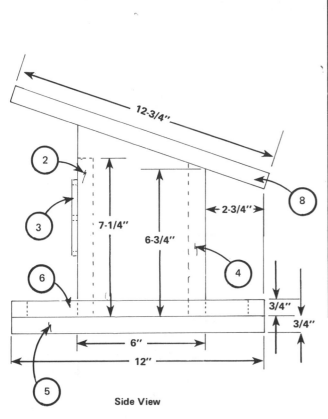

Side View

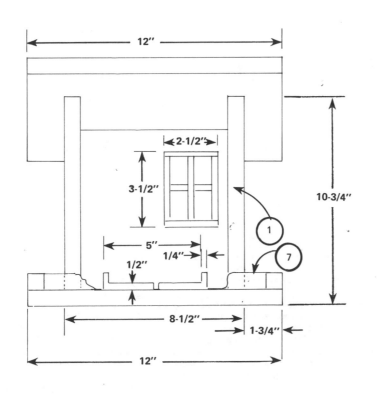

Front View

MATERIALS

Part No.	Pieces Needed	Size
1	2	3/4" x 6" x 10"
2	1	3/4" x 7" x 7-1/4"
3	cut from	1/4" x 1/4" x 20"
4	1	3/4" x 7" x 7-1/2"
5	1	3/4" x 12" x 12"
6	2	3/4" x 3/4" x 12"
7	2	3/4" x 3/4" x 10-1/2"
8	1	3/4" x 12" x 12-3/4"

Part 4 is longer than needed so the top bevel may be sized on assembly. Use water-proof glue and galvanized finishing nails throughout. Wood that works easily, such as pine, cypress, yellow poplar, or redwood can be used in this project.

INSTRUCTIONS

Cut the sides, parts 1. Be sure the slanted end is straight and smooth.

Cut part 2 to size and form the notches at the base. The openings should be large enough to allow bird seed to trickle through.

Cut the pieces for the "window" from the strip of 1/4 x 1/4-inch material and glue in place as shown. Then glue and nail part 2 between parts 1.

Add part 4 and saw the bevel at the top so it conforms to the slant on parts 1.

Size parts 5, 6 and 7. Assemble with glue and nails. Attach the two assemblies by nailing up through part 5.

Size part 8 and add to assembly by nailing down through the top.

Sand all edges and surfaces thoroughly. All corners may be rounded or left square.

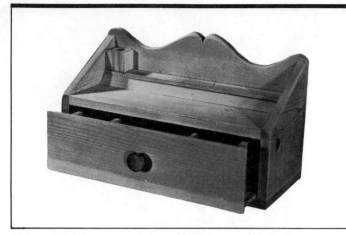

Kitchen Rack With Drawer

MATERIALS

Part No.	Pieces Needed	Size
1	1	3/4" x 10-1/4" x 18"
2	1	3/4" x 7-1/2" x 18"
3	2	3/4" x 6-3/4" x 9-1/4"
4	2	1/2" x 1/2" x 6"
5	1	3/4" x 6-3/4" x 16-1/2"
6	1	1-1/2" x 2" x 16-1/2"
7	1	1-1/2" x 2" x 2-1/2" (optional)

DRAWER

8	1	3/4" x 5" x 17"
9	2	3/8" x 4-1/8" x 6-1/2" plywood
10	1	3/8" x 6-1/2" x 16-1/2" plywood
11	1	3/8" x 4-1/8" x 14-1/4" plywood
12	2	3/8" x 4-1/8" x 5-5/8" plywood

No drawer pull is shown on the drawing but any of the ready-made wooden pulls available in hardware stores can be used.

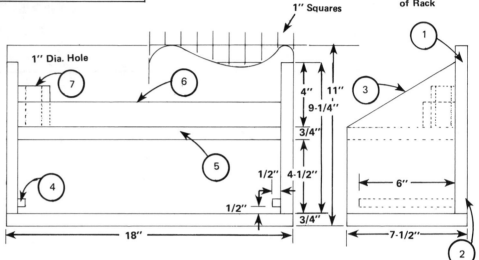

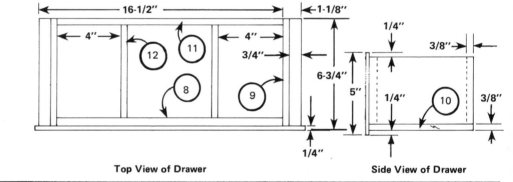

Top View of Drawer

Side View of Drawer

INSTRUCTIONS

Cut part 1 to overall size and lay out the design at the top. You can duplicate the shape shown on the drawing by using squares or choose your own design. The sweep of the curve is not critical. Cut out the shape with a coping saw and sand the edge smooth.

Size parts 2 and 3 and attach to part 1 with glue and finishing nails. Size parts 4 and attach as shown. These will keep the drawer from tipping when it is pulled out. However, these parts are not essential and may be omitted.

Cut part 5 and install. Be sure it is level and square to other pieces.

Cut part 6 to size and decide if you wish to

include part 7 which serves as a pencil holder. If you do, cut the piece to size and bore the 1-inch diameter hole. Notch part 6 to receive part 7 and install both pieces with glue and clamps. Nails are not needed here.

The front of the drawer, part 8, requires rabbet cuts if you make it as shown. An alternate method is to laminate a piece of 1/4-inch plywood to a piece of 1/2-inch plywood. Study drawing carefully if you decide to make rabbet cuts: the *width* of the cuts is not the same on all four edges even though the *depth* of the cuts is the same.

Cut parts 9 and attach to the drawer front with glue and nails driven into the shoulder of the

rabbet cut. Then size and attach part 10. Note that part 10 extends 3/4 of an inch beyond the drawer-sides.

Make part 11 and parts 12 and install with glue and brads.

Locate the center of the drawer front and install a ready-made, wooden drawer pull. The 16-1/2-inch length of part 10 will make the drawer fit snugly. Sand the outside edges a bit to make sure the drawer slide easily.

Drill two matching holes through the back of the project if you wish to place it on a wall. The unit looks well with a natural finish or stain. It may be antiqued if you wish.

Toy Truck

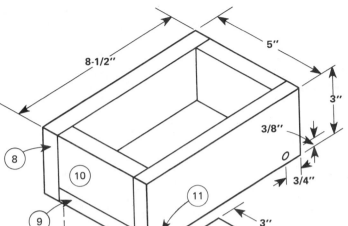

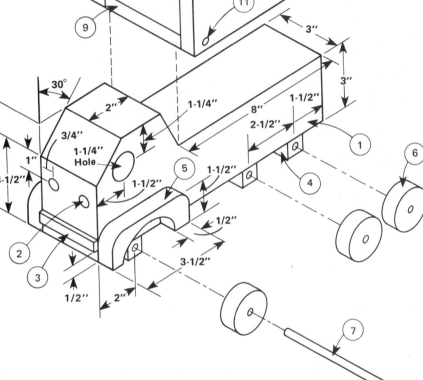

MATERIALS

Part No.	Pieces Needed	Size
1	1	3" x 5-1/2" x 12-1/2"
2	2	5/8" dia. x 1" dowel
3	1	1/4" x 1/2" x 3"
4	3	3/4" x 3/4" x 3"
5	2	3/4" x 1-1/2" x 3-1/2"
6	6	2-1/4" dia. x 3/4" thick
7	3	1/4" dia. x 5-5/8" dowel
8	2	3/4" x 3" x 8-1/2"
9	1	3/4" x 3-1/2" x 8-1/2"
10	2	3/4" x 2-1/4" x 3-1/2"
11	4	3/8" dia. x 1-1/2" dowel

Maple and birch are good woods to use for toys. Pine will do, even though it will dent during play. Use similar material throughout except for parts 2, 3 and 6. If you don't have a contrasting wood for these, stain the pieces a dark color before assembly.

INSTRUCTIONS

You can work with a solid piece of stock to make part 1 or you can laminate 4 pieces of 3/4-inch material. If you do the latter, cut the profile shape of each piece before you glue them together. Use a crosscut saw to shape the part if you work with solid stock.

Drill holes for parts 2 and glue them in. Either sand these flush or allow them to project.

Shape part 3 and attach it with glue and small finishing nails.

Shape up parts 4 and then drill a 1/4-inch hole through the center of each. This will be easier to do if you drill from both ends. Part 7 should turn easily in these holes, so test now with a length of dowel. If the fit is too tight, enlarge the hole by working with a small, round file or with sandpaper wrapped around a length of 1/8-inch dowel. Another way to assure a loose fit is to sand parts 7. Do not reduce

the ends since they must fit tightly in parts 6. Attach parts 4 with glue.

Form parts 5 and shape inside and outside curves with a coping saw. The outside curves are not critical, but the inside curve must clear the wheel. Attach the pieces with glue and two finishing nails.

Use a bit and brace to bore the 1-1/4-inch hole. You can drill a smaller hole if you lack a large enough bit, but not smaller than 1-inch.

Cut parts 8, 9 and 10 to size and assemble with glue and finishing nails.

Parts 11 are optional.

Attach this assembly to the body of the truck with glue and finishing nails.

Parts 6 can be shaped with a coping saw and

then center-drilled. You might be able to find a ready-made turning piece with a diameter that comes close to 2-1/4-inches. If so, all you have to do is slice off discs to form the wheels.

Cut parts 7 to length for axles and glue one end of each piece into one wheel. Pass the axles through part 4 and then glue on the second wheel.

Be sure all nails are set and concealed and all parts are very smooth. It pays to do a lot of sanding on individual pieces before assembling.

A natural finish will look good but do not use conventional sealers. Instead, rub in a generous application of vegetable oil with your fingers. Keep repeating the procedure until the wood will not absorb more oil. Then wipe with a soft, lint-free cloth.

Bobbing Robot Toy

MATERIALS

Part No.	Pieces Needed	Size
1	2	3/4'' x 2-1/2'' x 12''
2	1	3/4'' x 6'' x 11''
3	1	3/4'' x 6'' x 1''
4	2	3/4'' x 2-1/2'' x 4-1/2''
5	1	3/4'' x 6'' x 8''
6	1	3/4'' x 6'' x 2''
7	1	3/4'' dia. x 7-5/8'' dowel
8	4	4-1/2'' dia. x 3/4'' thick
9	2	3/4'' dia. x 2-5/8'' dowel
10	2	2'' dia. x 3/4'' thick
11	1	1/4'' dia. x 4'' dowel
12	1	3/8'' x 1/2'' x 6''
13	1	2'' dia. x 2'' dowel
14	1	3'' dia. ready-made wooden drawer pull
15	1	1/8'' dia. x 2'' dowel
16	1	short piece of 1/8'' or 3/16'' dowel for the robot's eyes and nose

INSTRUCTIONS

Cut parts 1 to size. Clamp together and lay out locations of holes for parts 7 and 9. Bore through both pieces so holes will mate exactly. Wrap a piece of sandpaper around a 1/2-inch dowel and enlarge the holes enough so a 3/4-inch dowel can rotate in them easily.

Cut part 2 to size and form the notch at the center of the rear edge. Attach to parts 1 with glue and finishing nails.

Cut parts 3, 4 and 5 and add to the assembly.

Cut part 6 to overall size. Use a plane to bevel one edge so the piece will slope back about 15 degrees. Add to assembly with glue and finishing nails driven at an angle along the front edge.

Make wheels, part 8, with a coping saw. Drill a 3/4-inch center hole through each.

Cut part 7 to length for an axle. Glue a wheel at one end, pass the dowel through the front holes in the body, and glue on the second wheel.

Study rear axle assembly on drawing and make parts 9, 10, 11, and 12. Drill 3/4-inch center hole and 1/4-inch hole in parts 10 so they will provide a tight fit for parts 9 and 11. Holes in part 12 should be a bit oversize.

Slip part 12 over part 11. Glue part 11 into both parts 10. This assembly is inserted in body from bottom. Both parts 9 are passed through the holes and glued to parts 10. Part 12 passes through the notch.

Cut part 13 and form a 1-inch center hole. Drill a 1/8-inch radial hole for part 15 and holes for pieces 16 you will use as the nose and eyes. Glue parts 16 into place, then glue on the drawer pull, part 14, which serves as the robot's hat.

Cut part 15 to length. This piece locks with a dab of glue at each end and passes through the hole in part 12.

See TOY TRUCK instructions for method of finishing.

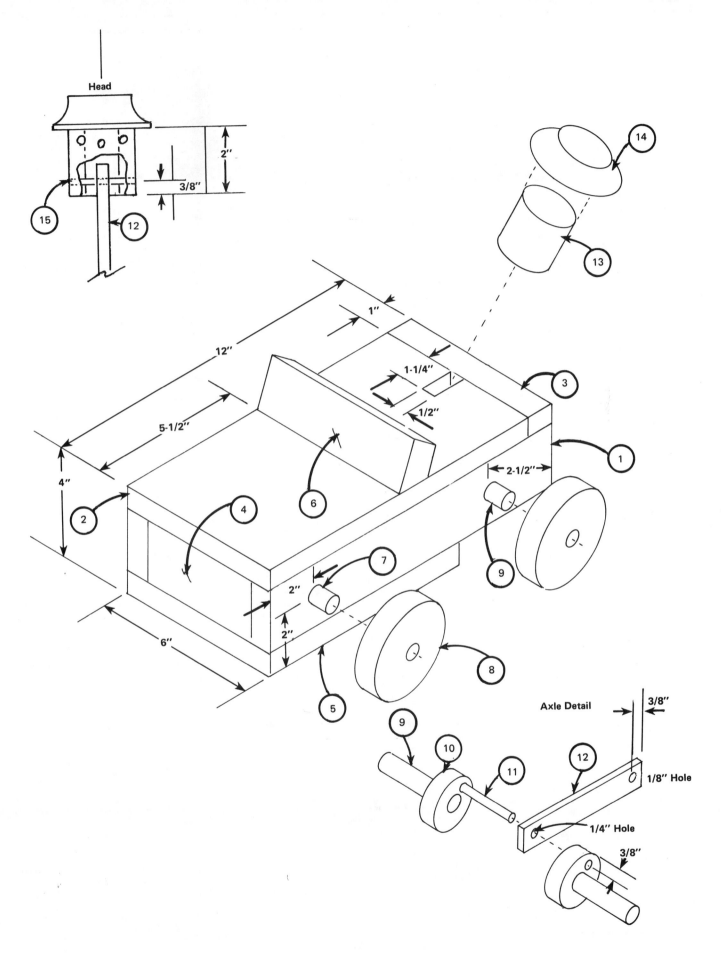

Head

2''

3/8''

15   12

14

13

12''

1''

1-1/4''

1/2''

5-1/2''

3

2-1/2''

1

4''

6

2

4

9

7

2''

2''

8

6''

5

Axle Detail   3/8''

9

10

11   12

1/8'' Hole

1/4'' Hole

3/8''

Toy Train

Part No.	Pieces Needed	Size
1	1	3/4" x 1-3/4" x 7-5/8"
2	1	1-3/4" x 1-3/4" x 2"
3	1	5/8" x 2-1/4" x 2-1/4"
4	1	1-3/4" dia. x 5-1/4" dowel
5	1	1" dia. x 1-1/2" dowel
6	1	3/4" x 3/4" dowel
7	1	1/4" dia. x 1-1/4" dowel
8	1	1/4" dia. x 1-1/4" dowel
9	1	1/2" dia. x 1" dowel
10	1	1/4" dia. x 1-1/2" dowel
11	2	3/4" x 3/4" x 1-3/4"
12	4	1-1/2" dia. x 3/4" thick
13	4	1/8" dia. x 1-1/4" dowel
14	2	1/8" x 3/8" x 5-7/8"
15	4	1/4" dia. x 3/8" dowel
16	2	1/4" dia. x 4-3/8" dowel

CAR

1	1	2" x 3" x 7-1/2"
2	1	5/8" x 2-1/2" x 7-1/2"
3	1	1/2" dia. x 1-3/4" dowel
4	2	3/4" x 3/4" x 2"
5	4	1-1/2" dia. x 3/4" thick
6	2	1/4" dia. x 3-5/8" dowel

INSTRUCTIONS

LOCOMOTIVE

Cut parts 1, 2 and 3 to overall size. Grip part 3 in vise and use a plane to shape the top contour. The radius of the curve is not critical as long as it is uniform. Finish with sandpaper. Assemble the three parts with glue and finishing nails.

Part 4 can be a large dowel or a section cut from a ready-made turning. If you wish to go all out, you can hand plane the cylinder from a 1-3/4-inch-square piece of stock. Plane off the corners until the piece is nearly round. Then finish with sandpaper. End by planing off a section so the part will mate with 1.

Cut parts 5, 6, 7 and 8 to length. Bore holes in part 4. Detail A shows a simple method for holding round pieces while drilling. Attach pieces with glue. Part 7 passes through part 6. You can make this a sub-assembly or drill for part 7 after part 6 is in place. Attach this assembly to part 1 with glue and finishing nails driven from beneath.

Cut parts 9 and 10. Drill through 9 and glue 10 in place. Locate the center at the end of part 1 and drill the hole needed for part 9. Glue part 9 in place. Be sure part 10 is vertical.

Cut parts 11 to size and bore center holes. Attach to part 1. Form parts 12, or cut from dowel or ready-made turning, and drill center holes. Drill holes for parts 13 accurately; they must set exactly on the center line of the wheels. Glue parts 13 in place.

Cut parts 16 to length. Glue one end in each wheel and pass the other end through the hole in part 11. Then glue on the other wheel.

Cut parts 14 and drill the holes that will mate with parts 13. The holes should provide a loose fit.

Shape parts 15. These can be cut from dowel or they can be square pieces. It is best to predrill holes through a single piece, then cut out separate parts.

Place parts 14 over parts 13. Put a dab of glue in the hole in parts 15 and add at the ends of parts 13. Part 14 must not be fixed in position.

CAR

Part 1 can be shaped from solid stock or made by laminating pieces.

Cut part 2 to overall size and shape as described for part 3 of the locomotive. Attach 2 to 1 with glue and finishing nails.

Locate and drill the hole for part 3. Shape the flat on part 3 by using a rasp or by making cuts with a dovetail saw. Drill the hole through the flat. Glue part 3 in place.

Shape parts 4 and 5 and cut parts 6 to length. Add these parts to the assembly in the manner described for the locomotive.

See TOY TRUCK instructions for method of finishing and for assuring free-turning wheels.

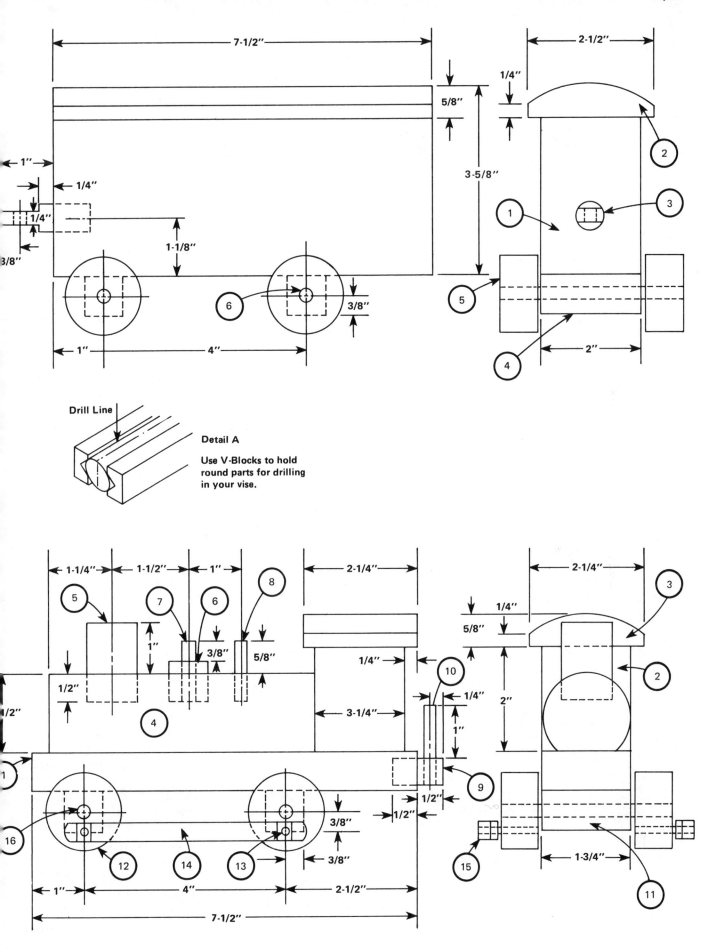

Drill Line

Detail A

Use V-Blocks to hold
round parts for drilling
in your vise.

15

Sharpening

I have said it before, but it is worth saying again: Sharp tools work better and are safer than dull ones. Dull tools require more power to use and are more likely to slip and mar the work or injure you.

An easy way to tell when a tool is dull is by holding it up to the light. Dull edges reflect light. If you can see a narrow white line or white spots along the edge of your tool, it probably needs sharpening.

The cutting tools you buy have edges designed to meet that tool's function. Axes need cutting edges that can withstand the force of striking the wood. Pocket knives need fine edges for scoring and cutting. Blade design is usually a compromise between efficiency and durability. When you are sharpening your tools, you should keep their function in mind. Too fine an edge can be as useless as one too dull.

Each tool has its own sharpening requirements, but basically sharpening is a two-step process: *shaping* and *honing*. Both are usually done *against* the edge. Shaping is done with a coarse stone or a grinding wheel, or in some cases, a file. A bevel is created along the cutting edge. Ideally, the length of the bevel should be twice the thickness of the blade. Too long a bevel makes a very keen, but very weak edge that tends to nick easily. Too short a bevel leaves too much bulk behind the edge and it won't enter the wood. Working with a coarse stone will produce a flat-ground edge. Sharpening with a wheel produces a concave bevel which is called *hollow ground*. Hollow-ground edges stay sharp longer than flat-ground edges.

OILSTONES

You will find two types of oilstones useful for sharpening in the shop. A small, fine-textured stone is for touching up edges and for sharpening small blades. Your fingers can provide all the guide you need for these stones. A small stone is also useful for those jobs where it is easier to move the stone than the tool, such as sharpening lawnmower blades.

A large, soft bench stone with coarse and fine surfaces on opposite sides can handle most other jobs. Artificial stones made of aluminum oxide are good for general work. The stone should be kept in a case to protect it from dirt and damage.

New oilstones should be soaked in a light, non-gumming oil, or a mix of equal parts oil and kerosene, before use. They should be kept well oiled and dust-free. After some use, a gummy residue may build up on the stone's surface. This reduces the stone's ability to grind and sharpen properly. A simple way to remove this gummy stuff is to *warm* the stone in an oven and then wipe off the oil that rises to the surface. Clean the stone after every use. Occasional cleaning with kitchen cleanser and a stiff brush can also help keep your stone in shape.

When sharpening, try to wear the stone evenly. An uneven stone can be ground flat by rubbing it with a mixture of 80-grit silicon-carbide powder and water. Mix the powder and water on a sheet of glass and gently rub the stone over it. Check the surface with a straight edge.

When using an oilstone, you first shape the bevel by pushing the cutting edge away from you across the rough side of the stone. The angle of the bevel depends on the tool you are sharpening, but it can be held either with your hand or with a guide. This is discussed below in the instructions for each tool. If you guide the blade with your hand, the blade will set itself. Gently shift the blade against the stone until both the heel and the toe of the bevel are in contact with it. This should give you the proper angle.

Honing or whetting is done on the fine side of the stone. Hone away from yourself with long, smooth strokes using your whole arm. The object is to grind an even edge. Once you think the edge is sharp enough, and you can tell by looking, make an additional pass with the blade laid on its back. This is usually enough to remove the slight burr that honing will leave.

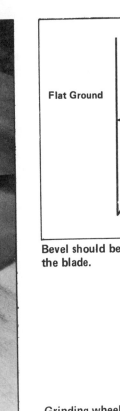

Bevel should be twice the thickness of the blade.

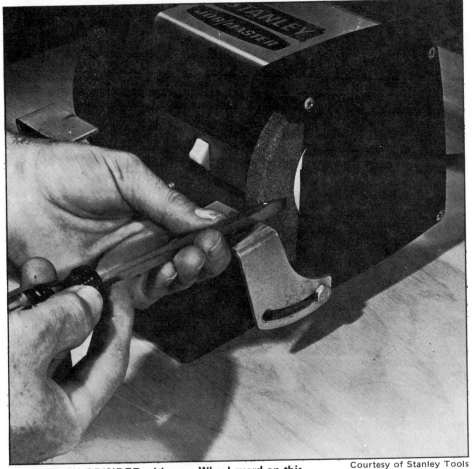

Courtesy of Stanley Tools

Use a BENCH GRINDER with care. Wheel guard on this machine was removed for the photograph. *Always* work with the guards in place, and *always* wear safety goggles.

Grinding wheels produce HOLLOW GROUND edges which stay sharp longer than flat ground. Tools such as axes are CONVEX GROUND, which combines toughness and sharpness. You should not attempt to shape an axe blade on a home grinder. They are not designed for that job and the wheel might shatter.

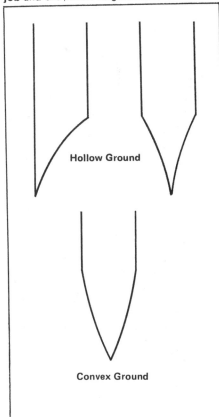

SHARPENING STONES used in the shop.

Frequent honing will not only keep your tools working well, it will cut down the need for grinding. In some cases though, you will save both time and effort by having your tools ground by a professional.

GRINDING WHEELS

In the past, grinding wheels were made of sandstone and kept wet to prevent overheating the work. Today, artificial stones made of dry emery or other substances are available. They are powered by hand or by motor. There is a great danger of overheating the blade with these dry wheels, which will cause it to lose its temper. The blade should be dipped in water frequently to prevent this. The advantages of a wheel are its speed and the fact that it produces a hollow-ground bevel.

If you do buy a bench grinder, be sure to read all the instructions thoroughly, especially those related to the soundness of wheels. Provide adequate lighting, use all the guards on the tool, and always wear safety goggles, regardless of how minor the grinding job may be. You should know that wheels that come with the tool are *not* made for side grinding. They will tolerate a minimum amount of touch-up work on the flat of a screwdriver blade, for example, but they are not meant to hold up under the pressure needed to shape the edge of an axe or hatchet. If you wish to do side grinding, wheels designed for that purpose are available.

Many bench grinders come with built-in adjustable guides for grinding bevels at the proper angle. Move the blade across the wheel from side to side in light passes and dip in water often. The resulting hollow-ground edge is easy to hone and should last a long time before it needs to be reground.

FILES

Some jobs, such as sharpening saw teeth, are best done with files. An 8-inch mill file and a 6-inch taper file are the most commonly used types.

SHARPENING PLANE BLADES AND CHISELS

The bevel on plane blades and chisels should be set at about 25 degrees. The bevel should be about twice the thickness of the blade, and it should be square to the sides.

Set the bevel flat on the coarse side of the stone and move it back and forth with a slight circular motion. Once the first bevel is shaped, repeat this procedure on the fine side of the stone, only this time lift the blade an additional 5 degrees or so. This will make a second bevel or cutting edge. When the blade is sharp enough, remove the burr by working the blade bevel up, flat on the stone in a circular or figure-eight motion.

A jig can be made to hold the plane blade at the proper angle for shaping. Make sure the blade and the stone are both held securely in place. Commercially made plane-iron bevel gauges and sharpening guides are also available.

Wood chisels are sharpened in the same way as a plane blade. First square the edge and then grind the bevel at a 25-degree angle. Grind until a burr appears, then clean off the burr with the bevel up. Cold chisels should be touched up often. It is also useful to grind a bevel around the butt end to help prevent mushrooming when you pound it.

SAWS

Sharpening saws is a job best left to professionals, but if you want to try or are just curious, here is the procedure. Steps involved are *jointing, shaping, setting,* and *filing.*

The first step is to examine the teeth to determine if they are of uniform size and height. If they are okay and just have dull cutting edges, you can go right on to the setting and filing steps. If they are not, you must start by jointing the blade. This simply means bringing the high points down to the level of the low points. Special clamps are available for holding the saw, but you can do the job if you place the saw between suitable lengths of wood and then grip it in a vise. Place a mill file flat on the teeth lengthwise and move it lightly to and fro until you have brought the top of each tooth to the same level. Don't allow the file to tilt as you work.

After the teeth are jointed, they must be shaped with a taper file to conform to crosscut or rip teeth—whichever type you are working on. Place the file between the teeth in the gullet and work straight across at right angles to the blade. Work with the file until you reach the center of the flat made by jointing. Then go to the adjacent gullet and file until the flat top becomes a tooth point. Repeat the procedure with all the teeth. When you are through, all the gullets should have the same depth. You *do not* do any beveling on the teeth during this initial filing operation. Its purpose is to *shape* the teeth.

After the teeth are shaped, they can be set. This means bending part of every other tooth to one side of the blade and the others to the opposite side. This, as I have explained, provides clearance for the blade in the cut. The amount of set varies: Softwood requires more set than hardwoods. The job can be done with an anvil or set block you make yourself, but it might be better to obtain a commercial unit, adjustable for amount of set. The tool is used much like a paper punch and does a lot to assure accuracy.

The final step is filing. Start with the blade clamped between blocks in a vise, teeth up with handle to your right. Take a few light passes with a mill file to flatten the top of each tooth as you

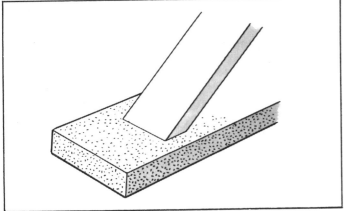

First work the blade back and forth with the bevel flat on the coarse side of the stone, then repeat on the fine side.

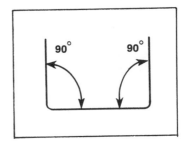

The bevel should be at right angles to the sides of the blade, but the corners can be slightly rounded.

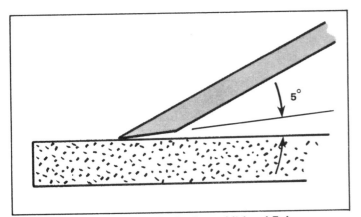

Repeat honing with the blade tilted an additional 5 degrees for final sharpening.

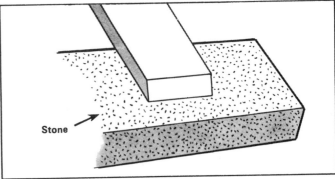

Remove burr with blade flat and bevel up.

An easy sharpening guide can be made by sawing a block of wood at the correct angle and nailing a guide strip on it to keep the blade square.

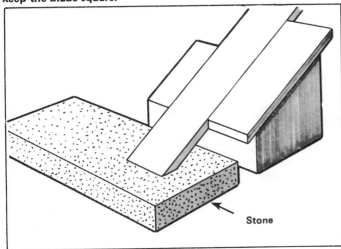

Another sharpening guide is just a beveled block with a wide recess to hold the tool square. The hold-down is secured with two screws and has a flat projection to fit the recess.

True the flat face of the blade on the fine side of the stone. Keep the blade flat and move it in a small circle.

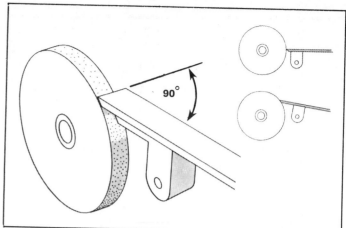

Sharpen plane or chisel blades on a grinder by first squaring the blade across the wheel, then shaping the bevel. Tilt the tool rest to the correct angle and keep the blade square to the wheel.

HOW TO SHARPEN A SAW

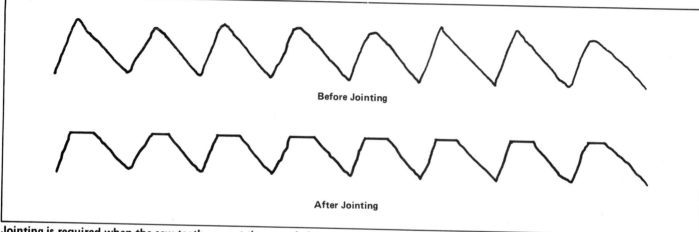

Before Jointing

After Jointing

Jointing is required when the saw-teeth are not the same height. High teeth are filed down to the level of the low teeth.

Place the saw between two boards and grip it in a vise for jointing. Place a mill file flat on the teeth and work along the blade with long, smooth strokes. You can make jointing more simple if you make the special holder for your file shown here.

For shaping, grip the saw between blocks of wood so that the tooth projection is minimal. Move the saw as you work so the vise always grips close to where you are working.

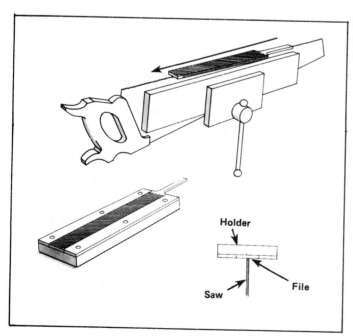

174

FILES TO USE ON SAW TEETH		
TYPE OF SAW	NUMBER OF POINTS	FILE
CROSSCUT	5 or 5-1/2	6-inch taper file
	6, 7, 8 or 9	4-1/2-inch taper file
	10 or 11	5-1/2-inch slim taper file
RIP SAW	4-1/2, 5, 5-1/2 or 6	4-1/2-inch taper file
	4 or coarser	6-inch taper file

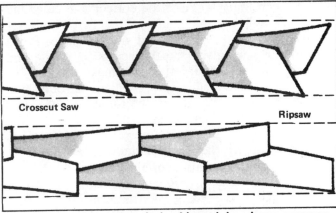

Crosscut Saw   Ripsaw

The points on alternate teeth should touch imaginary, common parallel lines on each side of the blade. If not, the teeth need setting.

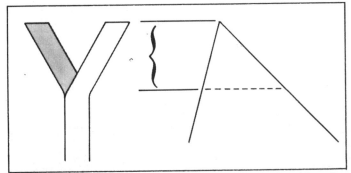

Setting means bending alternate teeth toward opposite sides of the blade. Never bend more than 1/3 to 1/2 of the tooth. Maximum set equals 1/2 the tooth depth. Excessive set can distort the blade and break teeth.

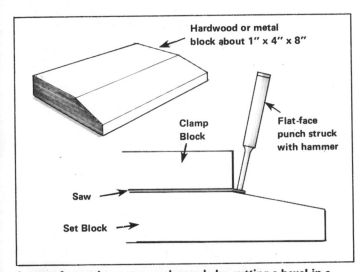

A gauge for setting a saw can be made by cutting a bevel in a block of hardwood equal to the angle of the set. The saw is clamped to the block with its points exposed over the bevel. A flat-faced punch and hammer are used to bend down alternate points. Then the saw is reversed and the procedure repeated on the remaining points.

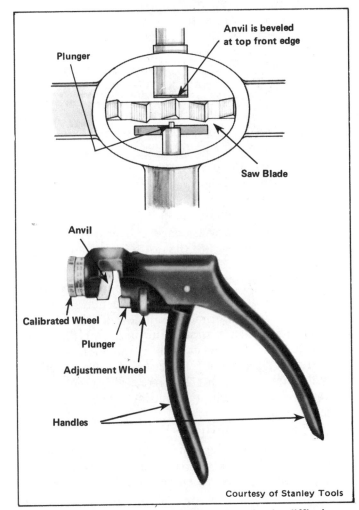

Courtesy of Stanley Tools

Adjustable SAW SETS are available which make the difficult job of setting simple.

did when jointing. Place the correct size taper file in the gullet on the left of the first tooth set toward you at the left end of the blade. For a crosscut saw, place the file across the blade and then swing it to your left until it makes a 65-degree angle with the blade. Keep the file horizontal and snug in the gullet. File on the forward stroke only until you have cut away half the flat on the tooth. Follow this procedure in alternate gullets until you reach the handle end of the saw.

Reverse the position of the saw so the handle will be at your left. Repeat the same operation, but start in the gullet on the *right* of the first tooth set toward you.

The only change you make when filing ripsaws is to file at right angles to the blade instead of at 65 degrees. Incidentally, you can buy special fixtures that clamp to the saw to give you the correct angle for filing automatically.

After all the filing is done, place the saw on a board and move a flat file very lightly once over each side. This is a little scary—it makes you think you are going to ruin all the work you have done. Actually, if you do it lightly just once, it will do nothing but remove the burrs left by filing and it will help to make a uniform set.

SCREWDRIVER BLADES

Screwdriver blades are best sharpened with a file or stone. A bench grinder is less useful because it produces a hollow-ground edge. You want to flatten the screwdriver edge and true its sides so it will fit properly into the slot in the screw head.

AUGER BITS

Special files are made for sharpening auger bits. Clamp the bit in a vise when sharpening. Remember, the spurs outline the hole and the cutting edges remove the waste. The inside of the spurs should be sharpened; *never* the outside. The cutting edges should be sharpened like a chisel with a bevel of about 20 degrees along their inside curve. Don't touch the outside curve except to remove the burr.

AWLS AND PUNCHES

Awls and punches can be sharpened by stroking them with a small stone while rotating the tool. The edge of a large stone can also be used. A grinder with a tool rest can be used, but apply only light pressure and rotate the tool as you grind. Maintain the original angle and restore the point.

KNIVES

Knives should not be honed on a wheel because their thin blades overheat quickly. Hold the knife on a large stone so that the second bevel is in contact with the stone. Stroke smoothly, edge

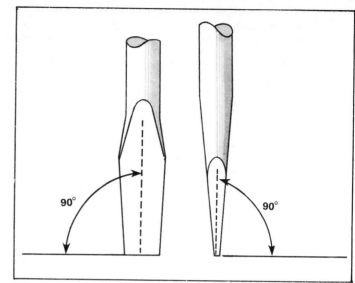

When sharpening screwdrivers, be sure to maintain the original width and thickness of the tip.

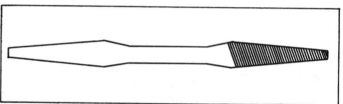

Best way to sharpen AUGER BITS is to use a file made for the purpose. Typical ones have cutting surfaces with safe edges at one end and cutting edges with a safe surface at the other.

Maintain the original bevel on an auger bit. File only the minimum necessary for sharpness.

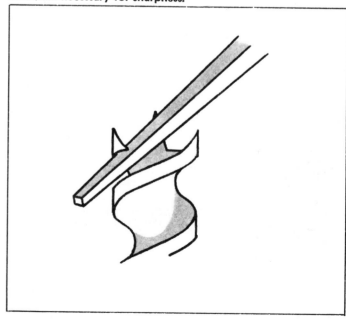

first. Then rotate the knife for the return stroke. Repeat until sharp.

SCRAPERS

Scrapers of all kinds, including cabinet scrapers, come with either flat or beveled cutting edges. The simplest way to sharpen them is to place the blade in your vise and stroke it at the proper angle with a smooth mill file. Each stroke should cover the full blade. The edge should then be honed by holding it square to the edge of an oilstone and stroking in both directions lengthwise. Any burr can be removed by laying the blade flat and passing it over the stone.

PLIERS

You don't actually sharpen pliers, but going over the knurled ends of their jaws occasionally with a triangle file will help them grip. Wire cutters in pliers should be filed straight across.

TIN SNIPS, SHEARS AND SCISSORS

The edges of these tools are beveled, not sharp. Use a flat file to shape their bevels. Hold the open snips in a vise and work them one blade at a time. Stroke across the edge away from you. Stroke diagonally across the entire edge.

FILES AND RASPS

You don't sharpen files, but you can prolong their life by cleaning them frequently. Filings wedge between the teeth and impair their cutting action A wire brush called a *file card* can be used to clean teeth. A piece of soft metal, say brass or copper, can be used to remove stubborn pieces.

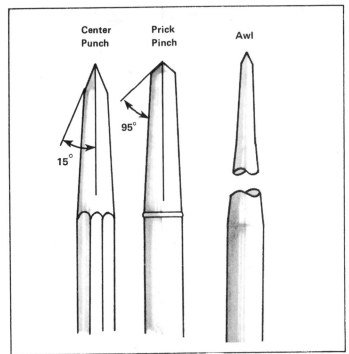

The points of an CENTER PUNCH, PRICK PUNCH and an AWL differ, but all are sharpened in the same way.

Sharpen points by stroking with a small, hard stone as you rotate the tool. On a grinder, use the tool rest to hold the correct angle. Rotate the tool and apply very light pressure.

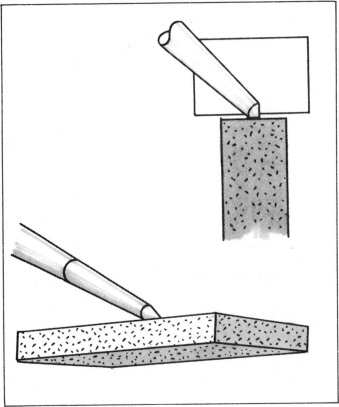

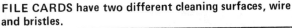

FILE CARDS have two different cleaning surfaces, wire and bristles.

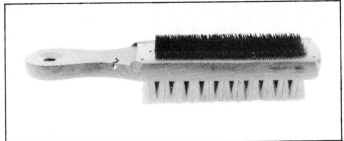

Shop Math

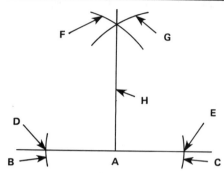

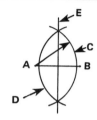

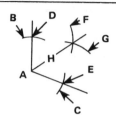

To construct a perpendicular to a line:
- Select base point for your perpendicular, point A.
- Strike arcs B & C equal distance from point A.
- Use points D & E as centers to strike arcs F and G with same radius.
- Line H drawn from point A to where arcs F and G cross is perpendicular to the base line.

To bisect a line:
- Strike arcs C and D from points A and B.
- Line E, drawn through intersections of the arcs, bisects line A-B. Line E is also perpendicular to line A-B.

To bisect an angle:
- Use point A as a center to strike arcs B and C.
- Use point D and E as centers to strike arcs F and G.
- Line H bisects the angle.

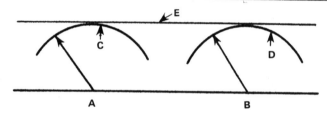

To draw a line parallel to a given line without measuring:
- Set a compass to the distance required between the lines.
- Strike arcs C and D from any two points A and B on the given line.
- Line E, drawn tangent to the arcs, will be parallel to the given line.

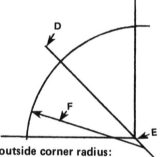

To construct an inside and outside corner radius:
- Bisect the angle, as with lines A and D.
- To round the corner, establish a center at any point on the line, and call it B. Use the distance from B to one side of the angle, C, as a radius for your curve.
- For an outside corner, establish a center at any suitable point, E, and use F as a radius.

Useful Figures

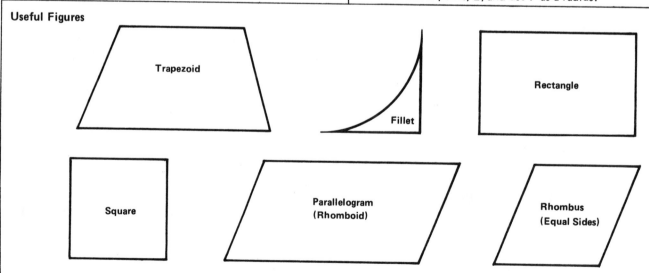

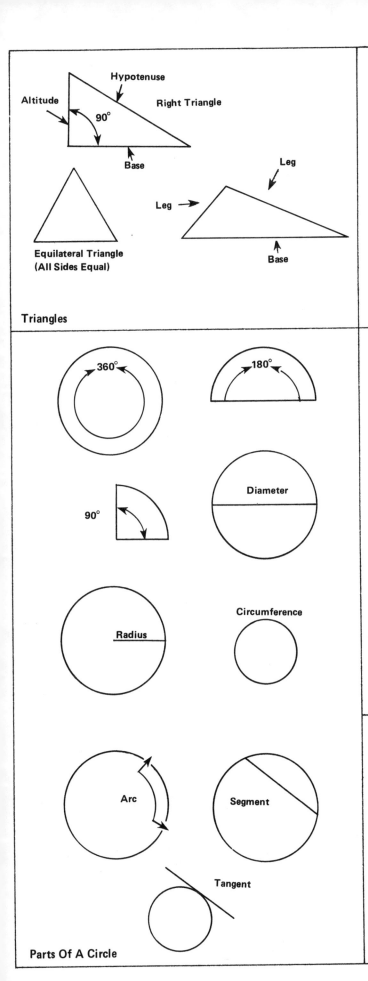

Triangles

Parts Of A Circle

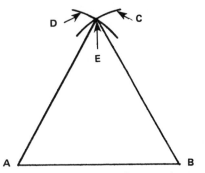

To construct an equilateral (isosceles) triangle:
- Draw base line to length A-B and set your compass to equal A-B.
- Use A as center to strike arc D.
- Use B as center to strike arc C.
- Draw lines from A and B to point E where those arcs cross.

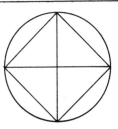

To construct a square in a circle:
- Draw perpendicular diameters and connect the ends of the diameters.

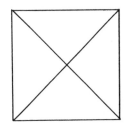 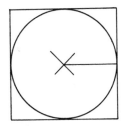

To construct a circle in a square:
- Draw intersecting diagonals. Use the intersection as the center of the circle.

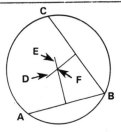

To find the center of any circle:
- Draw two lines, A-B and B-C, from the same point in any direction.
- Construct a perpendicular bisector for each of the line, D & E.
- The intersection of the perpendiculars at point F is the center of the circle.

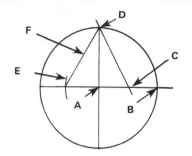

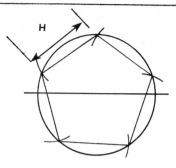

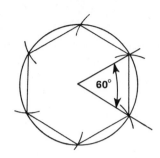

To construct a pentagon, a 5-sided figure:
- Draw perpendicular diameters and bisect radius A-B.
- Draw a line from C to D.
- Strike the arc E using the line C-D as a radius and C as its center.
- Set your compass to equal the distance from D to where arc E intersects the diameter.
- Use that setting to strike arcs on the circumference of the circle. The intersection of each arc and the circumference is the center of the next arc.
- Draw lines from point to point.
- H equals F.

To construct a hexagon, a six-sided figure:
- Set your compass to equal the radius of the circle.
- Mark six arcs on the circumference using each intersection as the center of the following one.
- Draw lines from point to point where the arcs cross the circumference.

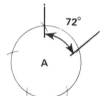 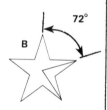

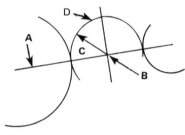

To construct 5-pointed star:
- Draw a circle that represents the overall size of the star and divide the circumference into 5 equal parts.
- Connect the points as shown.

To construct tangent arcs:
- Connect the centers of the given arcs with line A.
- Bisect line A between the two arcs to find point B and radius of the new arc, C.
- Use point B as the center for striking arc D.

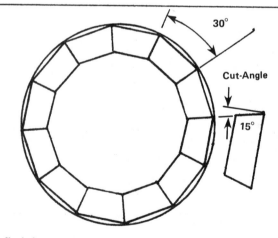

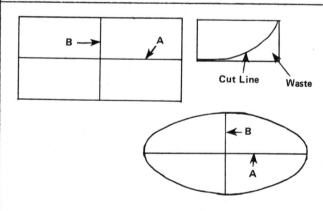

To find the correct cut-angle for a segmented form:
- Divide 360 by the number of pieces and then divide the result by 2.
- In this example, a 12-sided figure, 360 divided by 12 equals 30. 30 divided by 2 equals 15. The *included angle* of each segment is 30 degrees. The *cut-angle* is 15 degrees.

To make a pattern for an arbitrary ellipse:
- Draw a rectangle using the small, B, and large, A, diameters of the ellipse as dimensions. These will be the major and minor axes of the ellipse.
- Fold the paper on the small diameter and again on the large diameter. Draw and then cut a suitable curve.
- When you unfold the paper you will have the ellipse ready to transfer to the work.

THE DECIMAL EQUIVALENTS OF MOST COMMON FRACTIONS

Fractions	Decimal
1/64	.015625
2/64—1/32	.03125
3/64	.046875
4/64—2/32—1/16	.0625
5/64	.078125
6/64—3/32	.09375
7/64	.109375
8/64—4/32—2/16—1/8	.125
9/64	.140625
10/64—5/32	.15625
11/64	.171875
12/64—6/32—3/16	.1875
13/64	.203125
14/64—7/32	.21875
15/64	.234375
16/64—8/32—4/16—1/4	.250
17/64	.265625
18/64—9/32	.28125
19/64	.296875
20/64—10/32—5/16	.3125
21/64	.328125
22/64—11/32	.34375
23/64	.359375
24/64—12/32—6/16—3/8	.3750
25/64	.390625
26/64—13/32	.40625
27/64	.421875
28/64—14/32—7/16	.4375
29/64	.453125
30/64—15/32	.46875
31/64	.484375
32/64—16/32—8/16—4/8—2/4—1/2	.5
33/64	.515625
34/64—17/32	.53125
35/64	.546875
36/64—18/32—9/16	.5625
37/64	.578125
38/64—19/32	.59375
39/64	.609375
40/64—20/32—10/16—5/8	.625
41/64	.640625
42/64—21/32	.65625
43/64	.671875
44/64—22/32—11/16	.6875
45/64	.703125
46/64—23/32	.71875
47/64	.734375
48/64—24/32—12/16—6/8—3/4	.750
49/64	.765625
50/64—25/32	.78125
51/64	.796875
52//64—26/32—13/16	.8125
53/64	.828125
54/64—27/32	.84375
55/64	.859375
56/64—28/32—14/16—7/8	.8750
57/64	.890625
58/64—29/32	.90625
59/64	.921875
60/64—30/32—15/16	.9375
61/64	.953125
62/64—31/32	.96875
63/64	.984375
64/64—32/32—16/16—8/8—4/4—2/2—1	1.000

QUICK FACTS ABOUT METRICS

THE MOST COMMON PREFIXES
milli — .001 (one thousandth)
centi — .01 (one hundredth)
kilo — 1000 (one thousand)

RELATIONSHIPS
10 millimeters (mm) = 1 centimeter (cm)
10 centimeters (cm) = 1 decimeter (dm)
10 decimeters (dm) = 1 meter (m)
10 meters (m) = 1 decameter (Dm)
10 decameters (Dm) = 1 hectometer (Hm)
10 hectometer (Hm) = 1 kilometer (Km)

EQUIVALENTS
1 mm = .03937 inches
1 cm = .3937 inches
1 dm = 3.937 inches
1 m = 39.37 inches or 3.281 feet or 1.094 yards
1 Km = .62137 miles

ENGLISH EQUIVALENTS
1 inch = 2.54 cm
1 foot = 30.48 cm or .3048 m
1 yard = 91.44 cm or .9144 m
1 mile = 1.6093 Km

CONVERSIONS
mm X .03937 = inches
mm divided by 25.4 = inches
cm X .3937 = inches
cm divided by 2.54 = inches
m X 39.37 = inches
m X 3.2809 = feet
m X 1.094 = yards
Km X .621377 = miles

TO CHANGE A FRACTION TO A DECIMAL
• Divide the numerator by the denominator.
• Example: To change 3/16 to its decimal equivalent, divide 3.0000 by 16 which equals .1875.

Tool List

This list contains the tools you are most likely to need for home woodworking projects. Descriptions and tips about purchasing are given beneath their names. The page number at the right is the location in this book of more detailed information on that tool. Other tools are described in this book and they should be added to your kit as needed.

ADJUSTABLE WRENCH **106**
Holds nuts or bolt heads for tightening.

AUGER BITS **46**
Use with brace to form holes. Buy in sets that include 1/4 to 1-inch sizes.

AUGER BIT STOP GAUGE **51**
Adjusts to control the depth of holes.

AWL **53**
Marks dimension points or scribes lines. Makes starting holes for small screws.

BACK SAW **20**
Use with miter box and on any cut requiring fine cutting. A good size has a 14-inch blade with 13 PPI.

BENCH RULE **7**
Use for measuring and layout. Wooden rules are acceptable, but ends should be tipped with brass. Should be 1- to 2-feet long.

BLOCK PLANE **72**
For cross-grain smoothing and chamfering. Should be adjustable for fine or coarse work. Usually 6-inches long with a 1-3/8-inch cutter.

BRACE **44**
Use for driving auger bits. Also use with screwdriver bits and some drill points.

CABINET RASP **86**
For shaping and forming. A 10-inch half-round rasp is preferred.

CALIPER RULE **14**
Makes small inside or outside measurements. Used for checking diameters.

CHISELS **63**
Use for shaping and making joints. Best to buy in sets that range from 1/4 inch to 1-1/2 inches in 1/4-inch increments if you can afford to.

CLAMPS **96**
Clamps are useful for a wide variety of gripping chores. Your selection should include 2 each of 4- and 8-inch C-clamps and 6- and 8-inch handscrews.

CLAW HAMMER **34**
For driving and pulling nails. A 16-ounce weight is recommended.

COMBINATION SQUARE **8**
Use for measuring, marking and checking dimensions.

COMPASS OR DIVIDERS **13**
Use for marking arcs or circles and marking equal spaces.

COMPASS SAW **22**
Cuts inside and outside curves and cuts other saws are too large to make. Should have a 12-inch blade.

COPING SAW **22**
Cuts sharp curves, fine scroll work and internal cutouts.

COUNTERSINK BIT **50**
Use with a brace or hand drill to form seat for the head of flat-head wood screws.

CROSSCUT SAW **20**
Use for dimensional cuts across the grain. Good for working with plywood. Buy this saw first. Should have 10 PPI.

DOVETAIL SAW **20**
For precision sawing, especially for joints.

DUCKBILL SNIPS **106**
For straight or curved cutting on sheet metal.

EXPANSION BIT **46**
Use with a brace for drilling extra-large or special size holes.

FILECARD **177**
Use for cleaning files.

FILES **84**
Use for shaping, smoothing and sharpening. You should have a 10-inch smooth mill file, an 8-inch slim taper file, a 10-inch flat bastard file and a 10-inch half-round bastard file in your shop.

FLEX TAPE **6**
For measuring. Make sure yours locks in place and retracts automatically. Should have markings in 1/16ths of an inch on both edges of blade. Minimum length should be 8 feet.

FOLDING RULE **7**
Use for general measuring. A 6-foot length with an extension in the tip is a good choice.

FORMERS **88**
Cut and form wood. Available in many shapes.

HACK SAW **22**
For cutting metal.

HAND DRILL **44**
For drilling small holes. Points sometimes come with drill. Point selection should run from 1/16 to 11/64 inch in 1/64-inch increments.

KNIFE **63**
For marking lines, shaving wood or cutting thin material. Get one with replaceable blades.

LEVEL **14**
For checking vertical and horizontal surfaces. Should be at least 24-inches long. Some are equipped for checking 45-degree angles.

MALLET **36**
For tapping where a hammer would leave marks and for driving chisels. Models with either wooden or replaceable plastic tips are available.

MARKING GAUGE **12**
Marks lines parallel to an edge.

MITER BOX **26, 30**
Very convenient for making angle cuts. Make your own or purchase one of the commercial models.

NAIL SET **38**
Drives heads of finishing or casing nails below the surface of the wood. Most useful sizes are 1/32, 3/32 and 5/32 inches.

OILSTONE **170**
For maintaining edges on plane blades, chisels and knives. Should have coarse and fine sides.

PUMP PLIERS **106**
Gripping tool.

PUSH DRILL **44**
Use with points to drill small holes.

RIPPING CLAW HAMMER **36**
Use for heavy-duty nailing. 20 ounces is a good weight.

RIPSAW **20**
For making cuts with the grain of the wood.

SAFETY GLASSES **5**
Wear regularly to protect eyes from flying particles.

SANDPAPER **90**
For final smoothing and finishing.

SAWHORSE BRACKETS **145**
Quickest way to set up a work surface any where you are working.

SCREWDRIVERS **57**
Use for driving and removing screws. Set should include Phillips-head drivers.

SLIP-JOINT PLIERS **106**
Use for holding metal fasteners and for gripping round metal stock.

SMOOTH PLANE **70**
For smoothing edges and surfaces, for chamfering and beveling. Should be 10-inches long with a 2-inch blade.

SPIRAL-RATCHET SCREWDRIVER **59**
Drives screws quickly.

STEEL SQUARE **11**
For laying out, measuring and checking squareness.

T-BEVEL **14**
Use for laying out angles.

TACK HAMMER **36**
Best for driving brads and tacks. Buy one that is magnetic.

TORPEDO LEVEL **14**
Convenient for checking vertical and horizontal surfaces. Get one that is magnetic.

WOOD VISE **96**
For all types of holding jobs.

WRECKING BAR **43**
For dismantling wooden assemblies and removing nails.

Index

ACKNOWLEDGEMENTS
Thank You to the organizations that contributed to the fine photographs used in this book:

Adjustable Clamp Company
American Optical Corporation
Black and Decker Manufacturing Company
Disston Division, H. K. Porter Co., Inc.
Hand Tool Institute
Nicholson (The Cooper Group)
Oracle Road Lumber
Ronstadt's Hardware

Special thanks to the magazines that allowed me to reuse material originally created as articles:
Mechanix Illustrated
Popular Science
Workbench
Very special thanks:
To the Stanley Works who made available many of the tools in the book.
To W. C. Eymann, super-photographer and friend, who shot and printed many of the pictures.
And to R. J. DeCristoforo, Jr. for designing and building the projects.